# HARRY

# HARRY

## The People's Prince
### CHRIS HUTCHINS

**The Robson Press**

First published in Great Britain in 2013 by
The Robson Press (an imprint of Biteback Publishing Ltd)
Westminster Tower
3 Albert Embankment
London SE1 7SP
Copyright © Chris Hutchins 2013

ISBN 978-1-84954-547-1

10 9 8 7 6 5 4 3 2 1

A CIP catalogue record for this book is available from the British Library.

Set in Adobe Caslon Pro and Perpetua

Printed and bound in Great Britain by
CPI Group (UK) Ltd, Croydon CR0 4YY

For Mary Jarrett who inspired this book and
Gerri Hutchins who made sure it happened

# CONTENTS

# PROLOGUE

Harry has something very rare, very special – his mother's amazing charisma.
– 'Kanga', Lady Tryon

This is the story of Harry Wales. Harry is a daredevil pilot, soldier and bon vivant. Born into a dysfunctional family, he showed every sign of becoming a teenage delinquent, experimenting with drugs and drinking more than was good for him on his nightly rounds of clubs frequented by the more louche members of society.

He is better known as Prince Harry, third – soon to be fourth – in line to the British throne. But that's the family business. While courtiers make plans for his life, Harry Wales gets on with living it. He may be only a couple of lives away from becoming England's next king, but there are bad guys out there to be dealt with, and women to be loved.

His grandmother is the Queen and his late mother was the most famous woman in the world – for all kinds of reasons.

But Harry Wales is Harry Wales and not a day in his life is to be wasted. If anyone had good reason to keep it in the day, it's him. The past is the past and whatever the future holds will happen whether he likes it or not. As he was once heard to say: 'If I have one foot in yesterday and the other in tomorrow, I'm in the perfect position to piss all over today.'

I make no apologies for the frequent references to his mother – particularly in the chapters dealing with his early life – for it was undoubtedly Princess Diana who moulded Harry Wales, and just about everything that happened to her had a profound effect on shaping him.

Getting people to talk about His Royal Highness was never going to be easy. When they get to rub shoulders with a member of the Royal Family, the privileged ones often tend to consider themselves part of that circle and honour-bound to protect its members' air of mystery. One such person even quoted to me the words of the nineteenth-century essayist Walter Bagehot. He concluded that the monarchy's survival depended largely on its mystique and distance from the masses: 'Its mystery is its life. We must not let daylight in on magic.' Fortunately not every royal 'friend' had read Bagehot and the words on the following pages of the exceptions to his decree make fascinating reading.

Those who really know Harry Wales, however, placed no such restrictions on themselves. They saw the man as I did: an individual with a healthy mind who has overcome numerous obstacles on the road to becoming not just an interesting character but an inspirational man deserving of our attention who can comfortably withstand close scrutiny. I am obliged to those who shared their experiences of Harry so generously and I respect their wish in many cases to remain anonymous lest they be vilified by the Bagehot faction.

Now, let's get on with it.

*Chris Hutchins*
April 2013

# 1

# HARRY'S WAR

Travelling on the 10.45 train from King's Cross to King's Lynn, the Queen arrived several days early to ensure that her meticulous arrangements for the 2007 family Christmas at Sandringham had been strictly adhered to. The festive holiday for her twenty-eight guests should go without a hitch. A fastidious organiser, Her Majesty even used to insist on helping maids to make her sons' beds prior to their arrival for summer holidays in her castle at Balmoral, carefully placing favourite cuddly toys on Prince Edward's until he was in his early teens.

One by one the guests arrived on Christmas Eve, headed by Charles with Camilla who was enjoying her third yuletide at the monarch's country home after the Prince had made her both an honest woman and Harry and William's stepmother in April 2005.

Prince William had not been allowed to invite Kate Middleton because they were not yet married or even engaged; similarly, Prince Andrew had to restrict his female company to that of his daughters, Beatrice and Eugenie. Charles and Andrew's brother Edward, now the Earl of Wessex, arrived with wife Sophie as well as their daughter Louise and new son James. Princess Anne was accompanied by her husband, Timothy Laurence.

On arrival each paused in the grand entrance hall to admire the elaborately decorated tree – a Norfolk spruce taken from the 1,000-acre estate – before being ushered to their rooms.

Having changed into suitable outfits for tea, the guests assembled at precisely 4 p.m. to join the Queen and Prince Philip (who had celebrated their sixtieth anniversary the previous month) in the White Drawing Room where they enjoyed homemade scones and Earl Grey tea ('Is there any other kind?' Queen Mary once asked). Each of them was presented by the Master of the Household with a time-table and room plan so they would know where and when to marshal themselves.

Then it was time to place the presents they had brought for each other on trestle tables set up in the Red Drawing Room. Sections of the tables – laid out in order of precedence – had been marked off with tape showing where each family member's gifts should be placed. In line with German tradition, the presents were then opened, for the Queen has always regarded Christmas Day as being one for religious activity, rather than giving and receiving material things.

To please the Queen, the family always compete to see who can buy the least extravagant gifts. Having learned from an earlier mistake by Princess Diana, who had bought cashmere and other luxury presents, the Duchess of York once brought a pleasing smile to her mother-in-law's face when she gave her an ashtray which spun like a top to consume and conceal its contents. A non-smoker herself, Her Majesty said it was 'ingenious', which is more than she had to say when she opened Harry's gift to her one year: it was a bath hat bearing the slogan 'Ain't life a bitch!' Princess Anne hit the right spot when she selected a white leather loo seat which her brother Charles still uses.

Following the lengthy present-opening ceremony, those assembled moved through to the hall for drinks beneath the tree before going back to their rooms to bathe and change once more (up to five changes a day can be required on some occasions). As they sipped their pre-bath martinis – mixed to the servants' special formula – there was one question on everyone's lips: 'Where's Harry?' When someone joked: 'He's confined to barracks at Windsor, been a naughty boy', the Queen smiled. Only she, her husband and her eldest son were in on the secret.

While the Queen and her guests were beginning their festive celebrations, 2nd Lieutenant Wales was in fact more than 3,500 miles away in southern Helmand, the most dangerous province in war-torn Afghanistan, looking around the tiny room allocated to him in FOB (Forward Operating Base) Delhi; the ruins of a former madrasa, a school of Islamic theology once occupied by the Taliban. Even as Her Majesty's guests were plumping up the pillows on the four-poster beds in the eighteenth-century mansion's opulent suites, Harry – the first senior royal to fight on a battlefield since Queen Victoria's grandson Prince Maurice in the First World War – was checking out the blanket-covered cot he would sleep in for the next several nights.

For the formal Christmas Eve dinner at Sandringham – heralded (as are all the meals) by the sound of a gong at precisely 8 p.m. – evening dress is obligatory: black tie for the men, gowns and jewels for the ladies. In Helmand there was no such adornment for Harry: he wore full 'battle rattle', including body armour, over his camouflage fatigues, and helmet, and he carried his SA80A2 rifle and 9mm pistol together with the necessary ammunition at all times. Around his neck he wore a band to which were attached his ID tags and a small quantity of morphine in case of injury. While the royals looked out on the magnificent gardens beneath the windows of the Sovereign's palace-away-from-home, the Queen's grandson surveyed the rock-strewn desert which surrounded his quarters. A splash of orange here and there was the only evidence that this was the poppy breadbasket of the region but he was where he wanted to be: not for him the upstairs-downstairs, *Downton Abbey* kind of existence where the have-alls are waited on hand and foot by the have-nots.

And while the only 'enemy' the royals had to contend with was the band of photographers they referred to as the 'Nikon Army' kept more than half a mile away by officers of the royal protection squad, Harry knew that just a few hundred yards from where he stood was the real enemy, the Taliban – and they wanted him and his like dead.

'Within an hour of arriving here he crossed "no man's land" to meet the Gurkhas who were his men,' says Lt Colonel (then Major) Bill Connor who was there in his capacity as Lead US Advisor for the province, the man who would decide how American troops might be deployed to back up the British Army as well as Afghan soldiers. Connor was to become Harry's confidant and friend over the ensuing days and weeks.

> I couldn't believe it when he arrived at our tiny base. There was no special security detail, no SAS, he came in like a regular soldier and that's how he remained throughout his time there. This was a prince, the third in line to the British throne yet he made it known that he wanted to be treated just as the junior officer he was at that time. I called him Harry and he called me Bill although I was a major then and in the American military officers between different ranks normally call each other by rank or 'sir'.

Connor was wrong about there being no special security detail with Harry: six SAS troopers had in fact been detailed as his 'guardian angels' but they remained in Helmand on standby. They did not shadow him as armed royal protection officers had done all his life, but they were never more than a short Chinook flight away in case an unforeseen emergency involving the Prince arose.

There were few more dangerous locations in southern Helmand than FOB Delhi, and the sparse area between the base and JTAC (Joint Tactical Air Control) Hill where Harry was to greet his men was 'high risk' – in view of the Taliban snipers who, from time to time, raised their heads above the trenches and made full use of the mortars and missiles they were armed with.

'He went up there on to the hill without showing any sign of fear. I take my hat off to him,' says Connor, who at thirty-nine was sixteen years Harry's senior.

The men were mostly Gurkhas and they had no idea he was coming. When they came down from the hill that night they all wanted their pictures taken with him. He was happy to oblige but pointed out that the photographs were not to be seen by anyone until he had returned to the UK in March or April – not for nothing was he known as the bullet magnet. As it was, the Taliban would probably have been able to see the men lining up to have their pictures taken with him.

Clearly the enemy was unaware that the man being photographed shaking the soldiers' hands was an heir to the British throne or they would surely have stepped up their assault. Back in FOB Delhi he tucked into his army rations, enhanced with a little cooked chicken, before going over the instructions he had been given for his part in the war.

❦

It was a cold winter's night on the Norfolk estate and the two-bar electric fires placed in each did little to heat the enormous bedrooms where abundant blankets – but no duvets – were made available. Downstairs, however, roaring log fires kept the partying royals warm. There was no such luxury for Harry: 'It was bitterly cold and none of us got much sleep that night, including Harry,' says Connor. Much the same could be said by the royal guests since their hostess did not retire until past midnight and no one could leave the room until she had.

The following morning, as the Queen and her party braved the forces of the Nikon Army to be rewarded by cheers from a 1,000-strong crowd of well-wishers waiting in pouring rain to greet their arrival at the Sandringham Parish Church of St Mary Magdalene, Bill Connor and Harry stepped outside for morning exercises at their desert outpost:

We were actually working out when the Taliban opened up. It was one of those fire fights they regularly mounted from their trenches so close by. Harry and I made a run for the buildings – we had no body armour on, just our PT (physical training) kits.

It was like a 50s movie, a First World War situation with everybody in static positions. Every now and again they would pop their heads above the trenches and fire at us with machine guns and, of course, we would return their fire. You just never knew when it was coming.

Although they didn't celebrate Christmas as such because they were mainly Hindus, the Gurkhas put on some great entertainment for everybody that morning. There was one raucous game where they had to chase, capture and kill a freed chicken. Then they staged some very rough wrestling for us. As Harry said: 'God knows how they managed not to break any bones.' But the highlight was their wonderful bagpipe playing. Can't imagine what the Taliban thought of the Gurkhas' bagpipe music coming from FOB Delhi to greet Christmas.

The royals' lunch menu was the same as it has been for many years: clear soup, lemon sole, roast Norfolk turkey and a selection of cold meats arranged on silver salvers, followed by mince pies, Christmas pudding and custard. The fare was served by an army of liveried servants, the junior members of which having been allowed to have theirs at 11 a.m. while the butlers and footmen had to wait until 4 p.m. There is no record of what the royals discussed as they feasted, but there is some knowledge of what the servants were talking about below stairs: Paul Burrell and the pantry diary. In his tell-all book *A Royal Duty*, published in 2003, the butler had written about a temper Prince Charles had apparently flown into after being confronted by Diana with details of intimate lunches at Highgrove with Camilla Parker Bowles. How did she know about them? He demanded to know if Burrell had told her. No, was the answer, but he had recorded her name – along with all of Charles's celebrity guests – in the diary he kept in his pantry on each of the many occasions Mrs Parker Bowles had been there and Diana might have read that. The Prince angrily ordered him to abandon the practice, but the damage had already been done. This was the atmosphere Harry had grown up in and he was glad to be away from it.

Just as the royals had taken their places according to the Queen's seating plan, Harry and his fellow soldiers gathered in the dusty room that served as a mess. And there they looked hungrily forward to a treat of their own: 'A visiting brigadier had brought in a live goat for our Christmas Day meal,' recalls Bill Connor.

The Gurkhas offered Harry the honour of killing it … I'm not sure whether he did it or not but he certainly tucked into it along with the rest of us once it had been cooked and curried. I'm a Christian and I always say prayers before a meal. I'm not sure whether Harry did because my eyes were closed but he certainly kept silent during my prayers.

And just as the royals had opened their presents the previous afternoon, Harry and his new American buddy traded food from their respective MRE (meals-ready-to-eat) boxes: 'They had beans and stuff and we had spaghetti and chicken-type things. Their chocolate was a bit ordinary but we had name brands like M&Ms so those made a good trade.'

Harry – perhaps jokingly, perhaps not – said that celebrity chef Jamie Oliver should be flown in to do for the troops what he was trying to do to improve British school meals.

After sharing their curried-goat lunch – no silver salvers here, just disposable plates – Harry and Bill had their photograph taken together. It was a different story at Sandringham where the royals settled down to watch the Queen's televised Christmas message at 3 p.m. as they do every year. Her Majesty had chosen to highlight the needs of society's vulnerable – 'It is all too easy to turn a blind eye, to pass by on the other side and leave it to experts and professionals' – the woman on the 42-inch plasma screen (one of Sandringham's few concessions to modern technology) in front of them began. Towards the end of the speech, however, she had added some words that seemed aimed towards her absent grandson:

> And also today I want to draw attention to another group of people who deserve our thoughts this Christmas … those who have given their lives or who have been severely wounded while serving with the armed forces in Afghanistan … I pray that all of you who are missing those who are dear to you will find strength and comfort in your families and friends … Wherever these words find you, and in whatever circumstances, I want to wish you all a blessed Christmas.

Although he found himself in dangerous and extremely uncomfortable circumstances, Harry is unlikely to have felt disappointed about missing out on the royals' splendid occasion. He is as lukewarm as his mother about spending the holiday at the royal Norfolk estate: 'Diana told me she absolutely loathed being at Sandringham for Christmas,' said her friend 'Kanga' Tryon; '"So much stuff and nonsense," she would say.'

Certainly Harry's surroundings would have sent shivers through those closeted in one of the grandest houses in the land he called home. In addition to the buildings once occupied by the Afghan theology students, additional stone-floored quarters had been constructed with walls of earth-filled HESCO barriers, blast-proof wire cages filled with rubble and topped with corrugated iron and sandbags. Pear-sized stones were used to temper the ever-present desert dust but they proved to be of little use when the helicopters – like the one that had brought Harry in – descended. In one building where the brave Gurkhas (motto: 'Better to die than be a coward') slept, Harry was shown a hole in the ceiling where a Taliban missile had come through. 'Thank God the Gurkhas were up on JTAC when it came in,' says Connor.

There was probably more shooting going on at Sandringham on Boxing Day than in and around FOB Delhi. Following a sumptuous breakfast the royal party ventured out on to the estate where the men shot pheasants and the women – including the Queen – picked up the dead birds. It was yet another wet day: 'Bloody rain,' Prince Philip was heard to grumble. They could have done with some of it in Helmand Province where the shortage of water was always a problem.

Unlike most of the similar bases, FOB Delhi did have the luxury of running water, provided by a tapped well which somehow managed to feed rustic outdoor showers although, because the water was still frozen, use of it was forbidden before 11 a.m. each day. Harry was to admit later that he hadn't had a shower for four days or washed his clothes (including his underpants, he pointed out) for a week. He never lost sight of the fact that his home was no longer a palace with servants attending to every whim. Lance-Corporal Frankie O'Leary, a 21-year-old from Lewisham in south London, recalls:

He's one of those officers you can talk to, he's laid back and chilled out. Once a job needs doing he doesn't shout and scream at you, he just asks you to do it. It just makes you want to work for the man so you get the job done. That's the way he worked.

However, I noticed he had a nasty habit of leaving something just outside the bivvy [tent] when he got into his bed at night time and he would call someone over to say 'Can you pass me that?' But he always added 'please'.

Bill Connor, who is a lawyer and has since returned to practice in South Carolina, recalls the social side of his days alongside Harry in the war-ravaged territory:

He talked to me about London, the pubs he liked going to, his girlfriend and funny moments during his training or with his platoon. He was very proud of his Regiment, the Household Cavalry, and specifically his company. The Blues and Royals have hundreds of years of lineage and he wanted to uphold the traditions he felt were eroding. Like most junior officers Harry had his opinions on what his superiors could be doing differently.

We stayed off tabloid issues and rumours relating to the Royal Family. There was plenty of good-natured banter going on: once when we were discussing nationalities and Harry had said something, the company commander of the Gurkhas – a normally soft-spoken, intellectual English major, as I recall – yelled out to him, 'Shut up, you're a German anyway.' Harry took it in good part, in fact he laughed.

As indeed he should have: had the Queen's grandfather, King George V, not changed the family name to Windsor he would be Harry Saxe-Coburg-Gotha.

What he did not talk about was how troubled his romance was. For three years Harry had been seeing Chelsy Davy, the daughter of wealthy South African safari operator Charles Davy. He had met the feisty blonde, just a year younger than him, when he was working on a farm in Zimbabwe during his double gap year after leaving Eton. When their relationship ran into trouble because of the 6,000-mile gap between their homes, Chelsy agreed to move to the UK and enrolled on a law course at Leeds University.

Although barely 200 miles from London, the Yorkshire city might have been a continent away for all the good it did their romance. In two months, she complained, Harry ventured north to see her just twice and on the weekend she celebrated her twenty-second birthday, he chose to go to France to cheer on England in their Rugby World Cup semi-final. One graduate told a newspaper reporter that she had had difficulty making genuine friends and, used to the better things in life, was not impressed by the digs she shared with three others in a shabby red-brick terrace house where old mattresses were stacked in neighbouring gardens. Just eight weeks into the course and shortly before Harry left for Afghanistan, Chelsy's talkative fellow student reported, she had packed her bags declaring she could not stand the bitterly cold northern weather and was going home to Cape Town. It was said to have led to yet another blazing row with her royal beau. A war zone, Harry had decided however, was no place to display a broken heart.

As forward air controller, Harry's job in no man's land was to call in air support to bomb the Taliban attempting to attack forward positions. He had the momentous task of preventing friendly fire deaths as well as setting coordinates for the bomb drops that were to kill thirty members of the Taliban. On New Year's Eve – as the Bishop of Norwich, the Rt Revd Graham Jones, was chastising his royal congregation at St Mary Magdalene, during his twelve-minute sermon (he was allowed not a minute longer), about the ecological extravagance of Christmas lights – three 500lb bombs were dropped on Taliban bunkers by two US F15 jets, the first on Harry's say-so. The pilots Harry communicated with had no idea that the man they spoke to for hours each day was in fact the son of the heir to the British throne. Though news of the activity was relayed back to his seniors in London, his father was not informed; Charles was already north of the border preparing to celebrate Hogmanay with Camilla at his Scottish home, Birkhall, and had no great desire to know details of the war his son was fighting.

Passionate about his role in the war, he was frequently spotted by Connor studying air-support books 'even at meal times'. But he did not spend his entire period of service in Helmand poring over books or his laptop (watching a programme known as *Kill TV*). On New Year's Day he fired his first shots in combat from JTAC Hill, pumping rounds from a .50 machine gun in the direction of around twenty

Taliban who had been spotted approaching the British position. A shredded piece of sackcloth hanging in front of him provided the only cover.

Would men have died as the result of his machine-gun fire? 'It was extremely difficult to confirm Taliban "kills",' says Connor.

> We knew we were killing and wounding Taliban, usually at a distance of 0.5 to 1 kilometre away. However, we didn't walk up and see those we killed. We did see some places where the Taliban had not yet retrieved their dead but we could not go there. I say this because I am sure Harry and his men killed/wounded Taliban, but it would be extremely unlikely to have been able to confirm how many were killed.

Although during interviews at the time he was to remain tight-lipped about killing Taliban fighters, during his second tour of Afghanistan he made no bones about it: 'You do what you have to do – what's necessary to save your own guys. If you need to drop a bomb – worst-case scenario – then you will, but that's just the way it is. It's not nice to drop bombs. But, to save lives, that's what happens.'

His comrade-in-arms Bill Connor recounts his first experience of potentially fatal contact with the enemy:

> I can't speak for all the soldiers I commanded, and I'm sure they had varying emotions. Though I had been on prior operational deployments before Afghanistan, I didn't have to deal

with the 'killing' aspect of war until then. I wasn't sure how I'd react when I had to point my weapon with the intent to kill another human being. However, in my first major firefight (in Kandahar, before I went to Helmand) I remember the surreal feeling of being shot at when my small convoy was ambushed. I remember thinking, 'They're trying to kill me, and this may be my last day on earth.' That thought was extremely brief, because my training kicked in immediately and I gave orders directing fire at those who were attacking us.

Connor describes the fatal act in these chilling words, which perhaps offers a parallel of Harry's own feelings when confronted with a similar situation:

When I saw some of them killed in the fight … I honestly didn't have any guilt as they were trying to kill all of us. Harry never showed any emotions when he was doing his job. Part of war is suppressing emotions and he showed everyone he could do that… The bigger problem with guilt comes with those fights – and thank God we were not in them – in which the enemy used civilians as shields. I can imagine the times a soldier may have done everything 'right' by the rules of engagement and yet accidentally killed a civilian. Those would be the times someone would have a hard time putting the kill behind them. Again, through God's grace, I did not have to deal with any of those types of kills and, to the best of my knowledge, neither did Harry.

A serving soldier who was there with Harry puts it more bluntly: 'I don't believe he would have lost a moment's sleep over it. He's a professional, this is war and these men were coming to kill us. He used that gun in exactly the manner intended.' Harry, who handed his camera to a Gurkha soldier to film his introduction to live action, simply said: 'They poke their heads up and that's it.'

To think, just a few weeks earlier, he had been questioned by the police about the shooting of two birds of prey – a pair of rare hen harriers – on the Sandringham estate, an incident which made it necessary for the Crown Prosecution Service to announce later that it had found insufficient evidence to bring criminal proceedings against him.

In the village of Garmsir, Harry was back in the line of enemy fire again as he took part in routine patrols of the deserted, bombed-out streets just 500 yards from Taliban bunkers, nodding at locals as he walked through what had once been a busy bazaar: '[The locals] haven't a clue who I am, they wouldn't know,' he said, adding 'but I'm still a little bit conscious not to show my face too much.'

During long shifts in the battle group operating room he shared jokes and good-natured banter with a fellow redhead, Corporal Dave Baxter. 'He fixed my radio so he's a good guy to have on board despite he being ginger and me Irish.' Harry overheard the comment and joked, 'It's a lethal mix.'

Happy to be 'just one of the boys', Harry did much to boost his comrades' morale. Each day, after their pre-packed breakfast packs (while at Sandringham, meanwhile, they feasted on kedgeree), he organised a football kickabout using toilet roll wrapped in black gaffer tape as the ball. And when his unit found an old motorcycle in the desert during one patrol, he jumped on it and took it for a spluttering ride calling out, 'No brakes, no brakes.'

And despite the tension of ever-present danger he never complained – certainly not about being absent from home during the festive season: 'What am I missing the most?' he said in reply to one questioner,

> Nothing really. I honestly don't know what I miss at all: music, we've got music, we've got light, we've got food, we've got non-alcoholic drink. No, I don't miss booze. It's nice just to be here with all the guys and just mucking about as one of the lads.
>
> It's good fun to be with just a normal bunch of guys, listening to their problems, listening to what they think. And especially getting through every day, it's not painful to be here, but you are doing a job and to be with such fantastic people, the Gurkhas and the guys I'm sharing a room with, makes it all worthwhile. It's very nice to be a normal person for once.

He used some of the limited telephone allowance to call his grandmother, reassuring her of his safety despite the acute danger he and the fluid contingent of Royal Artillery soldiers he shared his quarters with were in. Other precious minutes were used talking to Chelsy, for whom he pined despite cooling off their relationship and his present location in the Afghan desert. It was hard to get mail to him but when one letter arrived he was particularly thrilled: it was from his brother. In it, William told him that their mother would have been 'so proud' of him. A Christmas card from his father did not arrive until early February – supplies had to take priority over mailbags and even the heir to the throne had no way of getting around that one.

His superiors' foremost concern was not that he would stop a bullet but that he might be captured. There could be no greater prize for the enemy than having not Harry Wales but His Royal Highness the Prince Henry Charles Albert David Windsor in their hands. Harry had some idea what to expect if the Afghans took him. Six years earlier, at the age of seventeen, he had volunteered to be the hostage when the Eton College Combined Cadet Force conducted an escape and evasion exercise. He had been 'captured' by five regular soldiers of the Royal Green Jackets, dressed as Taliban fighters complete with Kalashnikov AK-47 assault rifles, and taken to a barn in the Thames-side hamlet of Boveney. While other schoolboy cadets attempted to find and rescue him, he was hooded and submitted to twelve hours of intense inter-rogation and mind games. His captors moved him around to disorientate him, forced him to stand for long periods leaning on his finger tips against a wall, and made him kneel before them. While they shouted incessantly at him, 'mentally beating him to the ground', Harry would tell them only his name, date and place of birth. The rescue party was unsuccessful and he was released at 5 a.m. the next day.

The exercise prepared him for the cruel reality of capture, especially at the hands of al Qaeda, giving the young royal a small taste of what could lie ahead…

2nd Lieutenant Wales and his new friend Major Bill Connor were briefly parted early in January but reunited the following month for an operation in northern Helmand. 'The operations in northern Helmand, in between Musa Qala and the Kajaki Dam, were a different type of danger from Garmsir,' said Connor.

In these operations the UK forces [to which Harry was attached] were given the mission of isolating various small villages. The US forces [Bill was the senior American] had the mission of clearing the villages of Taliban. It's quite dangerous going compound to compound to clear Taliban. I recall that in the first compound we entered, an enemy fighter sprayed his AK-47 at us. Can't believe no one in our small group was hit. I can recall my heart racing as we cleared the other rooms while keeping watch over the hole that the Taliban fighter had crawled back into. We threw a grenade in the hole so I assume he was killed.

The sheer danger of this operation is emphasised further by Harry's American friend:

As I said, Prince Harry was with the UK forces with the mission of calling in air strikes and artillery. Considering all the restrictions due to the fact we were clearing Taliban from an Afghan village, he did an outstanding job. I remember, after the first day of fighting, he and I met up and he seemed pumped about the fact that we were taking the fight to the Taliban. His conversation led me to believe he wished he could join the Americans going through [all] the villages. Like me, Harry hadn't taken a shower in a week or more and had the dirty combat look. Harry was around Musa Qala in January 2008 and Taliban were still all over northern Helmand. Additionally during the fighting in the karez water system Harry was under constant threat of ambush as he moved from place to place.

By then, however, Harry had become a victim of his celebrity. He was later to discover that an Australian women's magazine, *New Idea*, had broken an agreed embargo and leaked news of his Afghan posting on its website. Harry was not told but his SAS guardian angels were alerted to the increased danger to which the celebrity magazine had exposed him. Miraculously, the news went ignored by the rest of the world's media (even CNN, not a party to the media agreement, knew he was there but suppressed the story after a call from the Palace press office) until it was picked up by one Matt Drudge and posted on his widely read news aggregate website, the Drudge Report. Drudge, a former shop assistant and the only child of Reform Jewish Democrats (his mother worked for Ted Kennedy) had previously undergone psychiatric treatment. He claimed to have been the man who broke the story of President Clinton's scandalous association with Monica Lewinsky, but he lacked both education and media experience, boasting that he had failed his bar mitzvah and achieved such a feeble high school graduation result that he reckoned it qualified him for 'no more than a post at 7-Eleven'. As a result of Drudge's website post, the Prince was recalled to Britain.

In general, Harry had a reasonable relationship with the media. He remembers being in his parents' limousine and hearing his father chastise his mother for waving to 'friendly' journalist James Whitaker as their car passed the ever-present bunch of media men. 'Oh, it's OK,' she said, 'James is friendly to us,' to which Charles replied sarcastically (according to royal protection officer Ken Wharfe, who was also in the car), 'That's all right then. At least they remind people we still exist.'

When Harry found out that his recall was down to Drudge's disclosure, he was furious. 'He was p****d off when he heard the [expletive deleted] Australian magazine had blown his cover on its pathetic website,' says one who sat next to him on the plane home.

It had put not just him but those of us around him in even greater danger than we already were. Then, when this man Drudge – 'Drudge with a Grudge' Harry called him – exploited a confidence which the rest [of the world's media] respected, we then saw that Harry had a temper to match his red hair. He'd kept his cool throughout but at this moment things went flying. And we understood it. He'd been doing such a great job and getting tremendous satisfaction from doing it.

To be honest, though, by the time this prat had blown his cover, hundreds of people already knew Harry was out there – he'd even done television interviews to be shown after he'd finished his tour.

Jon Snow touched on this when he declared on his blog:

I never thought I'd find myself saying Thank God for Drudge. The infamous US blogger has broken the best-kept editorial secret of recent times. One wonders whether viewers, readers and listeners will ever want to trust media bosses again.

Military bosses, however, do not like being disobeyed – even if it is an agreement with civilians rather than an order given to their soldiers. As Harry was being flown home the army's Chief of General Staff, Sir Richard Dannatt, said in a some-what reserved statement:

I am very disappointed that foreign websites have decided to run this story without consulting us. This is in stark contrast to the highly responsible attitude that the whole of the UK print and broadcast media, along with a small number of overseas outlets, who have entered into an understanding with us over the coverage of Prince Harry on operations.

According to subsequent remarks Prince Philip made to a royal protection officer, Dannatt was far less reserved when he telephoned the Queen to apprise her of the situation.

Once he had calmed down, Harry summed up his battle front experience saying he'd felt 'a bit of excitement, a bit of "phew" finally [to] get the chance to actually do the soldiering that I wanted to do ever since I joined up'. In what must have been an unguarded moment, however, Harry also said he had enjoyed being away from home: 'I don't want to sit around Windsor because I generally don't like England that much. It's nice to have been away from all the press and the papers.' Despite appearing, publicly at least, to get on with reporters and photographers, he had an innate mistrust derived from his mother's emotions and her fate, and it had an effect on his feelings about his homeland.

There was some comfort for Harry following his return, although he had to wait several weeks for it. In April he was promoted to the rank of lieutenant on completion of two years' army service. It boosted his pay by £78 a week.

The greater honour was to come, however. Less than two months after his promotion Harry was presented with an Operational Service Medal for his time in Afghanistan. His friend Bill Connor fared even better: in addition to being promoted from major to lieutenant colonel and awarded the Bronze Star for his service in Helmand and for being involved in direct fire operations against the Taliban, he received the Combat Infantryman's Badge. Later he was also awarded a valour medal from the US counter-terrorism Advisory Task

Force for actions during a substantial firefight in Kandahar. Both expressed their pleasure that the other's service had been acknowledged.

Harry's aunt, the Princess Royal, presented him with his medal at Combermere Barracks, which lies in the shadow of Windsor Castle. Princess Anne was overheard to remark to a girlfriend later: 'Well, at least when he goes on parade he will have a genuine medal to show for his bravery unlike two of my brothers.' (Charles and Edward presumably, since Andrew had earned his in the Falklands conflict.)

But the big surprise of the day was the presence at the ceremony of his on/off girlfriend Chelsy Davy who had returned to the UK to resume her studies in 'grim Leeds' after a sunshine break in South Africa. Seated beside Prince William amid the wives, girlfriends and children of other soldiers at the barracks and clearly aware of the media attention her presence would attract, Chelsy beamed with pride as Anne pinned the medal on Harry's lapel. The following day, to his obvious chagrin, Prince Charles noted that the presence of the 22-year-old Zimbabwean student accounted for hundreds of column inches in the morning papers, compared to his occasional line or two.

And later, following a parade through the streets of Windsor led by the band of the Blues and Royals, it was Chelsy who sat next to Harry at a service in the town's Holy Trinity church to remember colleagues who had fallen. Attractively dressed in a cream jacket and smart brown skirt, she stepped into a limo with him to return to the barracks for a reception attended by his comrades and their other halves, before retiring to the castle – a world apart from FOB Delhi.

Clearly Chelsy had forgiven Harry for neglecting her while she was in Leeds (it was not the first time she had chosen to overlook his bad manners). Her forgiveness on this occasion meant that they were once again an item: she had joined Kate Middleton the previous day at Cowarth Park to sip champagne and cheer on Harry and William who were competing in the Audi Polo Challenge.

Could Miss Davy be on her way to becoming Mrs Wales after all?

# 2

# A TRUE LOVE CHILD

Nothing upsets Harry more than sly insinuations that he was born to two people who did not even like, let alone love, each other. The fact of the matter is that he was very much a love baby. Lady 'Kanga' Tryon – a close friend and confidante of Diana's – said the Princess told her that Harry was conceived at Windsor Castle at a time when she and Charles were every bit the archetypal couple in love.

These were indeed happy days for Diana, and Lady Tryon's remarks made to the author just a few months before her death in 1997 go a long way to disproving the theory that Charles did not father his younger son. It was not until two years after Harry's birth that she took a lover, although by then Diana had had no less than seven advice-seeking discussions with the Queen about her fears for the marriage. Her Majesty summoned Diana for the first of those meetings – and Prince Philip, whom Diana did not particularly like, always insisted on being present – after a blistering row broke out on the night of Harry's christening of which more follows.

This marked a watershed in hostilities among the family. The Queen was frank with her daughter-in-law and, picking on what she regarded as Diana's unwise choices, told her she was misguided in choosing AIDS as a cause to support, although it is likely that the Palace realised that by doing so she had tapped into a well of unexploited popularity.

'Diana told me way back then that whatever happened between her and Charles she would never let go of her boys despite their obvious importance to the Royal Family,' said Kanga – a woman so close to Diana that she helped Charles choose her as his bride, ironically in league with Camilla Parker Bowles, in those days known as Kanga's twin-set-twin. 'She doted on those two, they couldn't have wished for a better mother but she gave Harry special attention because she felt he needed it. The royal court, the government, indeed the people, she said, would look after William.'

Kanga said that Diana told her about the Windsor Castle night of love over a 'tiddly' dinner at their favourite Knightsbridge haunt, the restaurant San Lorenzo.

She made me promise I wouldn't tell anybody at the time, not even Ant [Anthony, Lord Tryon], my husband. But she said she and Charles had been having a fantastic time. It was the Christmas of 1983 and everyone was in a party mood. There was lots of, shall we say, intimacy going on and she giggled like a naughty schoolgirl when she told me she had worn fake boobs at a party. She said it was the most romantic night of her life. He had given her a very special brooch for her Christmas present and had their bedroom filled with flowers. Then they all went off to Sandringham to shoot. Probably the last time she was ever to enjoy going to that house. She definitely was neither bulimic nor depressed at that time so you can take it from me: Harry was born out of love.

Of course we all know things went belly-up thereafter but I can assure you that those boys couldn't have wished for a better mother.

Praise indeed from the woman who at one time would dearly have loved to marry Charles herself (they had a brief fling in the 1980s) but Diana and Kanga had a common cause: both women by then had come to loathe the present Duchess of Cornwall, then plain Mrs Parker Bowles. They often met for lunch or dinner either at San L, as it was affectionately known, or in Diana's apartment at Kensington Palace where they exchanged cruel gossip about Camilla: according to Kanga Charles complained that the Parker Bowles home was 'a bit smelly' and that when Kanga asked him in a particularly indiscreet moment what Camilla was like to kiss he complained that she smoked too much.

☙

Harry Wales came into the world at 4.20 p.m. on Saturday 15 September 1984, nine days earlier than expected, putting an end to thirty-four years of the first two royal children being born a boy and then a girl.

With Prince Charles beside her in the royal limousine, Diana had been rushed to the grim-looking St Mary's Hospital in Paddington, a stark contrast to the magnificence of the 1,000-room Windsor Castle – Diana had adamantly refused to give birth in one of the royal homes. There, the Princess had been resting in preparation for the birth of her second child and had been 'putting up' with the morning sickness that troubled her through most of her pregnancy. Things had gone decidedly downhill in her marriage since the glorious night of Harry's conception described by Lady Tryon.

Never comfortable in such intimate situations, Prince Charles nevertheless stayed at Diana's side in the private but small and drab £150-a-night room in the hospital's Lindo Wing throughout the nine-hour labour, feeding her lumps of ice to suck and applying cream to her dry lips. Both were required to use a bathroom on the other side of the corridor. Delivered by the eminent gynaecologist Dr George Pinker (who did not approve of home births), the new arrival weighed in at 6lb 14oz and, as his nervous father was about to tell the world, the baby had light blue eyes 'and a bit of, er, brownish hair'. Diana was later to say: 'If men had babies they would only have one each.'

Charles telephoned his mother, in summer residence at Balmoral, with the news that all was well, then drove to Kensington Palace to tell an excited two-year-old William he had a brother. After telling his valet he needed a stiff scotch to overcome the stress he'd been through, he phoned a polo-playing friend to announce that now his second son had been safely delivered he would be available to play in the match at Windsor Great Park the following day.

Charles was happy, the Queen was 'delighted' and other members of the family were busy declaring that it was indeed a joyous time – at least all apart from Diana. As proud as any mother could be with a healthy newborn baby in her arms, she was suffering more than the physical pain of child-birth: she was secretly being treated for depression, certain in the knowledge that she had lost her husband's love. They no longer slept together and Diana told her voice coach, an American actor called Peter Settleton, that they managed to be intimate 'sort of once every three weeks'. The reason: Charles had returned to the arms of Mrs Parker Bowles and Diana was powerless to prevent it. She had not extracted a confession nor had he offered one but, as she was to say later, servants talk, policemen talk, even so-called friends talk.

While bells rang in churches throughout the land, she had to suffer alone the hurt of knowing that while the nation had a new prince, she had introduced a child into a dysfunc-tional family. Life was certainly going to be comfortable for Harry but never easy, she decided. She would have to work extra hard to try to turn that around. What a difference nine months had made.

The world, of course, was not to know what was going on in the hearts of the unhappy parents and it has to be remem-bered that Prince Charles is not a callous man and never has been. Because of his own strict upbringing – one psychologi-cal expert describes it as cruel – he has always had immense difficulty in showing normal affection to a woman. Because the Queen felt obliged to put her immense duty first, he grew up seeking motherly love elsewhere and eventually found it in the arms of his mistress rather than his beautiful young bride. One can only imagine how painful it was for both the Prince and Princess of Wales to watch people, not just in Britain but all over the planet, celebrating the birth of their child with their loved ones while they were compelled to live a lie.

And that was the state of the marriage when, the day after Harry's birth, Charles collected both his new baby and his wife – smiling and looking radiant as always for the photographers and the 2,000-strong crowd of onlookers – and drove them the short distance home to Kensington Palace in his blue Daimler. There he promptly switched cars. His polo gear already having been loaded into the boot of his Aston Martin, he set off for Windsor Great Park where his teammates showered him with champagne and hearty congratulations. All in all he had a good day, scoring a hat trick in his team's victory over Laurent Perrier. No wonder his son was destined to excel at the sport Diana always hated.

Harry's birth sold newspapers around the world. Harry Wales was a star from the moment he arrived in the world. All over Britain people were buying flags, hastily manufactured mugs and postcards as souvenirs of the kingdom's new arrival. In America, unscrupulous dealers attempted to sell sheets from the birth bed until the hospital was obliged to make it clear that sheets from the maternity ward were always incinerated regardless of the baby's identity. Within hours of his birth Harry souvenirs were as hot as Elvis Presley memorabilia. Gifts were bountiful, including £500,000 from his other grandfather, Earl Spencer, who acted like a man possessed. From an upstairs window at Althorp, his stately pile, he shouted news of the newly born child to visitors touring the grounds below and then phoned everyone he could think of to share his joy. Believing he had reached Prince Andrew, to the astonishment of the landlord the Earl even called the Duke of York public house in Windsor to tell him about the new arrival.

❦

Dressed in a white-laced gown, Harry was obliged to tolerate his first photo shoot when he was just five weeks old, but he was not fazed. The man behind the camera was no member of the paparazzi he would loathe in later life, but his great-uncle Lord Snowdon, a member of the 'Firm', or 'that fucking family' as Diana was to call it.

With Diana in agreement, Charles chose St George's Chapel, in the grounds of the castle where the baby was conceived, as the venue for Harry's christening instead of the Music Room at Buckingham Palace where most royal babies were baptised. The ceremony took place on 21 December and was conducted by the Archbishop of Canterbury, Dr Robert Runcie. Charles also chose the new Prince's names – though this time Diana was not in agreement. Charles's choice – Henry Charles Albert David – was too royal, said

Diana, to which Charles is alleged to have declared: 'Well those are the names he's going to have. You can call him whatever you [expletive deleted] want.' From that moment on he was never anything other than Harry to her, though when Charles chastised her on a later occasion for 'corrupting' the boy's Christian name she pointed out to him that an uncle of Charles's own mother had been affectionately known as Harry though christened Henry.

When it came to the godparents, Diana was adamant she had a say. She chose her chum Lady Celia Vestey, Lady Sarah Armstrong-Jones (daughter of the divorced snapper Lord Snowdon and Princess Margaret) and her former flatmate Carolyn Bartholomew.

Charles was permitted to choose three and he opted for his brother Andrew, then courting the soft-porn film starlet Koo Stark; Gerald Ward, a mega-wealthy polo player and farmer and once a suitor of Princess Anne's; and the perfectly decent artist Bryan Organ, whose 1981 portrait of Diana was his favourite.

Controversially, Princess Anne was overlooked, a turn of events that left her seething. Diana would not even have Charles's sister at the ceremony. She had also been over-looked as godparent to Prince William. Charles – who is godfather to Anne's son Peter and had promised his sister that he would reciprocate when the time came – had selected Princess Alexandra; his mother's lady-in-waiting, Lady Susan Hussey; his pal the ex-King Constantine of Greece; Earl Mountbatten's grandson, Lord Romsey; the South

African mystic Sir Laurens van der Post and the Duke of Westminster's wife, Tally.

The reason made known in royal circles at the time for Anne's exclusions was that it was because she had made Andrew Parker Bowles, husband of the much-unloved Camilla, godfather to her daughter Zara. There was certainly no love lost between Anne and Diana and they ignored each other whenever they found themselves in the same company. Prince Philip was incandescent with rage about Anne's exclusion and didn't have anything to do with his eldest son and daughter-in-law for weeks afterwards. But since it had taken him six weeks after Harry's birth to even call on the lad, he was not much missed. There was some consolation for Anne: clearly aware that she was deeply hurt by Diana's snub, Her Majesty subsequently gave her the highest honour a Sovereign can bestow on a female member of the family: she made her the Princess Royal.

Charles expressed his views on women, which some in the royal household considered controversial:

Although the whole attitude has changed towards what women are expected to do, I still feel all the time, at the risk of sticking my neck out, that one of the most important roles any woman could ever perform is to be a mother. And nobody should denigrate that role. How children grow up, what attitudes they have, are absolutely vital both from the social point of view and for the future. And all this stems from the social role the mother performs. I know it's awfully difficult these days because women want to work and have to do so to earn enough.

'How would he know?' Prince Philip said over lunch at the Cavalry and Guards Club with a trusted advisor and close friend of Harry. 'He and Diana even sleep in separate rooms when they are under the same roof,' Philip added – though he and the Queen had done so for many years, too. The christening did not pass without incident. At a celebration following the religious service, Charles complained to Diana's mother, Frances Shand Kydd, that her daughter had delivered a son with red hair. One who witnessed the altercation that followed said it was his clumsy attempt at being humorous (and remember, the affair with red-headed James Hewitt was a long way off) but Mrs Shand Kydd, who was known to enjoy a drink or two, told him in no uncertain terms that he should be grateful that her daughter had provided him with a second healthy son. After a half-hearted attempt to apologise Charles sloped off and his mother-in-law was virtually *persona non grata* from that point on.

The Queen had hoped that the arrival of her new grandson would cement what she saw as cracks rapidly opening in her son's marriage and she summoned Diana for a subsequent heart-to-heart, doing her best to soothe the Princess's troubled mind. But Diana was too fond of her own mother to be easily placated by her husband's and the rift was never properly healed. Furthermore, she told her mother-in-law, she was unhappy at the limited amount of time Charles spent with his children and that she had written to their private secretary, Edward Adeane, saying that in future His Royal Highness would not be available for early morning or evening meetings because he would be where he should be – in the nursery with their new baby.

However, Diana did accept one word of advice from Her Majesty. It was the Queen who told her that the infants should not be mollycoddled by way of compensation for their parents' growing indifference to each other: 'spare the rod and spoil the child' was the old adage of which she reminded her. Her Majesty's recommendation was well received by Olga Powell, who Diana had hired in late 1982 as a deputy to the princes' nanny, Barbara Barnes. Diana had always told her to be 'especially gentle' with Harry but now Mrs Powell had licence to be strict in a way that no royal nanny had previously been permitted. It did not go down well with Ms Barnes, the homely daughter of a forestry worker and she eventually quit her job, making it clear that she failed to understand why Diana interfered with her traditional nannying methods. The Princess blamed Barnes for being over-familiar with some of her own friends – especially those in the show-business fraternity – but Barnes already knew some of them from working for fourteen years for Lord Glenconner, who owned the Caribbean island of Mustique. In reality though, Diana was uncomfortable with the growing affection she saw developing between the ever-attentive 'Call me Baba' Barnes and her boys. And Baba would not be the last to suffer a similar fate for the same reason.

Two other nannies came and went: Ruth Wallace, an attractive and fun person who enjoyed a drink but could not stand the tension between her charges' parents and left Kensington Palace in 1990 to take a long trip up the relatively peaceful Amazon, and the motherly Jessie Webb who had previously worked for designer Nina Campbell. Charles did not like the fact that Harry was picking up cockney rhyming slang from Jessie and finally gave in to Diana's wish that Mrs Powell be made the principal nanny. Throughout, Diana regarded her more as a friend than a servant and Powell remained with her for fifteen years. It was Olga Powell, not butler Burrell, who was the true rock in the Princess's life, the one whose shoulder she could cry on in times of stress – and there were many such times to come.

Even Mrs Powell, however, found it hard to control Harry's excesses: she blanched on one occasion during afternoon tea at Windsor when he said to the Queen, 'Ooooh ... that's a pretty dress,' causing the monarch to blush. Although in normal life it would have been a perfectly reasonable remark for a small boy to make to his grandmother, the Queen is, after all, the Queen. Mrs Powell also blamed herself when Harry, covered in mud from his outdoor frolics, ambushed his formally attired father as he made his way across the lawn to a waiting helicopter of the Queen's flight. The young Prince jumped on Charles's back and yelled, 'Stay put. You're captured,' causing his father to tell his pilot, Commander Barry Kirby, that take-off would have to be delayed while he went back into the house to put on a fresh suit. Life for the Wales family, Mrs Powell complained at one point, was never going to be normal and she was told by a doctor treating her for stress (a common malaise in royal servant circles) that working for them was going to shorten her life. Nevertheless she stayed dedicated to the job for which she was initially paid £3,500 a year – £10,000 in today's money.

There can be no doubt that Harry Wales was born into a dysfunctional family. Apart from excess drinking there were accusations of sexual promiscuity which went as close to the top as it was possible to go. Princess Margaret's home on Mustique was little more than a bordello and her fascination with the private parts of a well-known London villain was the talk of the island. As for her husband, Lord Snowdon, most of the girls who worked in his Pimlico studio thought that he was gay to which he responded: 'I didn't fall in love with boys but a few have been in love with me.' In his 2009 memoir, *Redeeming Features,* leading British interior decorator Nicholas Haslam claimed to have had an affair with Snowdon (then plain Antony Armstrong-Jones) before the latter's marriage to the Queen's sister, and he also alleged that Snowdon had previously been the lover of another interior decorator, Tom Parr.

Although royal scandals abounded during his formative years and he, too, had his moments, Harry learned from an early age that there was much to do if he was to help repair the damage of the past. He was never likely to endorse the adage once expressed by his father: 'I've learned the way a monkey learns – by watching its parents.' Rather, Harry learned much by avoiding the mistakes he had witnessed his parents – and other relatives – making.

As and when Harry becomes a father himself, he is unlikely to put an infant through what I, as a journalist travelling with the royal couple, saw when he was taken to Italy by his parents on his first royal tour in 1985. He screwed his tiny face up in fear at the sight and the noise of the flocks trying to catch sight of the royal couple, but Diana had insisted the trip would help her baby 'get used to the crowds'.

In private, Harry showed his adventurous side from an early age. At just fourteen months he was allowed to share the saddle when William – who learned to ride at the age of three at his father's insistence – rode one of the two ponies Charles had bought him and, showing signs of demanding his own way, Harry threw a tantrum when it was made clear to him that he was too young to handle the horse on his own. To his mother's horror he made his first parachute jump at an early age, leaping from a kitchen table. Alas, his landing was not good and he sustained an injury which required stitches. The staff were sworn to secrecy about the accident; even some of their own team back at Buckingham Palace did not know about it. Harry, however, was proud to display his war wound at the Westminster Abbey wedding of his uncle Prince Andrew on 23 July 1986 and even declared that the jump had made him want to become a parachutist when he grew up. Even the memory of this minor accident would not daunt him when Diana's subsequent lover James Hewitt told him later that the average life of a paratrooper descending into combat was about four minutes. Even at that age Harry Wales knew no fear.

What he did know, however, was loneliness, something he experienced when, in September 1985, William went to nursery school. He wept buckets when he was parted from his brother, whose bed he had often crept into when he had 'bad dreams'. But his time at the same school would soon come.

# 3

# WHO AM I?

'Who am I?' a puzzled Harry asked his father after one of his first days at nursery school. He had himself been asked the question by a fellow pupil at the Notting Hill school, who merely wanted to know his name, but at the age of just three and struggling to integrate with strangers for the first time, Harry had begun to wonder what all the fuss was about whenever he was seen (and photographed) in public. The question moved Prince Charles to sit his younger son down and tell him exactly who he was.

It was a highly emotional encounter since the father had to tell his son that he was two people: to him, Diana and his brother William he was Harry, a much loved little boy who enjoyed playing with his toy soldiers and pretending to help out with the garden at their country home. But to the outside world he was something quite different: he was Prince Henry of Wales, fourth grandchild of Queen Elizabeth II and HRH Prince Philip, Duke of Edinburgh, third in the line of succession (behind his father and his elder brother) to the thrones of sixteen independent sovereign states known as the Commonwealth realms – not just the United Kingdom but Canada, Australia, New Zealand, Jamaica, Barbados, the Bahamas, Granada, Papua New Guinea, the Solomon Islands, Tuvalu, Saint Lucia, Saint Vincent and the Grenadines, Belize, Antigua and Barbuda and Saint Kitts and Nevis. He is also third in line to the position of Supreme Governor of the Church of England. He was always to be addressed as 'Your Royal Highness' and one day he would be a duke as well as a prince.

What he also told him was that his mother came from a family with grander heritage than his own. Charles's ancestral grandmother was a member of the Germanic House of Hanover, which didn't take over the British throne until the succession of George I on 1 August 1714, whereas Diana's family, the Spencers, date back to the 1400s as leading members of the British aristocracy, although they had started out in pre-Tudor times as sheep farmers – something Earl Spencer was reminded of while speaking pompously in the House of Lords. Spencer was interrupted by the Earl of Arundel who said, 'When the things of which you speak were happening, your ancestors were keeping sheep.' To which Spencer retorted, 'Yes, and when my ancestors were keeping sheep, yours were plotting treason.'

Diana's noble family descended in the male line from Henry Spencer who claimed to be a descendant of the cadet branch of the ancient house of le Despencer and the male-line ancestor of the Earls of Sunderland, the Dukes of

Marlborough and the Earls Spencer. In addition to Diana, another prominent member of the family was Winston Churchill, whose family had been linked to the Spencers by the marriage of Charles Spencer, 3rd Earl of Sunderland, to Lady Anne Churchill, daughter of the Duke of Marlborough. Althorp, where Diana is now buried, has been the family seat for 500 years.

Quite a lot for a three-year-old to take in and especially confusing for him when his mother challenged the grand-ness of Charles's proclamation by telling him he was a human being who was growing up in a position to help 'ordinary' boys – something Harry has never forgotten.

The Prince had arrived at 8.50 sharp for the first of his twice-weekly mornings (graduating later to five) in September 1987 wearing blue shorts, a blue polo sweatshirt and carrying a Thomas the Tank Engine school bag over his shoulder. Prior to leaving home he had cried about being separated from his mother despite an enthusiasm to follow in his brother's footsteps. But, placated by his police guard-ian, he dried his tears and grew excited by the waiting crowd of photographers, making faces at them before he stepped inside. Then, anxious to please, he had bounded forward to shake the hand of his headmistress but, following protocol, she reached over his head to shake the hands of his parents,. It was left to his father to pat him on the back and reassure a confused Harry that all was well. He had become accustomed to asking, 'What have I done wrong now?' whenever he was chastised.

Harry started his school life as a Cygnet. His coat peg was marked by a red card simply saying 'Harry', as he was to be known to the other children. The blue work smock hanging from it, however, was labelled Prince Harry. On either side were pegs for classmates Jessica and Beatrice. Harry had a picture of a duck above his peg, Jessica a deer and Beatrice a pen. Other classmates (none of whom are the source of information that follows) include Natasha, Lucy and Alexander von Preussen, who just happened to be the great-great-grandson of the late German Kaiser.

Diana was particularly pleased to see that Harry's classroom had a view of the garden and was decorated with pictures of balloons to illustrate different colours and numbers. There were shelves of games, farmyard toys, play bricks and a stack of children's books. Charles noted that this was a world away from the nursery in which he had spent his infancy. Nearby were classrooms for twenty-four older children – Little Swans and Swans – and the corridor was lined with school activity photographs, including one of the previous year's nativity play with Prince William playing the innkeeper.

Although Harry was showing early signs of being more of an outgoing boy than his brother, the experience of his first school days had clearly unnerved him. Still, the fatherly talk did much to boost his confidence and he went on to sing solo at the school's carol concert that term and to star in its nativity plays, lapping up the applause with which his performance was received.

One subject Charles always avoided, however, was the

unhappy family his sons had been born into. Although Diana did her best to shield her sons from marital tantrums, on the rare occasion he did witness her in a state of distress, her younger son would suffer worrying screaming fits and have to be calmed by his brother. It was of sufficient concern for her to discuss it with the psychiatrist whom she herself was consulting: Diana had to be told more than once that he would 'grow out of it'.

Whereas most of his playmates at Mrs Mynors' school lived in ordinary – if expensive – houses in the Chelsea and Notting Hill areas, home for Harry was the wing of a splendid London palace, built in 1689, where Queen Victoria was born and raised. Some say the Wales's wing was haunted by the ghost of a previous occupant but although Mummy was scared on the rare occasions she had to sleep there alone, Daddy had assured him there was no such thing as ghosts. Meals were usually taken in the nursery unless Diana was around; she would take him down to the kitchen and let him choose what he wanted for tea – fish fingers or beans on toast were the favourites and he delighted in eating them from a table covered in plastic 'so Mummy won't have to have the tablecloth cleaned'. Visitors greeted by the butler Harold Brown would be asked by Harry who they were and if they had to wait for Charles or Diana to appear he would invite them to follow him into the drawing room where his parents kept his favourite gadget – a video recorder used to tape favourite children's programmes he missed when he was at Mrs Mynors' school or travelling with his parents. If he considered them 'special' he would invite them to follow him up the stairs and show them his secret room – the nursery. Even then, Harry was never shy in the company of strangers.

When other children talked about their parents' weekend cottages in the country, Harry could boast about the nursery wing at a mansion estate in Gloucester, Highgrove, with its staff quarters, nine main bedrooms positioned above four grand reception rooms and a view of the spire and tower of Tetbury church as well as a working farm – 'Mummy doesn't have to go to Sainsbury's for our fruit and vegetables, we have our own farm.' Then there was Daddy's famous (though rarely seen) walled garden where Harry could copy his father with a set of toy gardening tools. It was in that garden that Charles and his younger son bonded, often sitting on a bench as the sun set, supping a tot of brandy or, in Harry's case, a plastic cup of orange squash. Halcyon days indeed.

'And who is that man who stands directly outside our play-room all day long?' one boy asked Harry. 'That's my policeman. My brother William has one too and Mummy and Daddy have several.' The boy who had asked the question was one of a handful of Mrs Mynors' pupils who subsequently formed what became known as 'Harry's gang', for he soon proved himself to be a natural leader even in the playground and espe-cially when it came to breaking rules. He also had no qualms about telling his new pals how generous his extravagant mother was: she bought him a child-sized police motorbike costing several thousand pounds – though somewhat less than the £60,000 she paid for a scaled-down Jaguar car for

William one birthday. And each of them got a £1,000 go-kart as compensation after they witnessed a particularly upsetting row between their parents. Their father – who had once been sent back on a family walk by his mother to find a dog lead he had dropped, being told, 'Leads don't grow on trees, they cost money' – was not pleased and pointed out to Diana how it would go down with the parents of one in four children in Britain living in relative poverty, but in her mind it made up for the paternal love her sons seemed to be going short on.

Harry had an easier infanthood than William as a result of an action taken by Charles and Diana before he was born. They had summoned a dozen or so editors to a meeting in an upstairs stateroom at Buckingham Palace. Whenever William was taken to the park, accompanied by nanny 'Baba' Barnes and a detective, the paparazzi would swoop. A curious crowd would gather around the Prince's pushchair and it was at these times that Charles and Diana felt their first-born was at risk from a possible kidnap attempt, even a terrorist attack. If newspapers, particularly the tabloids, stopped buying pictures of William's visits to the park, the paparazzi would move on and focus on another member of the Royal Family. Logical though this sounded to press officer Michael Shea and his royal clients, it was like asking a fox to walk past the open door of a chicken coop. Even if Fleet Street agreed, the paparazzi could still sell every picture to magazines in Europe and the United States.

After a briefing from Shea, the guests were split up into small groups while Charles and Diana 'worked the room' under the vigilant eye of Palace officials. 'If it doesn't stop we'll have to cancel my son's trips to the park,' Diana told one group. 'This would be a pity because I want him to mix with ordinary people. I don't want him to be brought up behind the Palace walls.'

Her voice was soft and well-modulated, not at all strident like most Sloane Rangers, who could easily compete against a combine harvester. Some sentences were punctuated by a nervous giggle. Nevertheless, it was evident that she was ill at ease and painfully conscious of her height, which, at six-foot-plus in shoes, made her very nearly the tallest person in the room. Much of her body language made her seem taller; she hunched her shoulders, hung her head and looked up, eyelashes fluttering, in the same coquettish way that made men swoon. She said in an aside to one of the editors, 'Oh my goodness, they're all so SHORT.'

On the other side of the room, Charles had seized the chance to give his views on intrusion. He became locked in conversation with David Montgomery, then editor of the *News of the World*, and it was apparent to those in earshot that he was becoming angry. Immaculately turned out, his hair neatly clipped and his cheeks glowing pink with the health of the super-fit and very rich, Charles kept his voice, and his composure, under control. But his cheeks turned a brighter shade of pink as he made some strongly held points about the reporting of his marriage. It was the trivia he found most offensive. What he ate for breakfast or what his wife bought when she went out shopping could be of no conceivable interest to anyone. Much to his annoyance, Montgomery listened politely but remained unrepentant. 'People are interested in everything you do,' he told Charles in a soft Ulster accent. 'We give people what they want to read.' The Prince did nothing to hide his annoyance at the response and made it clear to Montgomery that he and his fellow editors were there to listen to his and Diana's concern for their son's safety, not to hear what sounded like a sales pitch.

The experiment worked to a certain extent. There were no more park-walk pictures of William in the British papers and when Harry came along the editors kept to the code of conduct they had more or less agreed to at the Buckingham Palace meeting. To this day he is probably unaware of the crucial meeting his parents called that helped to spare him the fear of photographers instilled in William at a very early age. Still, their presence was enough of a disturbance to him that, when photographed re-entering Kensington Palace, he once used an expletive learned from his mother; Princess Margaret, who overheard the remark, was later to say to Charles, 'That boy should learn some manners or he will never be one of us.'

Despite Diana's generosity, several who knew the family at the time testify that Harry was even closer to his father than William was to their mother. Diana was never keen for either of her sons to risk their later lives with military careers, while Charles listened attentively to his younger son's admiration for the soldiers and their smart uniforms. Father and son sat together for a first viewing of the movie *Zulu*, the story of a small band of British soldiers who defeated thousands of Zulu warriors at Rorke's Drift in South Africa more than a hundred years earlier. Harry had to wait until he was ten before Charles took him to visit the Royal Engineers, one of the regiments involved in the Rorke's Drift campaign, but he never stopped reminding Charles of his promise to do so. The movie, which he watched every time it was shown on television, had sown the first seeds for his ambition to take part in what he considered a courageous adventure.

Furthermore he listened attentively to stories of the heroic war actions of the man Charles admired more than any other, his great-uncle and mentor Earl Mountbatten, Admiral of the Fleet and the last Viceroy of India. Speaking to this author six weeks prior to his death in 1977, Mountbatten had said,

> I do so hope that Charles gets married soon and has one or more sons. I have told him that, and that if and when they arrive he should steer them towards military careers. Serving their country is the best thing the family can do to sustain its reputation as rulers.

❦

With Charles having answered Harry's 'Who am I?' question, the Queen decided it was time she taught both boys something about what it was like to be royal and how to behave in the roles fate had carved out for them. She invited them to have tea with her once a week at Windsor Castle. Her Majesty made the occasions as informal as possible and during walks in the grounds deliberately stopped to chat to estate workers, showing the princes that they should never try to be 'too grand'. Although Charles and Diana were excluded from this regular event, Prince Philip would occasionally join them and lighten the atmosphere by pulling faces and telling reasonably funny stories he made up as he went along. Although they were never allowed to forget that 'Granny' was Queen and this was her castle, the weekly visits offered some relief from the growing tensions at Highgrove.

To the outside world they were the perfect family who had everything, but behind the scenes Charles and Diana were drawing further and further apart. Speaking frankly in the grounds of her Victorian mansion in Wiltshire Lady Tryon said one of the reasons the marriage was falling apart was that

> Diana will not make any effort to share Charles's hobbies or his other recreational pursuits: she makes it clear that she is not interested in fishing or polo, yet she had been more than happy to join him on the banks of the Dee and to cheer him from the edge of the polo field when he was considering asking her to marry him.

It's no wonder the boys enjoyed the calm behind the walls of Windsor Castle so much.

Always an adventurous boy, however, almost from the moment he could walk Harry took to exploring his parents' country estate. Walking hand-in-hand with his brother he would venture to the 900-acre farm Charles had bought to test his conservation theories and the princes would fearlessly chase the cows with sticks. The presence of armed police protection officers nearby ensured the boys were never in any great danger but, one said later, 'Harry was fearless even as a toddler. His mother would want to know how he had acquired the scratches and bruises he picked up on some of these expeditions, but all I could tell her was "boys will be boys".' She would hear that a lot in the years to come, as Harry demonstrated little of the caution his brother displayed. 'Being one of them' was never at the forefront of his mind.

# 4

# THE DIANA INFLUENCE

Harry's serene, pleasant and especially polite nature today owes much to the good manners instilled in him and his brother as small boys by their mother. Diana did a great deal to steer them away from what she considered the arrogant ways of some male members of her husband's family.

Staff at both Buckingham Palace and Kensington Palace remember Harry being particularly taken by his mother's friendly manner towards them and assert that he has followed in her footsteps despite the contrary behaviour of others that he witnessed.

'Diana would often bring William and Harry down to the kitchen to say thank you after a meal they'd enjoyed,' says Darren McGrady who moved from Buckingham Palace to be senior chef at Kensington Palace. 'Fergie – who was always trying to copy her – would do it with Beatrice and Eugenie but it was too late and [it was] so obvious that she was just trying to be Diana. Plus she'd get the names of the chefs wrong.'

On the occasions when Harry was in the royal kitchen with Prince Andrew, he would pull a face if his uncle behaved in a way that he knew Diana would regard as rude. 'Andrew always came straight to the point and [told] you exactly what he wanted,' says McGrady.

Whereas Harry had been taught to say, 'Please may I have…' Andrew would bark, 'Where are my mangos? I want my mangos!' Now there could be twenty chefs in the BP [Buckingham Palace] kitchen at the time and the chances are the one he picked on wouldn't have the faintest idea what he was talking about. His father was the same. Prince Philip would come into the kitchen and have tantrums telling people to 'fuck off' if he wasn't satisfied. […] He had that sort of temperament. Diana made sure her sons did not follow in those footsteps. She was always very polite and caring. At Balmoral she would ask after my family and how much I was missing them while we were up there in Scotland for long periods, and you knew she meant it whereas you got a clear impression that if the others did it they were just going through the motions, that to them we were just servants. I'm not surprised that Harry has turned out to be the same as Diana. She doted on him.

Harry's desire today not to get involved with the media any more than he has to owes much to the chatter and gossip he experienced when he was growing up. The journalist Tim Carrol, who was once sent by a newspaper to McGrady's home in Isleworth to check out a rumour that Diana was having an affair with the cook over candlelit dinners he prepared for her, says that when he expressed surprise at McGrady's candid – albeit negative – responses to his questions about his employer, McGrady replied,

> I didn't do it [break her confidentiality] until she did. She's on the phone to the *Sunday Mirror* every Tuesday morning. We hear her. When a story circulated about an alleged romantic interest in Prince Philip's life whose identity the investigating newspaper was unaware of, Diana said, 'I know who it is. Shall I tell them?'

Carrol used McGrady as a regular source and when McGrady didn't have the information the journalist required, he asked butler Paul Burrell to get the answers. For example, when Carrol phoned to check out a story that Diana might be pregnant again Burrell went to her bathroom and reported back that the Princess had taken her birth control pills right up to date.

If, when growing up, Harry needed any demonstration of his mother's common touch then he witnessed it when a butler named Jarrett died after forty-four years in royal service. The family sent a wreath, but Diana alone attended the funeral service. Two weeks later when the Queen was being served her breakfast by a butler she was not familiar with, she asked, 'Where's Jarrett?' On being reminded that he had passed away the never-unnecessarily-sentimental monarch said, 'Oh yes, of course he did,' and got on with her meal.

The arrival of 'Uncle Ken' in 1986 heralded a new era in Harry's life. Although he was only two, the youngster saw in Inspector Kenneth Wharfe – his and William's new police protection officer – a man who was neither royalty nor of the non-royal kind who would fawn over his parents or, indeed, over any member of the Queen's family. The straight-talking Canterbury-born policeman had joined the Metropolitan Police as a cadet at the age of seventeen and following training with the SAS was selected to join Scotland Yard's elite Royal and Diplomatic Protection Department, SO14. He was not to know that his job would involve far more than guarding the princes and later their mother.

By the time Wharfe was drafted in to protect Harry and William, the younger royal was already showing an adventurous side not seen in his brother. 'You never knew quite what to expect with Harry,' says Wharfe, whose first memory of the three-year-old was watching him trying to pull the stamens from a table display of lilies, managing in the process to bring the antique vase crashing to the ground in pieces while William peacefully played the piano on the other side of the room.

'Oh dear,' said Diana,

Harry's always having accidents, only the other day he was bounding on my bed and somehow managed to crash on to the bedside table. My framed pictures went flying and he even managed to break the glass of two of them. I'm afraid you're going to have to put up with his boisterous behaviour.

As Diana's mother-figure friend Lady Annabel Goldsmith recalls: 'Harry was always the more mischievous of the two.' That's a view reflected by the society interior director Nicky Haslam: 'Harry is obviously fun. He's sort of irresistible in his naughtiness and William seems to be good and rather more serious.'

Wharfe was more concerned for the family's safety than the Prince's 'naughtiness'. To this day Harry recalls being in a car with his mother, waiting to embark on a shopping trip. He heard the police officer instruct her to 'Fasten your seat belt, Ma'am.' 'Oh Ken, do I have to?' was her coquettish response. 'Only if you want the car to move as much as an inch from this spot,' the policeman replied. 'It doesn't go anywhere until everyone is strapped in – and that includes you.'

Wharfe knew that he had a difficult act to follow. Diana had been smitten by his predecessor, Sergeant Barry Mannakee, a married man to whom she turned as a source of emotional comfort when she realised that her husband had resumed his affair with Mrs Parker Bowles. Always a lover of soft toys, Diana gave pride of place on her bed to a brown bear Mannakee had given her. Charles never asked where it came from and she kept it there for a number of years.

Even when the servants were around, Harry's mother made no attempt to hide her warm feelings for the policeman. Once, as she was leaving for a dinner date, Diana wiggled her skintight-miniskirt-clad bottom at him and asked: 'Do I look all right?' Mannakee replied: 'Sensational, as you know you do,' adding, 'I could quite fancy you myself.' Diana giggled and said: 'But you already do, don't you?' A former palace aide confides: 'Everyone noticed that they just clicked. Whenever she had a problem she would go to Barry, always Barry.' The balding policeman had been an unlikely companion on Diana's endless shopping trips. They built up a bond on the Friday night drives from Kensington to Highgrove. 'They called them their M4 chats, after the motorway,' says the aide.

> She used to like his candid conversations. She found it and him very refreshing. Charles was away all the time. William was a toddler, Harry was a baby and she felt she had the weight of the world on her shoulders. She'd look at Barry being brilliant with her children and wonder why Charles couldn't be like that.

Soon Mannakee found himself coping with all Diana's emotional turmoil. On one engagement she threw herself into his arms and sobbed: 'I just can't go on any more. I just can't.' Rumours about the couple quickly spread around royal staff. 'It wasn't just talk, it was a forest fire of gossip about Diana and Mannakee,' said a family friend. 'Prince Charles couldn't just ignore it.' Mannakee was suddenly moved to duties well away from Diana and from that moment they never saw each other again.

Wharfe is certain that Mannakee's departure from Diana's service was brought about by the below-stairs telegraph.

Butlers, staff in general, had ownership of her, inside control. If they wanted to get rid of someone they could. And that's what happened to Barry. She adored him and she would invite him into her drawing room for afternoon tea – an unheard of practice for a senior royal. One servant would tell another and so on and sooner or later it reached [Superintendent] Trimming who, I believe, mentioned it to the Prince and Barry was out before his feet could touch the ground.

Wharfe is convinced, however, that the couple never had a sexual relationship: 'I asked her, "Did you fuck him, Ma'am?" "No," she replied, "you know I would tell you if I had, Ken. Charles got the wrong end of the stick."' That's not what she was later to tell James Hewitt when he asked her where the brown bear on her bed had come from and without hesitation she told him it had been a gift from Mannakee: in *Love And War*, one of the books he penned subsequently, Hewitt writes, 'I said it was a bit of a personal present to get from a bodyguard. She replied very simply, "He was my lover."'

Mannakee was killed in a horrendous accident on 22 May 1987, just eight months after his enforced departure from Kensington Palace. He was riding pillion on a motor-cycle driven by another police officer in Woodford, Essex. Their Suzuki GS400 was struck by a Ford Fiesta driven by seventeen-year-old Nicola Chopp who had pulled out of a side road into their path. Mannakee, a father of two, died instantly. Diana could not control her grief. 'Charles broke the news to her – albeit unemotionally – as they were on their way to France for the Cannes Film Festival,' adds the talkative family friend.

The Princess, in worrying screaming fits, immediately began trying to slash her chest and wrists with her jewellery. Charles did nothing to comfort her. Fortunately her lady-in-waiting was able to rearrange Diana's clothing to cover the cuts, bruises and tears in the fabric, but it was a close thing.

It was the kind of scene Diana, in her more volatile moments, did her best to shield her sons from. She was aware that Harry's screaming fits tended to follow her own low moments and that William was forced to calm his brother more and more.

Harry's distress continued even when he was asleep and he regularly wet his bed as well as suffering dreadful nightmares, even though Diana often slipped into his bed to comfort him. She was all too familiar with what it was like for a young one to suffer marital disharmony: she had cried herself to sleep at a similar age when her own father, the 7th Earl Spencer's son Johnnie, and her mother had screamed, shouted and even punched each other before heading for a bitter battle in the divorce court. Diana had found herself motherless after the then Viscountess Spencer lost custody of her and her siblings after her own mother, Lady Fermoy, sided with her son-in-law.

This was a situation Charles simply could not understand: how could he? If and when his own mother and her consort ever had disagreements they were never in front of the children.

As the rift between husband and wife grew wider, the rows got louder. When the Queen's former press secretary, Michael Shea, said of the couple: 'The only arguments they ever had were over the children,' Charles was heard to retort, 'Huh, the only arguments he was privy to, maybe.'

Diana did everything she could to compensate not just for the marital discord but also for the restrictions royal life necessarily placed upon her boys. There were trips to McDonald's (something Charles disapproved of, saying, 'I would never have been allowed to go to such places'), visits to the cinema ('Why? There's a perfectly good screen at BP and I can ensure you get any films you want'), sitting on Santa's knee at Harrods ('When the store was open to the public, for heaven's sake? What were you thinking of?') and excursions to theme parks where they could scream on thrill rides alongside the rest of the kids.

She could not, however, be with her boys when they were at school, but Ken Wharfe was and she relied on him to keep her up to speed with what went on, particularly with Harry at Mrs Mynors' infant academy. He brought home stories of the mischievous son's activities, which frequently had Diana curling up with laughter. There was the occasion when, during morning assembly, Harry persisted in tugging at the trousers worn by the piano-playing music master, Mr Pritchard. When the teacher finally lost his patience and demanded that Harry stopped pulling his trousers, the young Prince piped up, 'But Mr Pritchard, I can see your willy.'

Wharfe was not the only man to arrive on the scene in 1986, for that was the year Diana met the man who was to change her life – and Harry's: the dashing cavalry officer James Hewitt. It has to be said that Major Hewitt was an instant hit with her younger son. Although he still had his third birthday to come, the young Prince was already showing an interest in all things military, fascinated by 'Granny's soldiers' – as Diana said he called them – and was delighted when after bath time he and William were invited to come downstairs in their dressing gowns and tell 'Mummy's friend' about their day's adventures. But even more he wanted to know about what soldier Hewitt had to tell him about military matters. He had been 'excited' and 'frightened' in equal measure, Diana explained to Hewitt, when a cavalry colonel had bowed and yelled 'Sir' to him at the top of his voice.

Dining with a friend at the Tai Pai restaurant in Knightsbridge in late summer 1986, Diana had been bemoaning the fact that, having produced a second son, in the light of her loveless marriage she faced a stark choice: to enjoy some pleasure with the bankin', shoppin' and dancin' set, or to stay at home and turn into a palace couch potato. Three evenings later she accepted an invitation to a party in St John's Wood; this was the night she and Hewitt first set eyes on each other, contrary to subsequent much-quoted reports.

How Diana would have fretted had she known that her affair with Hewitt would eventually result in Harry serving on the front line of the world's most dangerous war zone. Hewitt claims she told him she would never be able to live with the thought of her sons ever being sent away to war. 'She said it wouldn't be fair to her as a mother,' he records.

> I pointed out that all soldiers had mothers. She was silent for a bit and then said that her sons were special because they were the only men in her life. I asked her how things were with Charles. She looked at me and I could see the pain in her eyes.

One of the first differences Ken Wharfe noticed about the two princes was William's inclination to conform, to obey, in sharp contrast to Harry's need even then to explore beyond the rigid boundaries of royal life. Wharfe recalls that on occasions when the elder boy told his sibling he was doing something he ought not to, Harry would reply, 'I can do what I like because I'm not going to be king. You can't because you are.' Noticing the distinction the two boys were making for themselves, Diana took to calling her second son GKH which she told him stood for Good King Harry.

'Yes, Harry was always the more adventurous of the two,' says Wharfe.

> Even when he was a small boy he showed signs of enjoying danger. He used to come to me in that little camouflage outfit Diana had had made for him – he never took it off – and ask me for 'assignments', saying that soldiers used them so

he needed to know how they worked. On one occasion I lent him a two-way police radio and told him to go and report to his aunt, Jane Fellowes, who lived in a lodge close by, well within the palace grounds. He duly did and radioed in: 'Ken, this is Harry reporting; assignment complete.' I then told him to go to the police officer on the gate and report back to me when he got there, but he didn't. I started to get worried when several times he failed to answer my call. Eventually he came in with the 'Ken, this is Harry' call sign. 'Wow, Harry,' I said, 'where on earth are you?' because I could hear traffic in the background. 'Just a minute while I check,' he said. 'Oh right, I'm outside Tower Records on the high street.' Needless to say my feet didn't touch the ground as I ran to fetch him. He was only doing what inquisitive boys of that age do, but of course Harry was no ordinary boy.

On another occasion Harry was being taught to drive (at no more than seven years old) in his father's Land Rover Discovery. When the lesson was over he demonstrated the kind of obstinacy which more than once had earned him a smacked bottom from his protection officer. Refusing an instruction to step out of the vehicle, he reached over from the front passenger seat and jammed his foot down hard on the accelerator, causing the car to plunge forward and crash into a stone wall. Miraculously there was no discernible damage to the vehicle but, had there been, how could anyone have blamed Harry? After all, as he pointed out later, it was the policeman who was in the driving seat when the accident occurred.

Of the frequent appearances by other men (and one woman) in the Waleses' marital home, Wharfe says that, while William could be circumspect, Harry – who often greeted surprised guests by wearing his American baseball cap back-to-front – was the one who assessed the visitors for their fun factor. And it was James Hewitt who always came top of the pops. By the time Wharfe had been drafted into royal duties by Scotland Yard in September 1986, Diana's affair with Hewitt was already well known and the policeman was urged to be as discreet as possible.

There was never any danger of the boys finding Hewitt in Diana's private suite since their own room was in the attic of Kensington Palace's apartments 8 and 9 and they were never allowed to go downstairs uninvited until their nanny – who was also in on the secret, as was just about everybody who worked at the palace – had made sure the coast was clear. There was one dangerous moment, however, when Harry was exploring his mother's dressing table and discovered a 'piece of treasure'. It was a gold fob watch inscribed with the words 'I will love you always'. 'Is this going to be Daddy's birthday present?' he asked. 'Yes,' she lied.

Harry liked his mum best when she was her normal self and never was the Princess more so than when she took her sons to visit her mother, Frances Shand Kydd, at the whitewashed farmhouse on the remote island of Seil, a few miles south of Oban, where she lived alone. There, when Diana washed up after their meals, Harry insisted on being 'dryer-up' of the dishes. There was no stress and there were no photographers since the visits *chez* Shand Kydd were always kept a closely guarded secret. Harry marvelled at the sight of his mother doing the domestic chores that over-attentive staff would never have allowed her to do in KP or at Highgrove. She even ironed Ken Wharfe's shirts and there was much laughter in the house when doing so on one occasion as the bath towel she was wearing slipped off and she was left standing naked for a few moments in front of her sons and the police protection officer. Harry laughed, William laughed and Wharfe politely turned away as she picked up the towel and re-covered herself.

Harry loved Grandma Frances not only for being 'normal' but also because she brought an atmosphere of calm with her when she came to visit the Waleses at Highgrove: Diana obviously thought the world of her and, despite their early differences, Charles respected Mrs Shand Kydd for not interfering, even though she was well aware of the extramarital goings on in both his and her daughter's life. Harry was especially fond of her for taking him on long walks when she visited, listening to his tales of adventure as they strolled through the countryside. Charles has his late mother-in-law to thank for teaching both his sons that they were human beings first and foremost, and royals second. When the royal yacht *Britannia* sailed close to Mrs Shand Kydd's home, taking the Royal Family to Balmoral where the Queen has spent her summer holiday every year of her life, they would assemble on deck and wave to Frances, who would stand at the edge of her oceanside garden to acknowledge the gesture.

'Oh,' Harry said to his mother one year, 'I wish we were going there for the hols.' Like his mother he was not especially keen on his other grandmother's castle and the formal welcome by its immense staff – seventeen gardeners, five cooks, four scullery maids and the sixty bagpipers who traditionally gave a noisy performance of what was definitely not his kind of music.

Although, through sheer determination, William was more knowledgeable than his brother when he was his age, soon after Harry joined him at the pre-prep Wetherby School the younger boy was reckoned to be the cleverer of the two and was quickly placed in the top group whereas William had to settle for a class with the averages. Harry was a chancer and if he didn't know the answer to a question he made one up and his guesses often proved to be right. Even in the playground he took chances, just as he was to do later in life when he gave no thought to the dangers of going to war. 'We worried about him a little,' says an ex-Wetherby teacher,

because he always did what he wanted with no fear of the consequences. When I warned him about walking in front of oncoming cars, he simply sniffed and said he wasn't bothered because they weren't allowed to knock him down. Has anyone told you about their go-kart adventures when they weren't at school? His mother told me that Harry was a particularly dangerous driver and had many a spill but she just laughed it off and 'made it better' by kissing where it hurt. She got Ken Wharfe to arrange a driving lesson for him from [Formula One driver] Jackie Stewart at Silverstone but, to Diana's amusement, he still went hell-for-leather and inevitably crashed on the bends. Charles eventually put a stop to it, the Queen having complained about the early-morning noise of the screaming engines beneath her bedroom window after, on one occasion, Diana had allowed the boys to take the karts with them for an overnight stay at Windsor. Diana wasn't happy about that. She was all for allowing the boys – especially adventurous Harry – their freedom. I was told later by someone I kept in touch with at KP that she even laughed it off when she heard Harry had had his first few puffs on a cigarette at the age of eight. It can't have pleased his anti-smoking father though and, of course, it led to a life-long habit.

Harry still smokes to this day, although he does his best to avoid doing so when there's a photographer around.

Although Harry's mother continued to be extremely generous to him and his brother (often to Charles's great annoyance), she never hesitated to put on her frugal face when others were spending money. On one occasion, after a shopping expedition to buy 'surprise presents' for the boys in Harrods, she went around the corner to San Lorenzo – the Italian restaurant run by her friend and 'fixer', the motherly Mara Berni. Prince Philip had previously tried to discourage her from frequenting the venue which, he said, he'd been reliably informed was 'over-priced and frequented by show-business hangers-on'. In defiance of his advice she arranged specifically to have lunch with a girlfriend there. Ken Wharfe who, as always, had seen her safely to her table, went back upstairs to maintain his protective stance in the entrance area which doubles as a bar.

Sipping an orange juice, he was informed by a waiter that Diana required his presence in the basement dining room: her friend was running considerably behind schedule and she wanted Wharfe to sit with her at the table. As she ordered her lunch, Ken was offered, and accepted, a bowl of pasta to keep her company. He had barely finished it when Diana demanded, 'And who's going to pay for that?' When Wharfe told her that he would be paying for the £11 starter himself, a suddenly cross Princess declared: 'And you'll put it on your expenses so the taxpayer will be paying!'

Having returned to his post by the upstairs bar, Wharfe was subsequently informed that his charge was ready to leave but did not require the limousine waiting outside for her with chauffeur Simon at the wheel. Instead she wished to go a few doors up the street to Kanga – the exclusive (and highly expensive) boutique owned by her friend, Lady Tryon. She picked out three dresses and asked her ever-present protection officer, 'What do you think of my choices?' Wharfe, somewhat surprised by the thousands-of-pounds price tags, asked on what special occasions she was going to wear them. 'Oh, I'm going to Pakistan with my friend Jemima [Khan],' she replied, adding, 'and there's bound to be one or two meetings with VIPs.' 'Oh,' said Ken savouring the moment, 'so the taxpayer will be paying.'

Diana learned much about penny-pinching from her husband. Once, on his farm at Highgrove, Charles was asked if he would make a small presentation to a policeman who had guarded his precious chickens for a number of years. The Prince grumbled but, sure enough, he was there on the day and made a glowing speech about the member of the constabulary who had done so much to watch over his treasured birds. Then he handed him a reward for his years of service: half a dozen eggs laid by the very same hens. Most of the royals – certainly the old-school ones – believe that they should receive valuable presents but not give them. It's ingrained.

When the Duke of Kent travelled to Poole Harbour to make a presentation he was rewarded by the owner of one boat with a handsome fleece made to his exact measurements. The generous donor had had two others made up to size – one for the Duke's accompanying private secretary and another for his policeman. Alas, the Duke was not happy when he learned he was not getting all three. When the policeman pointed out, 'You can only wear one, sir,' the minor royal replied, 'I know, but they make rather nice Christmas presents.'

Years later, following his departure from her service, Wharfe was photographed by the paparazzi talking to Diana in a London mews after she had spotted him and stepped out of her black Audi for a chat. Wharfe was astonished to see the pictures subsequently used in one newspaper with a headline suggesting the chance meeting was in fact a lovers' tryst. He sued and won damages but when he next saw the fabulously rich Princess she asked him quite seriously for her share. Noticing the surprise on his face she said, 'Well, they libelled me, too, but obviously I couldn't sue, so hand over my half please.'

However, Harry has always been generous and positively despised meanness. He frequently took toys to Wetherby to give to his special friends and was always popular as a result. To this day he donates money, in addition to his time, to charity and when there is a tab to pick up during nights out with his friends, he is the first to grab it.

❦

Harry and William acquired future playmates with the births of their cousins, Princesses Beatrice and Eugenie. Their Aunt Sarah gave birth to both at the Portland Hospital in London, Beatrice on 8 August 1988 and then Eugenie on 23 March 1990, a time when Fergie's marriage to Prince Andrew seemed to be sound. The same could not be said for the Waleses' union. Only days after the Queen had expressed her delight at the arrival of another grandchild, a member of staff walked into a room at Highgrove to discover Charles on his knees picking up broken glass from the floor – he and Diana had had another fight and this time their sons were close enough to have heard the screaming row. A maid, Michelle Riles, had once described the carnage she discovered in Charles and Diana's bedroom (he'd eventually gone to sleep in his dressing room) at Balmoral after what had obviously been a bitter confrontation. The maid (who had a fling with Prince Edward the same summer) said it looked as though the Second World War had just taken place but, fortunately, at that stage there were no children to overhear the fracas. Nor was either boy present in Japan when Diana came down the stairs to attend a reception in a red tartan Catherine Walker dress. She ran back to their suite when Charles told her, 'You look like a British Caledonian air stewardess.'

Harry later made it known to an army colleague that although he was barely five years old, he noticed a distinct change in his mother's mood when Hewitt was posted to Germany and subsequently to the Gulf, but that mood soon changed when she met a new man. It was in the summer of 1989 that Harry reluctantly acquired a new father figure in the form of James Gilbey, who used to refer to him and William (to their horror) as 'the lovebugs'. Harry did not like Gilbey and said he was 'no fun and a bit wet'. With Hewitt out of the country a lonely Diana had accepted an invitation to party with a couple of pedigree chums from the Gilbey and Guinness dynasties. The party was hosted by the former Julia Guinness, daughter of the brewing family. Julia was the sister of one of Diana's *bêtes noires*, Sabrina Guinness, who had had a passionate fling with Charles in 1979 that still rankled with Diana when they bumped into each other at the hairdressers soon after her marriage. 'Somewhat indignantly she asked me, "Is that who I think it is?"' says the hairdresser Kevin Shanley. 'I wish you had told me one of his exes would be here.'

Julia, on the other hand, was extremely popular with the Princess and she was happy to go to her party having been assured that Sabrina would not be there. One of the guests was Gilbey, a member of the Gilbey's Gin family, whose motto was 'Honour and Virtue'. Over a few drinks, Diana shared her troubles with the young motor trade executive. She was helpless and angry, desperately in need of a soulmate and Gilbey was the right man to listen: 'He makes a woman feel special – like she is the only person in the world who matters to him,' she told one confidante.

Gilbey, a darkly handsome Libran who had known Diana in her bachelor days, was shocked by the goings-on Diana revealed about her husband and the wife of Brigadier Parker Bowles, and how anxious she was to protect Harry and William from the looming scandal. Before she returned to the Palace, where her sons were sleeping soundly in the attic, Diana gave him her telephone number and urged him to call. He did and they met several times in the ensuing weeks. It wasn't long before the well-informed photographer, Jason Fraser, was on hand to snap her leaving Gilbey's one-bedroom flat in the early hours of the morning.

Harry, meanwhile was preoccupied with two big events – a party arranged for his fifth birthday on 15 September and his duties as a pageboy at the wedding of Diana's brother Charles to model Victoria Lockwood at St Mary's Church, Great Brington, close to the Spencer stately home Althorp House. The other pageboy was Alexander Fellowes, son of Viscount Althorp's sister, Lady Jane. Determined not to be outdone, Harry sat patiently for a fitting of his outfit, even though at one point he described it as a 'bit girlish'. He especially resented having to wear a dark green hat trimmed with burgundy taffeta and was amused by his mother's annoyance when his nanny had to tell Diana that someone had got his head measurements wrong and was hopeful he wouldn't have to wear it. To his great disappointment, the milliner Marina Killery was able to make some hasty adjustments to the dreaded headgear.

One of the few Diana told about Gilbey was her sister-in-law, the Duchess of York. By now, however, Fergie was having marital troubles herself: her sailor husband wasn't coming home on his shore leave but going to his old quarters at Buckingham Palace or Windsor Castle or spending time with Elizabeth Nocon, the wife of his photographic guru, Gene Nocon. Nevertheless, the Duchess had unexpectedly fallen pregnant with her second child and, working hard to promote her first two *Budgie* books, had little time to listen to Diana's woes. She was also about to embark on an affair of her own with Steve Wyatt, the stepson of American oil tycoon, Oscar Wyatt.

One week before Christmas, Prince Charles made one of the biggest mistakes of his life. Lying on his bed in the early hours of the morning at Eaton Hall in Cheshire, home of his close friend Anne, the Duchess of Westminster, he picked up his mobile phone and called Camilla. It was an X-rated conversation, picked up and recorded by a radio scanner and subsequently broadcast to the world. Charles and Camilla could no longer conceal their secret from the world at large and especially not from Harry and William.

Little more than a week later, Diana was caught in the same trap. It was New Year's Eve and she was at Sandringham with the Queen. Harry and William had been put to bed and her husband was downstairs with the other royals preparing to welcome in 1990. Quite alone, Diana dialled Gilbey's number. Gilbey was travelling to spend the night with friends near Abingdon when the call came through. He pulled into a lay-by on the downs near Newbury to listen as Diana began to pour forth her anguish, never knowing that Harry and William would hear what she had to say: 'I was very bad at lunch and I nearly started blubbing. I just felt really sad and empty and I thought, "Bloody hell, after all I've done for this f***ing family".'

Referring to her affectionately as 'Squidgy' (although he also called her 'darling' fifty-three times), Gilbey indulged in what can best be described as an intimate conversation with his princess, although it did not match the Charles and Camilla tawdry love chat. However, it made interesting listening for radio enthusiast Jane Norgrove, a 25-year-old typist who tuned in using a £95 second-hand scanner in her bedroom, recorded it and made it public, as did a second member of the public who picked it up on a further occasion – perhaps indicating a broadcast by an official source. Some suggest GCHQ might have had a hand, having already leaked the news that Fergie and her daughters had taken a 'secret' holiday to Morocco with Steve Wyatt.

Diana was staying at Balmoral with William and Harry when she was told that the following morning's papers would contain extracts – albeit censored ones – of what became known as the Squidgy tapes. In an effort to escape the inevitable storm breaking around her, Diana took her sons swimming at the Craigendarroch Hotel near the village of Ballater. As she tucked Harry into bed that night she told him that she would be all over the papers and on the television the next morning because someone had leaked the details of a 'silly' conversation she had had with the man she encouraged them to call 'Uncle James' – the name by which they also referred to Hewitt – at a time when she was cross with his father (Buckingham Palace initially tried to claim the tape was a hoax). No one will say how he and William took the news when they eventually were shown an article in *The Sun* head-lined MY LIFE IS TORTURE and read her miserable disclosure to Gilbey about their father: 'He makes my life real, real torture.'

Despite the Gilbey affair, Diana continued to exchange intimate correspondence with the distant Hewitt and, over-looking Harry's protests, took her sons on trips to the Devon home of Hewitt's mother Shirley – where they would have their most intimate letters sent. William remained tight-lipped but Harry said the visits were boring and he couldn't understand why they had to go all that way with their police-man in tow just to pick up some letters. After all, Auntie Shirley was no fun at all.

Harry's first experience of the death of a close relative elicited a strange response in the seven-year-old. Harry was on holiday with his parents and brother in the Austrian ski resort of Lech when news reached Ken Wharfe that Diana's father, the 8th Earl Spencer, had died. Charles had reluctantly agreed to switch their skiing holiday to Lech because she was still traumatised over the death in an avalanche of their friend Hugh Lindsay while skiing near Klosters – Charles's favourite. It had caused another row but Charles eventually gave in because, no matter where Diana would go, he wanted to be with his sons when they learned to ski. He would take them out on to the slopes early, leaving his wife to breakfast and gossip with her friends Kate Menzies and Catherine Soames in the restaurant of the five-star Hotel Arlberg.

Although he had been unwell for some time, Earl Spencer's death from a heart attack at the Brompton Hospital in South Kensington on 28 March 1992 was unexpected. Rumours the previous day that he had died were dismissed as nonsense by the family but proved to be startlingly prophetic. Who was going to tell Diana? Charles had received the news but was adamant that he was not the man to break it to her so the task was delegated to Wharfe. 'She was calm at first,' records Wharfe in his memoirs *Closely Guarded Secret*. 'She had not expected it, nobody ever does, however much they may have readied themselves for bad news. But before long her eyes filled and tears began to stream down her face.'

Charles did break the news to his sons, who had both been extremely fond of their maternal grandfather, but after some minutes of silent contemplation, always relaxed Harry was to ask, 'Does this mean we can't go skiing today?' The seven-year-old was focused – as he remains to this day – on what was to happen in the hours ahead. Grandpa Spencer had passed away yesterday.

In some ways it was a relief that Earl Spencer was no longer around to witness the painful scandals involving his daughter and son-in-law which were about to explode via the world-wide media. His grandchildren, however, were and it was never going to be easy for them. In September 1992, Harry was sent away to Ludgrove, an independent preparatory boarding school for 200 boys aged from seven to thirteen situated in the quaintly named parish of Wokingham Without, near the Berkshire town of Wokingham and close enough for Diana to collect him should he become the subject of too much ridicule as a result of the headlines she was now making daily. The headmasters Gerald Barber and Nichol Marston, as well as Barber's wife Janet found it necessary to assure Diana they would do all in their power to maintain his happiness 'in these difficult times'; but it was going to be no easy task.

It was on his first day at Ludgrove that Harry met the boy who would become his very best friend, Henry van Straubenzee. The two (along with William and Henry's elder brother Thomas) forged a close bond, often spending weekends at each other's houses and holidays together at a cliff-top house near Polzeath in north Cornwall. Thomas taught Harry and Henry to surfboard and they played French cricket on the nearby sandy beach. The Vans, as they were known, also stayed at Highgrove and Kensington Palace with their royal pals and even joined them on Mediterranean cruises when Prince Charles had the use of John Latsis's super-yacht, the *Alexander*. Apart from William, Harry had never had a friend as close as Henry van Straubenzee and, although he missed his mother's bedtime tales and his father reading him stories, the friendship made life a lot easier.

By this time, Harry had become a keen lover of fiction, in particular horror stories. One of his favourite books was C. S. Lewis's *The Lion, the Witch and the Wardrobe*, and he later starred in a student stage production of the tale. It soon became apparent that Harry's enjoyment of an audience was the start of an attention-seeking lifestyle. Unlike his brother he showed a liking for public adulation and a desire for fame. No wonder Harry was destined to become the life and soul of every party he went to.

Although he struggled in many of his academic classes at Ludgrove, he excelled at sport, not surprisingly because the school had an excellent sporting reputation having been founded exactly 100 years earlier by Arthur Dunn, the noted footballer of his day, who was then succeeded by two England international football captains: G. O. Smith and William Oakley. The well-known cricketer Alan Barber had been headmaster in the years preceding Harry's arrival.

Although by now he was enjoying his schooldays, Harry looked forward to short breaks with his father and was particularly pleased when he and William were invited to join a shooting party with Charles and the children of sixteen of his friends at Sandringham for a few days in November 1992. Diana, however, had other ideas: she made it clear that she didn't want to go and had her own plans: she was going to take her sons to spend those days with the Queen at Windsor. The argument went backwards and forwards through private secretaries until Diana took her lawyer's advice and wrote a letter saying that she did not feel the atmosphere at Sandringham would be conducive to a happy weekend for her sons. What she meant was that she did not wish them to spend time in the company of Camilla who would almost certainly be there.

That was it, Charles decided. He'd had enough of her game-playing and it was time to call it quits publicly. He informed his mother but, at the time, she was distraught by the millions of pounds' worth of damage caused by the fire that had devastated large sections of Windsor Castle. Its most ancient parts built by William the Conqueror in 1066, it was the favourite of her residences and had been in constant use throughout the ages. Diana and her tantrums would have to wait.

But not for long.

# 5

# GETTING THE NEWS

In 1992, Harry Wales was already at his desk for the morning's school work at Ludgrove when he was told his mother was on her way to see him. Fellow boarder William had already been informed. This was serious. Diana never paid them surprise visits. Both boys were already waiting in a private study room when the Princess arrived. She was nervous and constantly stroked her handbag arm as she waited for the master who had conducted her to the room to excuse himself and leave, firmly closing the door behind him.

She began by telling her sons that there was to be an announcement the following day, a very sad announcement. The Prime Minister was to inform Parliament and thereby the nation that she and their father were going their separate ways. The dream marriage was over.

Though it did not come altogether as a surprise, William took the news badly. He cried and promised her his undying support and Diana cried too, assuring him that despite their differences she and her father still loved each other.

Always the more soft-hearted of the two, in a way William became her partner in sadness, and it has to be said that she unloaded her troubles on him somewhat, which surely did the boy no favours. When she told him that she expected to be stripped of the 'Her Royal Highness' tag once the marriage was officially ended, more tears poured down his cheeks as he told her, 'Don't worry, Mummy, I'll get it back for you when I am king.' Harry didn't care too much about such things. He recalls his mother saying that when the Duke of Edinburgh once told her that if she didn't behave they would remove her title, she had replied, 'My title is a lot older than yours, Philip.'

As a measure of his love for a woman he called his 'second Mum', Harry went to his room, sat down at his desk and wrote a heart-breaking letter to the nanny he called Granny Nanny – Olga Powell – explaining to her in the straightforward manner that was becoming his style, what was going on. Not a woman known to shed tears easily, Mrs Powell said she wept for a day when she received the letter and never failed to cry when she read it again and again.

Despite his tender age, Harry was far more philosophical about the situation than his brother. As Paul Burrell puts it, 'he was far more outgoing and pragmatic'. Diana wasted no opportunity to tell her friends at the height of her troubles that Harry would see no problem in 'taking on the job' and that she considered her younger son was far more suitable to be king than the elder one. Having named him Good King Harry, in order to placate a young boy envious of his brother's ultimate destiny, she was now suggesting that he actually should become monarch. He was strong enough, she felt, to cope with the traumatic episode that was about to affect all of their lives. William, she feared, would be damaged by it, perhaps for life: '[William] doesn't want to be king and I worry about that. He doesn't want his every move watched,' she said. During a flight home from visiting soldiers in Germany, one seated close to them says he clearly heard Diana ask Harry how he would feel if he had to take William's place and be the next king. After a few moments of uncharacteristic deep thinking, the young Prince replied, 'I shall be King Harry. I shall do all the work.'

Proving the stronger of the two in many respects, Harry asked Charles repeatedly if there was anything he could do to 'make Mummy and Daddy happy again' even though Diana had told him as well as others that there were times when she could not even bear to be in the same room as his father.

So that they could see the confirmation of the end of their parents' relationship for themselves, Harry and William were asked to join their headmaster Gerald Barber in his study to watch the then Prime Minister John Major announce the couple's official separation to a hushed House of Commons on 9 December 1992. Diana, who remained indoors at Kensington Palace that day, smiled when she heard Major deny there was any plan for them to divorce since she and Charles had already decided dissolution was inevitable once the public had accepted that they were no longer living together. Diana was furious, however, when she learned that Charles had gone alone to see the Prime Minister to discuss the divorce; he was in fact following protocol to resolve constitutional issues which did not affect his wife. (Diana later complained that Major offered her ambassadorships by way of consolation, but always failed to deliver; she had been inspired by the good works being done by then President Clinton's wife Hillary, with whom she lunched at the Washington home of Katharine Graham in 1994.)

In truth, both boys had come to realise that the end was near when Charles and Diana whisked them off for what turned out to be a disastrous cruise on a yacht belonging to the self-made (and generous) Greek shipping billionaire John Latsis, a man who had befriended Charles many years earlier. It was far from a happy holiday. Diana had gone only under duress, having given in to a plea from the Queen to give the marriage one last try. But such was the depth of her anguish that after one blazing row with her husband she went missing, sparking fears she might have jumped overboard. It was Ken Wharfe who found her hiding under the tarpaulin cover of one of the ship's lifeboats. She was weeping uncontrollably and it took Wharfe some time and many consoling words to persuade her that Harry and William needed her even if her husband didn't. Suicide was not an option. Made aware of what had happened, William took himself to an area of the ship where he could be alone; it was Harry who gave her strong comfort and did his best to assure her that he hoped they could still be a family.

Harry telephoned his mother three days after the parliamentary announcement and asked her if she would come back to Ludgrove to have tea with him and William. To his delight she agreed and took the opportunity to meet with their teachers to talk about something other than separation and divorce – their educational performance. To her disappointment she learned that, despite his brilliant start at the school, Harry had begun to slip back, showing little interest in several of the subjects he was being taught. She took her son to one side and told him that they still had more, much more, than most people. Determined to prove her point she subsequently took them to a shelter in Westminster to which she was in the habit of paying unpublicised visits. Sister Bridie Dowd took them through to meet a number of the homeless men who took refuge there. The boys stayed for almost two hours talking to their new 'friends' – one of whom showed them some card tricks – and they promised to call again. Diana's experiment to show her sons that the rich and famous they mixed with were only a small proportion of the world's population had worked and they never forgot it.

Harry, more than William, quickly grew to accept his family's situation and in many ways maintained an even closer relationship with his mother than he had prior to the break-up of her marriage. During the Christmas of 1993, he and William had a party at Bill Wyman's Sticky Fingers restaurant on Kensington High Street. Using his mobile phone Harry called Diana to say what fun they were having. She was attending with Charles (although neither spoke to the other) the annual Kensington Palace staff Christmas dinner at Simpson's-in-the-Strand. Before Harry was halfway through telling her what he had phoned to say, she said, 'Stay there, I'll be right over,' and immediately left the grand restaurant to be where she knew she would be more welcome and wanted – the former Rolling Stone's burger bar on the other side of the West End.

She fought hard to have Harry and William stay with her at Kensington Palace for Christmas but her in-laws would not hear of it. The young princes had to join the traditional royal celebrations at Sandringham but although William knew the Queen had to be obeyed, Harry tried to defy the royal decree and urged his mother to go ahead with her yuletide plans – she had already bought tickets for the three of them to go to the pantomime at the London Palladium. By now under severe pressure, she agreed to go to Sandringham but stayed just twenty-four hours before flying to New York where, she said, the people were more friendly. Harry was desperate to go with her but she was obliged to leave him with his father for the rest of the holiday. Two days after Christmas he went missing and was eventually found in a wood on the Sandringham estate. Between sobs he told the estate worker who found him that he was missing his mother.

One of the more controversial developments of the split was that Charles hired, at a salary of £18,000 a year, a new nanny for the boys while they were in his care – 27-year-old Alexandra Legge-Bourke (known as Tiggy), the daughter of a former Royal Guards officer turned merchant banker, William Legge-Bourke. Her mother, the Hon. Shân Legge-Bourke, was, along with her sister Victoria, lady-in-waiting to Princess Anne. This was no motherly Cockney professional child minder who liked a tipple, but an aristocrat in her own right who could and would stand up to Diana – they had both learned the rules of life at the same Swiss finishing school (Institut Alpin Videmanette). In turn Diana insisted on retaining Olga Powell for when the boys were with her. The Princess was never fond of Tiggy and found every opportunity to criticise her – not least when she learned that the new helper had allowed Harry puffs on the cigarettes she constantly smoked in his presence. When she saw a photograph taken on the ski slopes of Klosters of Charles giving Miss Legge-Bourke (whom he had known for many years) an affectionate kiss, she told a friend: 'Huh, he's never been known to kiss Olga.' That single kiss led to a rancorous feud between the two women. It began with gentle mocking. Diana told Harry: 'You know why she's called Tiggy, don't you? It's after the Mrs Tiggy-Winkle character invented by Beatrix Potter. Isn't that funny?'

It got worse, much worse. Coming from a rich land-owning family, Legge-Bourke was reported as saying she gave them, 'What they need at this stage – fresh air, a rifle and a horse. She [Diana] gives them a tennis racket and a bucket of popcorn at the movies.' According to Diana, the nanny her husband had hired against her wishes took the princes on a two-day visit to her parents' home in Wales. During the trip she took them to the Grwyne Fawr reservoir in Monmouthshire, allowing Harry to abseil without protective headgear, any advanced training or even the necessary permit, headfirst down the 160-foot dam wall that was holding back 400 million gallons of water. The incident was photographed by a passer-by and his picture ended up on the front page of the *News of the World* under the headline MADNESS! Another photograph circulating at the time showed Harry on the Queen's Balmoral estate shooting rabbits through the open roof of a moving car with Tiggy at the wheel, a cigarette dangling from her lips. One report Diana received suggested that Harry had been seen driving down the lanes of Balmoral with Tiggy smoking in the back seat, but the Princess could not prove this. Furthermore, she was speechless when she learned from Ken Wharfe – who severely admonished the boy for the offence – that during a scheduled flight Harry had placed his hand down Tiggy's top to touch her breasts. It didn't help matters when Diana was assured that Tiggy had laughed it off, saying: 'Boys will be boys; I suppose he's got to learn.'

That incident actually caused a blistering row between Tiggy and her normally supportive employer, Prince Charles. Although hurt, she soon recovered whereas Harry was angry at his father for 'picking on her' and refused to talk to him for days.

Under Tiggy's free-spirited guidance, Harry became even louder and more self-confident while William retreated further into his shell. Harry and Tiggy would have pillow fights and engage in mock battles on the sofa. This woman was fun and despite his young age Harry clearly had a crush on her. He did everything he could to impress Tiggy which was just what Charles had wished for when he told her that he wanted them to enjoy their young lives in a way that he had never been allowed to, although he did warn her to be cautious when anyone likely to report back to Diana was around.

And what a sound piece of advice that turned out to be for when she saw, or at least thought, that she was losing her sons – especially Harry – to the boisterous, fun-loving, if slightly unorthodox, Sloane, Diana reportedly composed a set of rules: 'Miss Legge-Bourke will not spend unnecessary time in the children's rooms. She may not read to them at night, nor supervise their bath time or bedtime. She is to carry out a secretarial role in the arrangement of their time with their father [and] that is all.' In another she instructed: 'Miss Legge-Bourke is to stay in the background on any occasion when the boys are seen in public. She is neither to be seen with them in the same car, nor to be photographed close to them.' Apparently Charles told Tiggy to ignore the eccentric instructions.

But it was that ski-slope kiss in 1995 that festered in Diana. She became convinced that the new royal employee was having an affair with the man she was still married to – a view confirmed in her mind when she saw Tiggy wearing a diamond fleur-de-lis brooch of the kind that Charles had given to previous girlfriends. Diana had one herself. Things came to a head at the Christmas party for St James's Palace staff in the Lanesborough on Hyde Park Corner. Flushed with the success of a trip to New York where she had received the Humanitarian of the Year award from the United Cerebral

Palsy Foundation and made a triumphant speech declaring 'Today is the day of compassion', she bore down on Tiggy and said in as sarcastic a voice as anyone can remember her ever using: 'Hello Tiggy, how are you? So sorry to hear about the baby.' The insulted nanny fled the room in tears and returned to the safety of Kensington Palace where she could be with Harry and William.

The implication that Tiggy – who Diana referred to as 'the woman who looks like a man' – had aborted a child fathered by the heir to the throne was a serious sign that Diana was losing it. As for Tiggy, the following morning she decided she had had enough: she instructed libel lawyer Peter Carter-Ruck to write to the Princess's law firm, Mishcon de Reya, accusing her of circulating 'malicious lies which are a gross reflection on our client's moral character'. The Queen's private secretary Robert Fellowes wrote to Diana telling her that the allegations against Tiggy were completely unfounded – on the date of the implied abortion the nanny was at Highgrove looking after Harry who, despite his tender years, could have been called as a witness against his mother had the case gone to court. Diana was furious but she wasted no time in settling, telling one close to her, 'The bitch can have all the money she wants, but never my sons. I gave birth to them, they belong to me.' For his part, Charles took steps to ensure that Olga Powell was back in overall control and despite her stern nature and their affection for Tiggy, Harry and William were glad that that war at least was over. The row between people they were both so fond of had disturbed them deeply.

Harry, however, was particularly upset by another very public episode. With ever increasing paranoia, Diana realised that the family now thought of her as the enemy and Tiggy, the woman she regarded as her own most bitter rival, as a friend. Despite settling with the nanny, her façade was beginning to crack and, far from seeing her as an enemy, the Queen described Diana to a regular companion as 'not a well woman'. Her Majesty's insight had already been proved when just five days after the twelfth anniversary of her wedding, Diana had taken Harry and William to see *Jurassic Park*. When photographer Keith Butler snapped their picture as the trio left the Empire cinema in Leicester Square, she dashed up to him and, standing on tiptoe to confront the six-foot-three-inch-tall cameraman, screamed: 'You make my life hell.' Passers-by gazed in amazement at the sight of the Princess of Wales, fetchingly dressed in black blazer and silk trousers, brushing tears from her eyes as she stormed off down the street ahead of her sons and their detectives. The mask had slipped. Butler, one of the paparazzi's shrewdest operators, had crossed the line; he admitted later that 'she was clearly very distressed', but evidently failed to recognise that he was the cause of her vexation that night.

Diana retreated to Floors Castle, the Scottish home of the Duke of Roxburghe, where her old friend Willie van Straubenzee was staying. When the press followed, her fury returned. Once the Queen learned about the Leicester Square incident and the fact that Harry had burst into tears and even screamed at the sight of his mother's anger, she telephoned

Diana and insisted that she return and seek help for her public display of anger, however righteous it was. The two women had kept each other at arm's length since Diana spent what turned out to be an innocent night at Gatley Park, the home of the Lord Lieutenant of Hereford and Worcester, Thomas Dunne and his wife Henrietta. The Dunnes had not been in residence as they were away shooting, but their son Philip was at home. And Diana, although separated, was still very much married to Charles, who had his reservations about Diana's apparent attraction to the dark and handsome merchant banker. Her Majesty had a long memory and recalled previous incidents reported to her by royal protection officers, including the time Diana disappeared from Highgrove for an entire weekend and couldn't be traced. The monarch had been particularly disturbed by reports that during an official visit to Portugal with Charles she had flirted with both Prime Minister Aníbal Cavaco Silva and President Mário Soares.

During earlier disagreements between the Queen and Diana – the latter of whom had the previous year threatened to walk out once Harry started boarding school – Diana had stood her ground but this time she knew Her Majesty would not tolerate any argument. The Queen more or less ordered Diana to seek further therapy. The Princess obeyed and for a time it appeared to work. Encouraged by her American pal, Lana Marks, she set about an amazing PR operation to demonstrate to the world that she was not the broken woman who had caused such a much-publicised scene in public, but one very much in charge of her life in general and her sons in particular. She took Harry and William, along with Mrs Powell, on holiday to Nevis, an exotic island in the eastern Caribbean, one of the sixteen sovereign states that make up the Commonwealth to which both boys are heirs to the throne.

It was Ken Wharfe who had suggested Nevis after he had ruled out her first choice, drug-swamped Jamaica, as being too high a security risk. On a reconnaissance visit to Nevis he had discovered the Montpelier Plantation Inn owned by an English couple, James and Celia Milnes-Gaskell. The first few days of the holiday were idyllic: intricate arrangements had been made to ensure that no one – particularly the press – knew where the Princess and her princes had gone and they were able to sunbathe and swim from a deserted beach watched over by Wharfe and three other Scotland Yard policemen, each armed with a Glock self-loading pistol. The Milnes-Gaskells reckon it was one of the happiest times in Diana's life, a time when she strongly re-bonded with her sons.

Harry, nevertheless, preferred to spend as much time as he could at the nearby (and larger, much to Diana's annoyance) beach house occupied by their police protectors. Encouraged by them to find diversions from what he considered to be his mother's girly company, he was the one who came up with the idea of the Nevin Giant Toad Derby. With the help of his brother and the Milnes-Gaskell children he managed to capture a dozen of the creatures and then, having selected the most athletic-looking toad for himself, invited the adults to place bets on the others. He made quite a few dollars that day and it gave him an entrepreneurial sense that continued to develop and, in later years, would influence his choice of friends.

Soon after her return Diana took Harry and William to Thorpe Park, the adventure centre in Surrey to which she had introduced them two summers earlier as her shaky marriage continued its helter-skelter descent. But on this later occasion she was a changed woman: Daredevil Di, wet hair slicked back as she thundered down the rides in black trousers, leather jacket and suede ankle boots. 'This,' she said 'is what the boys need – especially my danger-loving Harry!' While other pleasure-seekers had been astonished to find the royal trio in their midst, the half-dozen freelance photographers and a television crew showed no such surprise, having been tipped off in advance. Harry, clad in jeans and bomber jacket waved to them as he shot down Thunder River getting soaked in the process. One photographer, particularly familiar with the trio, said it had been made clear to him that this was a major PR exercise:

I don't want to risk money-in-the-bank jobs by ratting on my source. Let's just say no one from Thorpe Park had told me they would be there and Diana wasn't surprised to see me and the other snappers. Harry seemed to know exactly what it was all about and played his part to perfection.

The PR operation was far from over: the following day Diana took her sons to lunch in Knightsbridge at San Lorenzo on

Beauchamp Place, a short thoroughfare of bijoux shops in Knightsbridge where her friends, the Italian owners Mara and Lorenzo Berni, made her feel nothing if not wanted, needed and loved, and once again the forewarned paparazzi were there in force. Despite the mischievous spring in her step as she approached the restaurant, Diana, dressed in a figure-hugging navy blue suit with a skirt short enough to be called eye-catching, paused at the doorway with her sons, both smartly dressed in jackets and ties. All three displayed broad smiles for the photographers (although, according to the waiter who served them, Harry's briefly turned to a frown when he was told that fish fingers were not on the menu). Diana had clutched the hand of each son as she descended the nine stairs to the basement level, aware that all eyes were on her. As she made her way to her usual table beneath the potted palms she made a point of pausing to greet those she knew and to make sure Harry and William cheerily acknowledged them too – especially the photographer Terry O'Neill, of whom she was particularly fond: 'How are you today, Terry? Did you enjoy the motor racing?' – a reference to their last encounter at Donnington Park a few days earlier. She and the boys were warmly greeted by Mara. On this one occasion the trusted owner knew not to hand her the personal mail that Diana had regularly delivered to the restaurant – she did not trust the Palace postal system with intensely private items. Lana Marks had done her work well. The year 1993 may have been Her Majesty's *annus horribilis* II (Andrew, her favourite son had acrimoniously separated from his wife

Sarah Ferguson) but Diana was determined to make it a recovery year for herself, a year in which she would happily withdraw from public life, declaring, 'Being a princess isn't all it's cracked up to be.'

It had been four months since the Prime Minister announced the official separation of the Prince and Princess of Wales, and his suggestion that Diana could still rule as queen since one day her son would be king had disappeared into the mists of antiquity. But Diana knew that, barring a divorce, there was still a possibility of it happening. Queenship was something she had been prepared to sacrifice to gain her freedom from the nightmarish life she had lived as a royal. As Mara Berni was to say later, 'Charles did choose right. He chose the perfect future queen. The trouble was that, unlike other royal wives, Diana was not prepared to look the other way while he two-timed her. I feel so sad for those boys, especially Harry who in my opinion is the more vulnerable of the two.'

Diana had declared, 'I'm just myself.' That was a statement that earned her brownie points from many but was not enough to silence her critics once the Squidgy tapes of her conversation with Gilbey, with whom she had frequently sat at the same San Lorenzo restaurant table, had exploded the convenient myth of 'Shy Di'. Nevertheless she was carefully changing every aspect of her life which failed to comply with her new image, even to the point of having speech therapy so that she would sound, as well as appear, more confident. Harry said to her on one occasion, 'Why are you talking like

that?' Even at his tender age he had noticed that the whin-
ing accent on the Squidgygate tape – heard by millions via a
playback telephone line *The Sun* had helpfully installed – was
in the process of disappearing. She didn't tell him that she
had been receiving the speech therapy as part of the improve-
ment agenda. The new accent, a cross between *Howards' Way*
and *Howards End*, added a modern, composed touch to her
outwardly calm exterior.

The difference in her was as clear to see as it was to hear
and the San Lorenzo diners made an adequate preview audience for yet another facet of her performance as a liberated
woman. 'She took everyone's breath away,' says Terry O'Neill.
'She looked so beautiful; she looked a million dollars, she was
radiant – and she knew it.' Under the watchful eye of Ken
Wharfe – who had been reinstated at Diana's insistence after
being removed when it was established that he had set up
rendezvous between her and Gilbey – her sons, the perfect
extras for such an occasion, ate a hearty lunch aware that
their mother was as happy as they had ever seen her. It was
the perfect way to spread the word that, whatever else was
wrong with the Royal Family, Diana was in sparkling form
and Harry and William were the loves of her life.

After the jolly lunch the young princes flew to Balmoral
to join their father for what remained of the Easter holiday,
leaving Diana to begin a new chapter in her social life. It
might have been the end of her royal life but for her sons
it was just the beginning of theirs. In August 1995, at the age
of just ten, Harry undertook his first official engagement

attending the fiftieth anniversary of VJ Day at the Cenotaph, proudly saluting officers in the military parade. It was one of the most important ceremonies in the royal agenda and his father had made him acutely aware of Lord Mountbatten's part in it, to the extent that Harry even passed on to a school chum Charles's disgust that President Clinton had referred to it as 'The End of the Pacific War'. How proud Mountbatten would have been of this boy.

Harry was so excited about the prospect of his role in the ceremony and so impressed with the event when it happened that he paid no attention to a new friend who had emerged in his mother's life – the eminent heart surgeon Dr Hasnat Khan, who might have become his stepfather had circumstances transpired otherwise. Diana originally met Khan in Australia in 1989 but it was six years later that she fell for him during a chance encounter in a lift at the Brompton Hospital where she was visiting a sick friend. As they stepped away from the lift she told her companion Susie Kassem, a retired magistrate and hospital visitor, that she thought he was 'drop dead gorgeous'. On several occasions she tried to phone him but when he did not take her calls she began to write to him at the hospital and, although a modest man who shunned the limelight, he finally agreed to meet her. Paul Burrell would be sent to pick him up from The Anglesea Arms, a pub close to the hospital, and transport him in the boot of his car to Diana's quarters at Kensington Palace.

It was the beginning of the end of the Princess's affair with James Hewitt and Harry was not pleased. Hewitt was a soldier, Hewitt was fun. The Pakistani doctor was pleasant and polite but he was no brave warrior, no role model. Aware that Khan did not meet with her younger son's approval, Diana played it low key. He and William were not invited downstairs to the Kentucky Fried Chicken meals she sent out for and she certainly did not tell her sons that she had asked a friendly Catholic priest they knew as Father Tony if he was prepared to secretly marry her and the Muslim doctor – a request that was turned down in no uncertain manner. They did not breakfast with Khan on the occasions he stayed overnight at the Palace and Diana had to leave early for engagements. To her he was 'Mr Wonderful'; to them he was 'the doc' – or sometimes something ruder although they never said it to his face.

Meanwhile, Harry was facing a problem of his own: he was about to be separated from his best pal. William was off to Eton and he would be alone at Ludgrove for the next two years. The worry did not stop him mischief-making, however. There was no other suspect when an American woman visiting Highgrove accepted a pint of beer and discovered halfway down it that she had swallowed a goldfish.

Meanwhile, Diana was once again becoming distracted. Falling deeper and deeper in love with Khan, she did everything possible to get him to make the relationship permanent: 'She was very much in love with him,' says her friend Rosa Monckton. 'She hoped they would be able to have a future together. She wanted him to marry her.' But the dedicated surgeon, in fact, had no wish to join the royal circus – for him it was a very private affair. Or so he thought. Khan was furious when he discovered later that reports of their 'secret' romance had been the result of his telephone being hacked: 'I feel as if I've been robbed,' he said, after police told him that his name and phone number were eventually found in paperwork uncovered during the Operation Weeting hacking inquiry. He stated later that the Princess told him it was nonsense to suggest Prince Charles resumed his relationship with Mrs Parker Bowles only after their marriage foundered irrevocably: 'Diana had every reason to believe that Charles and Camilla never stopped seeing each other,' he says. Although she desperately wanted to become Mrs Khan she knew it was impossible because she could never have taken her sons to live in Pakistan, even though she had visited Khan and his parents there and began to study the Koran. Torn between her lover and her boys, she made the most painful decision of her life, arranging to meet the doctor in Battersea Park for what turned out to be their final encounter. 'When she came back to Kensington Palace she was streaming with tears,' says one close to her.

When Harry saw her red-faced he was desperate to know what had happened, but all she could do was hug him. She was sobbing her heart out when her hairdresser Natalie Symons arrived on the morning after the break-up and discovered the Princess had not even applied her mascara – always her first task of the day.

Now Harry was showing signs of increased anxiety and, while a marriage counsellor might have been a more suitable expert to guide a mother through this emotional maze, Diana poured most of her troubles out to the psychiatrist she had been seeing through the early days of her marriage. He warned her of the damage all this confusion could be doing to her sons:

> I told her this would not be good for them, particularly for Prince Harry, who was already a fighter, and that this might well affect him in later years. I never met her younger son but from what she told me he was already starting to rebel. She said he loved his father and admired James Hewitt but it was obvious from what she told me that when other men came along he started to get not just confused but angry and she was especially worried that Harry was showing signs of the kind that lead in adult life to aggression and addictions of various kinds.

Alone at Ludgrove after William had left for Eton, Harry received another surprise visit from his mother. He was playing football when she arrived and sat alone on the sidelines until the game was over. The two went for a walk. 'What now?' he thought, remembering her previous 'surprise' visit when she had brought the dreaded news of her separation from his father. She wanted him to know that she had given an interview to Martin Bashir for a special edition of

*Panorama* which would be shown on television the following week. Harry groaned: already sad about the loss of his brother's companionship, he now faced the prospect of his mother pouring out the troubles of her marriage to the world. Although he was only eleven he could see that she was opening up all the old wounds he thought had begun to heal. She asked him to watch the programme as it would explain many of the things he had not been able to understand – hurtful things.

Like William in his room at Eton, Harry did watch the programme and, according to one in whom he confided the following day, he certainly did not enjoy it, although he blamed Bashir for asking 'such personal questions' on a television programme broadcast globally. His mother, however, held nothing back about her own infidelity as well as that of her husband. While William listened in silence twenty miles away, Harry, according to a Ludgrove teacher who sat with him through the transmission, grew ever angrier as Bashir grew increasingly intrusive and the Princess responded beyond the interviewer's wildest hopes. Both boys learned things they would never have imagined possible. Did their mother really make herself vomit because of their father's behaviour with 'Auntie PB' as they called Camilla at that stage? Did the people really believe she was stupid because she hadn't passed any O levels and that she was as thick as a plank? Did Daddy's friends really say that she should be put in a home for unstable people because she was 'a basket case'? Had she really never met Andrew Morton, whose book she had told them was very unfair? Was she really having an affair with 'Uncle James' [Hewitt]? Had she lied to them that AIDS patients were suffering from cancer?

The red-headed Prince stormed from the room angrily. Mummy really had never told them much of this and, according to a friend of Camilla's, he said she shouldn't have told the world. He loved his Mummy, but he loved his Papa too. When it was over, sensitive William just sobbed. The Queen was absolutely livid – her family was falling apart. Her sister Margaret had divorced Lord Snowdon, Princess Anne had dumped Mark Phillips and Prince Andrew's marriage to the former Sarah Ferguson was falling apart. 'Do the younger generation have no discipline?' Her Majesty was heard to say.

And why had his mother spoken out in the most public manner possible when constantly claiming that she wanted more than anything for her private life to be kept that way: private? Lady Tryon said it was Diana's obsession with the media (though the obsession was reciprocated) that most annoyed Charles.

When the princes went to Scotland to be with their father, so did the photographers. He had plenty of opportunity to be with them, with his arms around them, with them smiling at him just as they had smiled at her. But he wouldn't play Diana's game; he's too much of a gentleman. When he came in from fishing one day, I asked him how it had gone and he said, 'Terrible! I only got twenty minutes in because the press were so awful.' He had Harry with him and he could have taken the chance to turn it into a photo call, but he's not like that and he never will be, no matter how powerful Diana gets by using the media … How can you treat two boys like Diana did? They suffer. No marriage is perfect but we make them work just so we don't cause pain and suffering. Not Diana; she thinks only of herself and her amazing publicity campaign.

Harry never forgave Kanga for having been so outspoken and Charles had to explain to her that she was unlikely to see the boy again.

Long before the public realised it, Diana had been living the life of a separated woman. There were girly trips to Paris – the first in the company of two friends, Hayat Palumbo and Lucia Flecha de Lima. She had met Lucia, the 52-year-old wife of the Brazilian ambassador to Britain, during a tour of Brazil two years earlier. Lady Palumbo was the wife of Lord Palumbo, a controversial figure in property development who Harry had often heard his father curse. Harry sulked when his mother returned from jolly lunches behind the pink geraniums at the Kaspia restaurant near Berkeley Square with the friends of hers he knew his father did not approve of. During a second visit to Paris (which was supposed to be kept a close secret although she had an aide tip off the photographer Daniel Angeli) she met with President Mitterrand – a meeting which boosted Diana's self-esteem so much that she vowed to return as soon as possible for a more private visit. No one could have imagined what would befall her the next time she visited the French capital.

Diana and Charles's marriage was finally ended in August 1996. Harry was greatly relieved – seeing his parents part was far less painful than witnessing their often silent war. She was, as she had warned William, stripped of the 'Her Royal Highness' title and was henceforth to be known as Diana, Princess of Wales. She also lost the services of a full-time police bodyguard. Ken Wharfe was a thing of the past.

Harry was particularly amused when her new policeman turned up in disguise and driving an old Toyota. Diana would no longer have police protection other than when she attended public events, for which purpose the retired Royal Protection Squad officer Colin Tebbutt was engaged. Tebbutt told Harry he wore disguises because pursuing photographers were likely to recognise him even when they were travelling in his 'old banger', which Diana – instantly recognisable herself, of course – named 'the Tart Trap'. She always sat in the front whereas other royals insisted on riding in the back of limousines transporting them. Princess Margaret had always called him by his surname and would yell out 'Wireless!' when she wanted the radio turned on. Harry and William called him Colin and never asked for anything without saying 'please'. They liked Mummy's new, albeit occasional, bodyguard.

She had more time for the boys when her charity commitments were pared down from around a hundred to six, but on her own instigation she mounted an anti-landmine campaign, telling her sons that war was wrong. Harry was not so sure: if he was going to be a soldier, there had to be battles to fight.

# 6

# LOSING MUM

The summer of 1997 could not have had a happier start. On the first day of July Diana celebrated her thirty-sixth birthday and the morning began with a call from Harry: he had gathered a group of his classmates together to sing 'Happy Birthday' down the phone to her. In return she had a surprise for him: they were all going on holiday together to the south of France. Mohamed Al Fayed – a close friend of her stepmother Raine Spencer – had invited them to spend time with him and his young children, Jasmine, Karim, Camilla and Omar, at his palatial French home, the Villa Castel Ste-Thérèse, set in a ten-acre estate high on the cliffs above St Tropez. What's more, he had spent more than £10 million on a new yacht, the *Jonikal*, with the royal holidaymakers in mind. After all, they no longer had the royal yacht *Britannia* and this was his chance to put two fingers up to the Establishment which had always rejected his attempts to enter its midst. He even had his own photographer on standby to take pictures of him with Harry, William and their mother.

He had another 'treat' in mind: his son, Dodi, would be joining them although no one was to mention the model Kelly Fisher whom the playboy had left behind without any explanation. Al Fayed was matchmaking and he badly wanted Diana in the family.

Harry did not like Dodi – the pseudo-film producer he nicknamed 'Sister' for some obscure reason – any more than he liked Al Fayed's son Omar, whose 'arse he kicked' according to one of the bodyguards who witnessed 'a severe altercation', but the jet-skiing, scuba diving, barbecues on the private beach and trips on the *Jonikal* made up for his displeasure to a certain extent. Still, he was acutely aware of the Fayeds' fawning attention to all three royal guests. The constant circling of bodyguards in speedboats did more to alert the paparazzi than it did to put them off.

At night – when she was not being pursued by Dodi – Harry sat with his mother for long talks. Things had been going on which he did not understand. In particular he wanted to know what had happened to her friendship with Elton John, of whom he was particularly fond but with whom she appeared to have had a spectacular falling out. Suddenly the radio would be switched off when one of his records came on; magazines featuring the musician were consigned to the waste bin.

Harry was bemused – she had always spoken highly of the star and praised his work, especially his enormous charity efforts. But the two had had a bitter spat and now, in the heady atmosphere of the French Riviera, Diana decided it was time to tell him what had gone wrong. Elton was a very close friend of Gianni Versace and had been helping the designer put together an impressive coffee table book showcasing all of his products. There was to be a launch party for it and Elton wanted her to be there. She said she would think about it but, having examined some of the book's content, had decided that she could not be associated with it: what would her boys think when they saw the nudes and sexual innuendo Versace had chosen to include in the glossy publication?

She told Harry that the two of them had exchanged angry letters over the matter and she had begun hers by coldly addressing her old friend as 'Mr John'. Then why, Harry wanted to know, after Versace's murder on a Miami street, had she travelled to his funeral on Elton's chartered jet? The answer was simple: she needed a lift. He was puzzled when he watched television coverage of Versace's funeral service and saw her comforting 'Mr John' in a way that suggested they had never exchanged a cross word.

During the holiday she also tried to make him understand why she had developed the deep hatred she obviously had for Tiggy, the nanny she knew both boys were extremely fond of – a fondness which brought out an irrationally jealous streak in their mother. Harry especially enjoyed memories of long walks and deep conversations with Tiggy, whom he had come to regard more as a sister than a nanny.

The previous month Diana had given the Fourth of June celebration at Eton a miss because, she said, she had not wanted to steal the spotlight. She was horrified to learn later that William had invited Tiggy in her place and, moreover, that the former nanny had gone armed with supplies of champagne which she handed out freely – many of them to people Diana was friendly with. Harry asked her if it was true his mother had referred to her as 'a bitch' and Diana reportedly replied, 'Well she is. She gets ideas above her station.'

Her behaviour was beginning to confuse him and he was particularly concerned about the sudden presence of Fayed Jr in her life. Dodi had described himself as a film producer since stumping up the money for the movie *Chariots of Fire* sixteen years earlier, but he had taken no creative part in the making of the film. Harry grew deeply suspicious when Fayed arranged a disco for him and William at which there were a number of scantily clad young girls. No, one of them told Harry, they had never met Dodi before, but they had been recruited by two of his 'team' who were scouting the beach at St Tropez for some girls who would like 'some fun' with their boss's guests.

The trio returned to London in the Harrods jet on 20 July. It was Charles's turn to have custody of his sons, so Diana bid them an emotional farewell before they left for Balmoral. She was not to know she would never see them again. Happy to be away from the Fayeds, they enjoyed lunch with the Queen Mother at Clarence House to celebrate her ninety-seventh birthday before boarding *Britannia* for its last ever cruise to the Western Isles before decommission.

'This is a real ship,' Harry told his father, 'not like Mr Fayed's – his is a boat.' And when it came time for a photo call in return for a promise from the press to leave them alone for the rest of the holiday, it was Harry who came up with the idea of climbing down a salmon ladder on the Dee and beckoning to Tiggy at the top who was smoking one of her trademark cigarettes. The photographers were delighted and Charles amused, but when she saw the pictures Diana was not so impressed.

Left to her own devices the Princess soon became bored 'cooped up in Kensington Palace'. When Dodi Fayed phoned offering to take her on a Mediterranean cruise onboard the *Jonikal* – it was his father's suggestion, he assured her – she accepted. She had enjoyed his company on the earlier holiday and had become quite attracted to him but assured her close friend Rosa Monckton that it was no more than a holiday romance and that in fact she was embarrassed by Dodi's conspicuous spending on gifts for her – she was, after all, still getting over the break-up of her relationship with heart surgeon Hasnat Khan, whom she had desperately wanted to marry. The pair set off on 31 July for Corsica, where they began a cruise to Sardinia. To Diana's surprise, Mohamed Al Fayed was not there; in fact, apart from the staff, it was just her and Dodi. This was no simple pleasure trip, it was a love cruise. Dodi was courting the woman his father longed for him to marry and, according to a member of the crew, the magic seemed to be working, although I am told that Dodi remained in secret contact with Kelly Fisher throughout. The Fayeds made much of the supposed romance: when Dodi said he would never have another girlfriend, it was in a supposedly private conversation with none other than the Harrods press spokesman Michel Cole. It came as no surprise when the remark was relayed to a hungry press contingent.

However, the magic seemed to have worn off by the time they flew to Paris: Diana realised that she was being manipulated by the storekeeper and his son. She had also grown tired of Dodi's personal habits and was desperate to see her sons again. So, early on the evening of 30 August, after Dodi had disappeared into the bathroom and locked the door behind him, as Diana said he frequently did, fearing that he had returned to his old cocaine-using addiction, she telephoned her sons from the Imperial Suite of Al Fayed's Hôtel Ritz. It was a joyful conversation: no one could have imagined it would be their last.

Dodi had a plan for the night. He summoned driver (not even a qualified chauffeur) Henri Paul from the bar where he had been consuming copious quantities of his favourite Ricard pastis, a powerful aperitif, and ordered him to drive himself and the Princess to his personal residence in the city. Their bodyguard Trevor Rees-Jones made no attempt to have them don their seat belts (he was saved, though seriously injured, by the front seat air bag) and they set off at high speed on what would be a fatal journey. Diana, who was inclined to be superstitious, might not have been surprised that it was the thirteenth concrete pillar of the tunnel below Pont de l'Alma which her car crashed into at 68mph killing her, Fayed and Henri Paul.

Harry and William were in bed asleep in adjoining

bedrooms at their grandmother's castle – the Queen's Scottish home which Diana had so hated – when a red-eyed Prince Charles went first to William's room at 7.15 a.m. to break the dreadful news to his elder son. There was no easy way to put it: the boy's mother was dead and now they had to go next door and tell Harry. The three of them wept and wept and wept, but despite his own grief, William did all he could to try and comfort his younger brother. Harry, however, was beyond comfort, inconsolable even when the Queen tried. Her Majesty had been woken at 1 a.m. by her private secretary Sir Robin Janvrin after he received news from the British embassy in Paris that the Princess had been involved in a serious road crash in a Paris tunnel. She summoned Charles who called his deputy private secretary Mark Bolland and asked him to find out how serious the accident was. After a number of calls to the Paris police, Bolland called back with the news: 'Very serious.' Diana's injuries were critical: Charles's first thought was that she might be brought home brain damaged or paralysed. How was he going to tell the boys?

It was shortly after 3 a.m. that Sir Michael Jay called to tell him that Diana was dead; Charles hadn't even known that his former wife was in Paris. He wondered how he could possibly explain all this to his sons as he walked at sunrise on to the moors surrounding the Balmoral grounds.

Consumed with grief himself, he broke the news as gently as he could. Harry had had a bad night after arguing with his brother about Dodi – the man he disliked so intensely. 'Is Mummy really dead, Daddy?' were, Charles recalls, the first words he managed between sobs. In response the Prince could only nod and hug his son.

But this was Sunday and there was no way the Queen was going to allow her family to miss the day's service. The boys were told to get dressed and be prepared to face a much bigger crowd than usual at Crathie Kirk. William and Harry looked numb, frozen in tragedy, in the back of the black Daimler that was transporting them. Princes Philip and Charles wore kilts as tradition demanded, and stern faces. By order of the Queen there was no reference to Diana in the morning's prayers. She may have been their mother but Diana had ceased to be a member of the Royal Family and the Queen declared what had happened in France to be 'a private matter'. Instead of being obliged to take a commercial flight to Paris from Aberdeen, Charles was, however, permitted to use an RAF plane to bring Diana's body home from the French capital, but he had to use all his persuasive powers to get his mother to allow the coffin to be taken to the Chapel Royal at St James's Palace rather than the Spencer home.

What appeared to be the senior family members' virtual indifference to the tragedy caused Harry to continually ask his father the question: 'Is it true that Mummy is dead?' Finding it hard to believe that she was no more than injured, he begged to be allowed to help bring her home. The Queen remained in Balmoral for days, keeping Harry and William with her, permitting them to read a selection of the letters of sympathy that were flooding in. Initially she also resisted all pleas to have the flag over Buckingham Palace fly at half-mast – it had never happened before other than following the death of a monarch. Not one to shed a tear over the tragedy, Princess Margaret complained about the smell of the thousands of bunches of rotting flowers laid in tribute in the gardens beneath her apartment at Kensington Palace.

When Diana's coffin was transferred early one morning to Kensington Palace, the Queen Mother, who had always tolerated her, sent her page William Tallon (better known as Backstairs Billy) to place flowers on her behalf but when he returned later he noticed that the casket had been lowered. When he asked why, he was told that Prince Harry was waiting for a last look at his mother's body so he could be assured she was no longer alive, but he was not yet tall enough to view it in its former position. Finally convinced, he placed a card in her hands on which he had simply written 'Mummy'. Earlier he had insisted his father take him out to join the crowds viewing the flowers and reading the cards. Charles was visibly saddened but Harry was positively excited as he read out some of the heartfelt messages written to his mother and drew his father's attention to a number of them.

The funeral arrangements, however, caused further contention. Charles had asked his sons to walk with him behind the coffin-bearing gun carriage, drawn by six black horses to Westminster Abbey, but William adamantly refused, declaring he had no wish to march 'in any bloody parade'. 'I'll do it, I'll do it, Daddy,' Harry said. But it was the Duke of Edinburgh who persuaded the older boy to join them, saying, 'If I walk, will you walk with me?' William respectfully agreed and Philip helped the young princes hold back the tears by keeping them in conversation pointing out the London landmarks they were passing. As the procession passed Buckingham Palace, Philip pointed to the balcony where the Queen led other members of the Royal Family in bowing to the cortège.

Harry still believes that it was the Duke's rare display of compassion that helped him get through the funeral service even when his uncle, Diana's brother Charles (by now the 9th Earl Spencer), who had already blamed the press for causing the tragedy, seemed to be firing a shot over the Royal Family's bows when he said in his eulogy: 'I pledge that we, your blood family, will do all we can to continue the imaginative and loving way in which you were steering these two exceptional young men so that their souls are not simply immersed by duty and tradition...' In a sentence that directed aristocratic disdain to the ruling family, he declared that his sister 'needed no royal title to continue to generate her particular brand of magic'. There was no mention of his rejection of Diana's plea to return to Althorp when her marriage collapsed citing 'unwanted intrusion' as his reason, even though she made it clear that she was in desperate need of the kind of privacy she believed only her family home could offer.

In initially blaming the media for causing the crash, Spencer was presumably unaware of how his sister had acknowledged her debt to the British press after they honoured the agreement she and Charles had reached with them at the meeting in Kensington Palace. The editors had kept their promise to abide by their wishes. Spencer seemed to blame the entire media for the crazy paparazzi chase by continental photographers and the actions of Fayed's intoxicated driver. It did not endear him to the British media.

It was more than two weeks after the funeral that Harry and his brother were given details of the Paris tunnel accident – and then nothing was held back. The drunken chauffeur, the defective limousine, the bodyguard who had not protested against the route that would inevitably lead to a paparazzi chase as well as his failure to insist that his charge put on the seat belt that might have saved her as Ken Wharfe says he would have done. But, above all, it was the part played by Dodi Fayed – as anxious to impress his father with a royal match as he was to win over the Princess – that earned Harry's wrath: 'It must have been Sister's fault!' he repeated over and over. Harry grew even more furious when Al Fayed inflamed the situation by suggesting that they had both been murdered and, at one point, suggested that Prince Philip was involved in the plot. 'Who would want to kill Mummy?' the young Prince asked his father at one point. The Royal Family, having had enough, removed the 'By Appointment' logo Harrods had been able to display for many years. It was an unsavoury battle which lasted years before Al Fayed finally accepted that the deaths had been the result of an accident for which his son was partly to blame.

Harry was the member of the family who suffered most from Diana's death. William's looks, easy charm and academic superiority were always going to make life smoother for him. Harry made up for it by going at everything at the double. He was his fragile mother's son with all of her charged emotions, many of her fears and much of her paranoia. Charles began to allow them greater freedom and encouraged others to befriend them to an extent he would never have experienced at their ages. Tiggy, once Diana's bitter enemy, became Harry's substitute mother. At Charles's invitation, the former nanny was invited to stay with them at Highgrove while they were given time off school to grieve. She spent every waking hour with them going through many of the thousands of letters of condolence they had received to show how much their mother had been loved. William wanted to reply to them all – an impossible task – but Harry just wanted the comfort the second most important woman in the world to him had to offer.

He also received close comfort and attention from his late mother's sister Lady Sarah McCorquodale who turned up at Ludgrove on the morning of his thirteenth birthday with a PlayStation, the gift Diana had planned to give him. Sarah and Diana's other sister, Jane, phoned him every day in a compassionate bid to help him recover from his great loss.

In an effort to relieve Harry of his grief, Charles arranged for Tiggy to take him and school friend Charlie Henderson on safari in Botswana on his half-term break from Ludgrove – time he would normally have spent with Diana. Charles chose Africa so they could meet up on his breaks from various engagements there – plus he had a special surprise for him when they joined up in Johannesburg: Harry's favourite group, the Spice Girls, were in town for a concert and Charles had arranged for Harry, who played their records incessantly, to meet them. Once in the city, Harry rarely left his father's side. The two spent an hour talking in a suite at the new Hilton Hotel and when Charles went outside to shake hands after declaring the building open, he was surprised to hear the crowd shouting, 'Harry, Harry'. He looked up to the balcony of their suite and saw his younger son snapping pictures of him. 'He's right there,' Charles cheerfully told those who hadn't spotted the Prince. Later Harry emerged into the world's spotlight for the first time since his mother's funeral. Smartly dressed in a dark-blue two-piece suit – Charles had told him he could go in jeans but the young Prince, rapidly becoming PR conscious, said he considered it would open his father up to criticism of being a 'Diana imitator' – the two of them went to the concert where he met his heroines backstage. Needless to say they – 'Baby Spice' Emma Bunton in particular – made a great fuss of him (although he seemed more interested in the sexily costumed Geri Halliwell) and for the first time in weeks he was seen to smile.

To Harry's delight that was not the end of the trip: Charles took him to the remote settlement of Dukuduku where father and son both sampled the local beer – something Charles, now a single parent, would never have allowed in the days when he played the role of stern father. They also called on Nelson Mandela, who gave Harry several gifts which he added to the Zulu souvenirs he had already acquired on the trip. With one exception – a Zulu bracelet which he gave to Tiggy – he still keeps his 'Africa collection' in his room at Highgrove alongside his Arsenal scarves.

The trip proved to be a strong re-bonding experience for father and son and Charles was determined to repeat it when he took Harry and William on an official visit to Canada. Although he had fears that the boys would be overwhelmed by the attention they were obviously going to get, they were delighted by their reception from a screaming crowd of what can best be described as 'royal fans'. It is interesting to note that Harry enjoyed the adulation and collected a large batch of newspapers adorned with front-page photographs of himself, his brother and his father. William was somewhat more reticent, aware that this was what he would have to experience for the rest of his life and acutely conscious of how much his mother had secretly resented public adulation. From the window of their suite at the Waterfront Hotel in Vancouver, Harry pointed out to his brother a group of screaming girls holding aloft a banner that read 'William, I'm the one for you'. At that time William was easily the more attractive of the two and, rather like Paul McCartney when he stood alongside John Lennon, was the one the fans were screaming for – but this did not deter Harry. He was perfectly happy to settle for his brother's cast-offs if necessary, but it proved not to be so; when they arrived in the town of Burnaby he discovered that pupils at the high school they visited had formed a Harry fan club. Charles was pleased with the Princemania he witnessed. During years of walking with his ex-wife through crowds like this he had come to accept, somewhat reluctantly, that the person they had come to see was Diana. But this was different: after everything he and the boys had come through he was happy to take a back seat and watch their popularity grow. Acceptance had become his byword and when the young princes' photographs dominated the front pages, he knew that the editors were giving the public what they most wanted to see and read. His superstar sons were a breath of fresh air on what otherwise might have seemed a rather stuffy and formal visit. When Harry turned his baseball cap back and called 'Yo dude!' to him, Charles's response – 'Really, do you have to do that?' – was more of a gentle admonishment than the strict reprimand he might have given in earlier times. Indeed, it was William who seemed more concerned at Harry's response to the adulation than their father, according to a veteran British journalist covering the tour. 'I could see that William was wise enough to see what lay ahead. Everything these boys did would be subject to close public scrutiny, and that meant things bad as well as good.' How right Harry's subsequent activities were to prove him.

Some months after their Johannesburg meeting, the Spice Girls turned up (by helicopter, of course) for tea at Highgrove which Harry – in William's absence – hosted, serving the girls coffee and cakes and offering them wine from his father's cellar, all the time regaling them with praise for their hit records, several of which he knew by heart. The young Prince did his best to entertain the girls by reprising some of his own stage performances, in particular loudly repeating the battleground speech from Shakespeare's *Henry V*, 'Cry God for Harry, England and St George!' Although it went largely unnoticed by most, a disloyal servant claims that the Prince paid little attention to 'Posh Spice', Victoria Beckham, who had initially refused to leave the helicopter because of the high wind blowing outside. Nevertheless, it was a big day for the publicity-hungry group too as they reflected on leaving the royal home with goodie bags containing, among other things, free samples of the organic food and drinks sold by Charles for his charity under the Duchy Originals label.

Once the Spice Girls had departed, Harry told his father that the day had been the second best in his life. When Charles asked him what had actually been the best day, the young fan replied: 'The first time I met them.'

Such acts proved that Charles had mellowed – even the feud between the Windsors and the Spencers seemed to have run its course and, in a bid to show that he would not let such a war between the families harm his relationship with his nephews, Charles Spencer declared that he had reached 'an understanding with the Prince of Wales'. For his part, Charles, who always hated confrontation, said in moderate response, 'Both boys are coping extremely well – perhaps better than anyone expected.' That said a lot about royal blood: they had learned from an early age that they had to present a certain veneer regardless of what they were feeling inside.

Despite what Spencer thought of him, Charles had firmly established himself as the man in his sons' lives and, as Harry has noted in more recent times, he began to 'chill out', taking them on the sort of outings that Diana would have taken them. There was a visit to one theatre to see the children's classic *Doctor Dolittle* and another to watch Barry

Humphries's performance as the outrageous Dame Edna Everage. Whereas in the past the Prince might have frozen at the Australian comic's remarks about the young princes dressing up in women's clothing, he laughed hysterically and the boys joined in. Back at St James's Palace, where Charles was now living, Harry charmed the staff with samples of the comic's performance, telling one servant that Humphries had picked out a large woman seated on the front row of the audience and said to her, 'What a lovely dress, beautiful material – you were lucky they had so much of it.'

Although Diana would always be at the front of their minds, with their father's help they were clearly learning to overcome their grief. Unable to deliver it personally because it occurred in term time, Harry was the one who sent a bunch of flowers to be placed on Diana's grave on the first Mother's Day following her death. Soon after Charles gave in to his younger son's wish to visit the grave on an island at Althorp, the Spencer estate which the heir was never overly keen to visit. It was all part of the healing process and Charles made further efforts to satisfy one or both of his sons' desires whenever his own duties permitted. He even cancelled one long-standing engagement to take Harry to France to watch England play against Colombia in the World Cup. That day David Beckham became his newest hero after the player scored his first ever goal for England with an impressive free kick. Charles was pleased he had taken the day off from royal duties for he was able to witness a further stage in his son's recovery from the tragedy of losing his mother so publicly and at such a young age.

Charles was happy because his sons – particularly Harry – were happy. They were bonding in a way that would never have been possible while the Prince and Princess were at each other's throats.

Just one feud remained (and still is) unresolved: that concerning the book written by Paul Burrell, which he called *A Royal Duty* and which was serialised in the *Daily Mirror*, then edited by Piers Morgan. The servant made a fortune by revealing the secrets Diana had trustingly shared with him, even reproducing private letters she had written to him at times of great stress, irrationally suggesting in one that Charles was planning for her to die in a road crash, and in another that her husband had put her 'through hell'.

It was more than her sons could stand. Despite their tender years Harry and William sat down together and compiled a statement:

> We cannot believe that Paul, who was entrusted with so much, could abuse his position in such a cold and overt betrayal. It is not only deeply painful for the two of us but also for everyone else affected and it would mortify our mother if she were alive today and, if we might say so, we feel we are more able to speak for our mother than Paul. We ask Paul please to bring these revelations to an end.

They were no longer boys to be toyed with and their message to Burrell was also a signal to the media world at large.

# 7

# OFF THE RAILS

One troubled year and two days after Diana's death, Harry joined his brother at Eton. Because he was born in September – on the cusp of the academic year division – he had been able to spend an extra year at Ludgrove in a bid to improve his disappointing academic performance. The exceptionally high standard of learning at Eton was always going to be a challenge for him for, like his mother, he was no academic. Diana had considered two other options – Radley College in Oxfordshire and Milton Abbey in Dorset. Harry, however, wanted to be at Eton because William was there and had been for two years. And anyway, it was close to Windsor Castle where the Queen always spends weekends and even though he was a boarder at the college it was comforting to know his grandmother was nearby and that at weekends he could easily walk and have tea with her, as William often did – resisting the taunts of local yobs who were always on the warpath for the Eton 'toffs'.

Prince Charles had his own doubts about Eton: he had wanted his sons to go to Gordonstoun in Scotland where he, his father, two uncles and two cousins were all educated. But the Spencers had always favoured the Berkshire college that Diana's father and brother both attended.

If Charles was still miffed about the choice he did not show it when he and Harry arrived in a Vauxhall estate car and posed briefly for photographers in heavy rain. On arrival Harry was wearing a favourite light-green sports jacket but that was soon to be swapped for the unique Eton uniform (black tailcoat, waistcoat, white tie and the stiff collar he used to complain made his neck sore) which dates back to the nineteenth century.

Father and son stepped into Manor House to be greeted by housemaster Dr Andrew Gailey, a kindly Irishman, and his wife Shauna who entertained them along with the other new boys and their parents. There they were joined by the no-nonsense house 'Dame' or matron, Elizabeth Heathcote, who made her authority known by instructing the Prince to sign the entrance book. Next, Harry was taken to his room which, he was happily assured, would be cleaned and tidied by a maid, a girl who would also make his bed and attend to his laundry. Looking out of the room's ivy-covered window he noticed that some of the press photographers were still lingering below and Harry, being Harry, obliged them with a bonus picture by waving to them.

His royal protection officer was duly installed in the next room with instructions to report to his superiors if Harry continued to show the worrying signs of distress he had suffered since the Paris car crash. Watching over his younger brother was also a task allotted to William who was lodged close by in the same house. After a year that had tested his parenting skills to the limit, Charles was all too aware that his younger son was particularly vulnerable and the special tasks entrusted to the policeman and the sibling were never going to be easy ones for them to accomplish.

Founded in the mid-fifteenth century by King Henry VI, Eton has a formidable reputation for producing great men. No less than eighteen British prime ministers, including the Duke of Wellington, Horace Walpole and Harold Macmillan, and writers George Orwell, Henry Fielding, Aldous Huxley, Percy Shelley and Ian Fleming did their learning there. Most leavers go on to university, one-third of them to Oxford or Cambridge. All this was well above Harry's intellectual level.

The college has a language all of its own. William taught him that the cricketers are known as 'dry bobs', rowers as 'wet bobs' and those who go in for neither are 'slack bobs'. Lessons are 'divs' and teachers are 'beaks'. Boys who merit positions of special responsibility are marked by different colour waist-coats, trousers or buttons. Fees for the 1,300 or so pupils are now in excess of £30,000 per year. Harry was spared the process of acting as a servant to any of the older boys by the relatively recent abolition of the fagging system, and by the time he arrived the thrashing of offenders with a birch rod while they were stretched over a wooden block had also been done away with. Nevertheless, he managed to annoy several of his fellow pupils by going out of his way to demonstrate that he was just one of them, when he was clearly not. This proved to be quite a problem in the ensuing months and he had difficulty in making friends. He won several over, however, when he demonstrated in more than one playground fight that he had fists as good as the best of them, a fact that was noted in an early report to his father along with a mention of his 'aggressive' play when he was on the football field. This one was not to be messed with, was the message, although his bravery when taking on boys bigger than himself was a good indication of what was to come in later years. It was, however, to cause him a nasty injury when, during a soccer match, he collided with another player while jumping to head a ball and landed flat on his back. He suffered such pain in his arm that it was thought he had fractured it. His arm was put in a sling but even that did not prevent him thumping a pupil who dared to laugh at his predicament.

His enthusiasm for Eton's fearsome Wall Game (where two teams of ten players wrestle and push a ball in a scrum along a 110-metre wall for the chance to have a shot at a garden wall or tree), which had caused fatalities in the past, was a sure sign that he feared nothing or no man. To the Palace's dismay he was photographed on crutches after kicking in a window following a particularly strident row with another pupil over a girl they both fancied. He soon became a familiar figure in the matron's office. After persuading a local barber to give him the same haircut that Michael Owen, his football hero of the day, was currently sporting – a 'skinhead' – the Palace had to plead with Fleet Street editors not to publish photographs of him taken in the streets of Eton and Windsor looking just like any other delinquent on the hunt for female fodder.

His behaviour was a concern for all, but there was light at the end of the tunnel, as one (now retired) housemaster relays:

> We used to say that Harry was like a firecracker and when other pupils saw him coming they used to pass a by-now familiar warning: 'Don't light the blue touch paper', in other words don't give him the slightest excuse to vent his spleen. He needed some outlet for his anger and he found it when he discovered the Combined Cadet Force. Eton has a long-standing military tradition and he became an enthusiastic recruit of the well-disciplined Force. That, for a while, curbed his frustration and diverted much of the aggression he had been displaying outside the classroom. We knew then that he was destined for a career in the military, where he could channel that aggression usefully.

Never a truer word…

Nevertheless, it was hard to reconcile the image of a grief-stricken Harry standing behind his mother's coffin with Harry the Hellraiser who emerged during his time at Eton. One balmy summer evening he was being driven along King's Road, Chelsea, in a 4x4 with his bodyguard and some friends on their way to a party. Music blared from the vehicle's sound system as it pulled up at traffic lights next to an open-topped sports car. Harry lowered his window and began lobbing chips into the other car to the obvious annoyance of its driver. When a newspaper columnist upbraided Harry in print for being a lazy, disdainful and privileged yob, Paddy Harverson, Prince Charles's then spin doctor, wrote an angry letter to the paper:

> Like any other nineteen-year-old fortunate enough to be able to spend time travelling and working abroad, Harry should be allowed to benefit from his experiences without being subject to this kind of ill-informed and insensitive criticism.

Despite Harverson's protest, Harry would be the first to admit that from an early age he was a seasoned imbiber of vodka and it was not for nothing that he earned the nickname Pothead Harry. Unfortunately he was often 'out of it' in public: on one occasion it was left to his younger cousin Beatrice to restrain him when, dressed in jeans and wearing a reversed baseball hat, he lost it during a wild scene at a party in the Chinawhite marquee after a Guards Polo Club event, lobbing water and cans of Red Bull at his friends. The contrast between his overwrought excitement and Beatrice's ladylike dignity could not have been more pronounced.

Chinawhite owner Rory Keegan says:

> The princes were young men growing up. They were not doing anything wrong. They had a right to have fun. Couldn't we let them have their youth without invading it at every turn? Harry doesn't have a bad bone in his body and it's important to us to protect him.

Harry's first serious experience with alcohol had come about during the Mediterranean holiday with his mother and brother as Mohamed Al Fayed's guests in July 1997. Each time the yacht pulled into a port, Harry would go ashore with whoever he could round up from the small cruise party and, as Diana herself was later to put it, 'got into mischief'. One of those who went along told his own father that they all felt 'happily squiffy' after sampling a local brandy.

Things were to take a turn for the worse, much worse. Harry and his brother had helped arrange a Highgrove party ahead of their father's fiftieth birthday. The outside of the house had been decorated with wildflowers and Greek statues had been erected in the Prince's favourite spot – his beloved walled garden. The boys had gone to great lengths to persuade Camilla to join the gathering to show they bore her no ill feeling. Guests included the actors Rowan Atkinson, Stephen Fry and Emma Thompson, whom he and William had persuaded to stage some comedy sketches poking fun at their father along the lines of Atkinson's Blackadder – charging the audience £30 a head for the pleasure. The young hosts had also chosen the musical entertainment – including remixes of DJ EZ and Norris Da Boss Windross, neither of whom most of the guests had ever heard of. The finale of their 'sounds' programme was the '70s hit 'Y.M.C.A.' by the Village People, which the guest of honour was obliged to dance to. Although he had no idea of the gay connotations Charles was instructed by his sons to try and imitate their movements. It was not long into the night, however, before a drunken fourteen-year-old Harry stripped completely naked and ran around the surprised – to put it mildly – distinguished guests. One present says:

> Charles was visibly shocked, in fact he turned crimson but he told a group of us later that it was just teenage high spirits and he himself had done much the same. It was the only time in my life that I didn't believe him.

More than one so-called royal watcher suggested that a likely reason Harry had become so inebriated was Camilla's presence. They could not have been more wrong for by this time both boys had accepted Mrs Parker Bowles's part in their father's life and they were happy that she made him happy, especially since he constantly reminded them that he had truly loved their mother. No, Harry's drunken behaviour was a sign of things to come and there never had to be a reason – he drank when he was happy, he drank when he was sad. He just liked the effect.

On another cruise in August 1999 – this time with his father – he drank heavily aboard John Latsis's yacht, the *Alexander*. He was often found weeping for his mother in the arms of Tiggy but such emotional demonstrations owed much to the alcohol he had put away.

During a shooting party on the Duke of Westminster's estate he was sick across the bar at the Duke's home, Eaton Hall in Cheshire, and a disgusted member of the catering staff was ordered to clean up after him while the 'legless and speechless' Harry was put to bed. The same year he threw cider bottles and drunkenly abused teenage girls while holi-daying at the Cornish resort of Rock. One of the girls he targeted said, 'He was vomiting behind the wall. He's one of the most revolting people I've ever come across.'

Invited to Spain the following year to play in the annual Sotogrande Copa de Plata polo tournament, he spent his nights in Marbella clubs, often staying at his table until the cleaners arrived around dawn.

The big trouble started once he joined William at Eton. Fellow students swear he did not drink during term time but made up for it when he invited a number of them to Highgrove during the school holidays. He founded Club H with a well-stocked bar in the cellars (converted in Charles's time to a bomb-proof shelter) and it became the venue for wild parties with various mind-altering substances reportedly being handed around. All the new friends he had made at Eton were welcome with one exception: a particular boy, who was gay, had become infatuated with Harry, would follow him everywhere and wrote him 'affectionate' notes, becoming the bane of the Prince's life as a result. According to another student:

Harry has nothing against chaps who bat for the other side as long as they don't try and involve him. This particular fellow persisted, he would not leave him alone. I think Harry was too nice to tell him he simply wasn't interested, that he liked girls too much to be interested, but on the second occasion that he turned up at Club H bringing a bunch of flowers – most people brought a bottle – he was asked to leave. In fact he left Eton soon after. Harry was sad about that, too. He hated the thought of being responsible for someone else's academic downfall, but if it hadn't been him it would probably have been someone else and they were more likely to have given the chap a good hiding.

Girls as well as drugs were allegedly brought to Club H by Harry's long-standing drinking buddy (still to this day) Guy Pelly, then a nineteen-year-old student at nearby Royal Agricultural College in Cirencester. Harry's chat-up line for the girls he met in surrounding pubs and clubs was, 'How would you like to come back to my palace for a drink?' – a close runner-up to the *Playboy* boss's immortal 'Hi, I'm Hugh Hefner'. He had fewer problems than most men of his age in getting the girls to accept his invitation to party. Although she never went to Highgrove one 24-year-old, occasional model Suzannah Harvey, accepted the seventeen-year-old Prince's invitation to 'step outside', during a hunt ball at Badminton House and was later to tell her story to a Sunday newspaper showing how wild he was when it came to necking and fondling members of the opposite sex.

All went well at Club H when he and William had Highgrove to themselves but when Prince Charles was in residence he made it clear that the noise emanating from the stereo sound system below stairs was intolerable. A new venue had to be found.

Just six miles from Tetbury lies the Wiltshire village of

Sherston and in its midst sits a particularly attractive Cotswolds pub, the Rattlebone Inn. The sixteenth-century pub is named after eleventh-century Saxon warrior John Rattlebone, whose ghost is said to haunt it, and it had a fine reputation, as indeed it does today having been restored to respectability since what is referred to locally as the Harry episode.

When Harry and his cronies discovered the pub (William was away on his gap year around this time) it was about as decadent as could be. Underage drinking was rife, late-night lock-ins were a regular thing for those who wanted to get drunk after hours, cannabis was openly smoked at the bar and behind a hut at the back of the building a dealer sold cocaine although, by all accounts, the quality of the product was not the best. According to the *News of the World* one of Harry's acquaintances, 29-year-old John Holland, who was caught in a sting, made it known that in addition to supplying weed he was able get cocaine for £30 a gram but he had to go to Shoreditch in London to get it. Even so, it was half the price charged in the West End.

The centre of entertainment at the Rattlebone was a pool table and it was often the scene of many altercations. Harry was involved in at least one scuffle with two men during a particularly raucous game and he was thrown out after calling the pub's French chef, François Ortet, a 'fucking frog'. Younger than most of the Rattlebone's customers, Harry was especially vulnerable but royal protection officers were loath to shop him to his father for fear of losing his all-important trust in them.

Reports at the time suggested that it was the staff at Highgrove who informed Prince Charles of Harry's pot-smoking after they smelled the substance in his room and in the cellar. In fact the truth is far more sinister: unbeknown even to the Prince's policeman, MI6 had been watching a Pakistani youth who was a regular at the pub and whose mobile phone was being monitored by GCHQ – the government's listening post, located just thirty-five miles from the Rattlebone at Cheltenham – as part of an anti-terrorist operation. The MI6 report to intelligence chiefs included details of what was going on with the third in line to the throne and was secretly conveyed to Charles in much the same way as news of the Duchess of York's secret flight to Morocco with her then lover Steve Wyatt was leaked from GCHQ to a journalist, effectively putting an end to the Yorks' marriage.

Whether or not MI6 ever nailed their suspect in Operation Cotswold Pub, no one will say but one thing is for sure – Harry owes a great deal to that watched man; indeed, the surveillance of one Pakistani individual may have saved his life, for when Charles was given the details of the report in which his son was so damningly named, he acted without hesitation. Harry was summoned to his father's side and asked point blank if he had been taking drugs and mixing in drug-taking company.

Realising the game was up, Harry came clean. Yes, he told his father, he had been smoking cannabis; yes, he had been drinking too much and yes, some of his more unsuitable friends were into heavy drugs (in fact three of the thirty of those closest to him already had criminal convictions). And yes, again, much of his bad behaviour could be attributed to such indulgences: when, for example, he threw to an aide the skis he was due to return to a hire shop in Klosters, growling, 'You take them back,' he was suffering from a particularly punchy hangover. Charles's belief that Harry's drinking until he was sick was just a phase he was going through, was shattered in an instant. His distress was clear in a telephone call he then made to his close friend Gerald Grosvenor, the Duke of Westminster, who responded by saying that he had frightened his daughters, Lady Tamara and Lady Edwina, off drugs by taking them to a rehab centre in Liverpool to see for themselves the horrors of addiction.

Next Charles had a heart-to-heart with his adolescent son explaining that a fondness for alcohol had long been some-thing of a problem in both families. The Queen Mother was known to enjoy her daily tipples, Princess Margaret drank a bottle of whisky a night and four sons of King George V all had alcohol problems – the Duke of Windsor, his brother King George VI and the Dukes of Kent (who was also addicted to cocaine) and Gloucester. Furthermore, both of Diana's parents were fond of the bottle – Earl Spencer's fondness for more than the odd dram was cited when he was accused of cruelty during his divorce from Diana's mother who herself was given a driving ban for driving under the influence – and her sister Sarah was expelled from school for drinking vodka. It was William who heightened the alarm first raised by the MI6 report when he discovered that Harry had gone out of his way to befriend Camilla's son Tom Parker Bowles who had been arrested in 1995 for being in possession of marijuana and ecstasy and had admitted using cocaine. The Prince's erratic behaviour on some occasions suggested that he might have tried mind-altering substances, and more than once Charles had to tell him to calm down when he inexplicably went wild – often in front of photographers who were by now ever on the lookout for instances of the young man they now tagged 'His Royal High-ness' going crazy. From the smells often thought to be coming from Harry's room at Eton, he got a different nickname from his fellows: Hash Harry. Certainly there was a culture of joint-smoking behind the college's hallowed walls at the time so no one could be certain which room the smells of weed being used emerged from, but Harry was high up on the list of suspects.

Something needed to be done: acting on Gerald Grosvenor's advice, Charles remembered a drink-and-drug rehabilitation centre in south London he had officially opened the previous year. He summoned his former equerry Mark Dyer and acquainted him with the situation. Harry should be taken there to see what terrible harm the substances could do – and left there if necessary. He couldn't take him himself for fear of the publicity such a visit would arouse, but it was no problem for Dyer. One school of thought suggested that Dyer did it on his own initiative without consulting Charles but he would never have done that. Charles was fully informed throughout and was a party to later disclosure of the visit.

In the event it took just a one-day visit to the Featherstone

Lodge rehab in Peckham, one of London's toughest areas, to convince Harry that he had embarked on the road to hell. His escort, or 'buddy' for the day, was a chap of similar age to himself who was addicted to heroin. Initially embarrassed to be there at his father's command and as a potential inmate, and after being shown a room he might one day be required to occupy for an extended period of recovery, Harry sat in on groups where inmates poured out their sorry tales. He met men of his father's age who had lost everything – homes, wives, children and careers – as a result of drinking the way he had started to: a girl from a respectable middle-class family who had turned to prostitution after a cannabis habit had led to harder drugs, a crack addict who collapsed in a West Kensington crack den and was told: 'Get out, we don't call ambulances around here, we put bodies on skips.'

A counsellor had relayed to him the Japanese definition of alcoholism: 'The man takes a drink, the drink takes a drink and the drink takes the man.' He was told that only he could say whether he had reached the stage of alcoholism or addiction which demanded giving in to the craving every time the thought came into his head, but if he had there was no cure, only a treatment and the treatment would involve regular attendance at meetings of Alcoholics Anonymous and/or Narcotics Anonymous. When he asked if that would be for the rest of his life, he was given a simple answer: 'Yes, if you like happy endings.'

There was one moment of laughter when he heard an old

drunk declare: 'Giving up drink is easy, I've done it hundreds of times.'

Despite that moment of light relief, Harry left Featherstone Lodge pale, shaken and clutching a handful of literature about the illness he was showing early signs of suffering from. The realisation that despite his highly privileged background and lifestyle, his fate lay in no one's hands but his own made tough hearing for a man who was used to being take care of. If he wanted recovery, he had to work for it. If he didn't want to be sick and put to bed at anyone else's party, he had to learn to say 'No'. And above all he had to choose the company he mixed in: 'stick with the winners' was to be his new motto.

In the early days those winners were his father and brother. His weekend passes were limited and strictly monitored and that Christmas he was made to spend the entire break in the company of Charles and William. When, during one fireside chat, his father told him of his own teenage drink scandal, it sounded pathetic: Charles had gone into a pub on the Isle of Lewis with four other boys during a sailing trip to Stornoway and ordered a cherry brandy, the only drink he could think of when encouraged by his companions to 'have something'. How Harry would have sniggered, considering the quantity of hard liquor he was putting away.

When the story broke shortly after Christmas, praise was subsequently poured on Charles for his responsible action in ordering Harry to the rehab, but all was not quite as it seemed. Charles's media manipulators were subsequently accused of shamelessly using the story of Harry's disgrace for his father's benefit. Charles's former spin doctor Mark Bolland (Harry named him Lord Blackadder) was obliged to pour cold water on reports that he had leaked the exclusive 'Harry's drugs shame' story to his holidaying friend Rebekah Wade (now Brooks), then editor of Rupert Murdoch's scandal-obsessed *News of the World*, in order to show Charles as a loving and caring father who would go to any lengths to do the right thing. Privately Charles admitted that his policy of giving advice instead of imposing rules had not worked, that it was far too lenient, but that did little to enhance Bolland's denial that any such funny business had gone on. In any event, Charles got the praise, the *News of the World* got its scoop (and under the terms of a tight media agreement to leave both young princes alone at this delicate stage in their lives, that could not have happened without royal assent) and Bolland had good reason to resemble the proverbial cat with the cream. A remarkable development followed when the Press Complaints Commission, which had always regarded the protection of children's privacy as a priority, backed the newspaper's decision to publish the story. Some regarded it as no coincidence that the boss of the industry's self-regulating body, Guy Black, was Bolland's live-in partner and the two men had been on holiday with *News of the World* editor Rebekah Wade the previous summer.

Regardless of how the story had been broken, the Queen insisted on a public statement being issued. It read: 'The Queen shares the Prince of Wales's views on the seriousness of Prince Harry's behaviour and supports the action taken. She hopes the matter can now be considered as closed.' A spokesman for Charles declared, 'This is a serious matter which was resolved within the family,' adding somewhat optimistically, 'It is now in the past and closed.' Some hope! Tony Blair – whose own son Euan narrowly escaped being arrested for being drunk close to 10 Downing Street – got in on the act too: '[The Royal Family] have handled the situation quite properly: they have done it in a very responsible and, as you would expect, a very sensible way for their child.'

Nevertheless the episode was not forgotten at Eton where Harry's hopes of becoming a prefect, as William had been, were dashed. One teacher says:

The prefects are the twelve elite pupils at Eton – they have to be considered popular, responsible and mature for their age. One of a prefect's duties would be to catch pupils slipping out to drink in pubs illegally. His housemaster had put his name forward but in view of the scandal the outgoing prefects, who picked their successors, said it would be ridiculous to elect Harry Wales in view of the offences he had admitted to.

William was extremely popular and a deserving choice. Harry's also popular. But basically he is seen to be of a different calibre, a bit of a naughty boy.

There was some saving grace – in his final year he was made house captain of games having excelled in physical sports, particularly swimming and athletics.

As for the Rattlebone Inn, it was soon under new management and a local man was successfully prosecuted after pleading guilty to supplying cannabis in the pub's toilets, though it had taken a newspaper sting to catch him. The police said they had no intention of charging the Prince over allegations that he smoked the drug there and that, like the First Family, they considered the matter closed. As for Harry, he was removed from the pub for a second time, this time not by the management but by his father.

It was during his time at Eton that Harry's honesty was put to another severe test. On one occasion his father's press secretary Sandy Henney received a call from a Highgrove gardener: Charles's beloved moorhen had been shot, would she be so kind as to pass on the bad news to His Royal Highness? Knowing how fond he was of the bird, the already-overworked Henney refused to inform the Prince herself but told the gardener to call HRH direct. Charles was mortified when he got the news and immediately demanded to know where his sons – who had been at Highgrove that weekend – were when the shooting occurred. When he was informed that they were in the vicinity of the crime scene, the pond, he said they had to be questioned by their housemaster, Andrew Gailey, who was to ensure that one of them came clean. When Dr Gailey told them their father was upset because his beloved moorhen had been shot, William said, 'Which moorhen is that, Dr Gailey?', at which point Harry cut in with: 'The one you told me not to shoot.' Harry was given twenty-four hours to phone his father and own up, which he did, saying, 'I'm so sorry Papa, it was me, I shouldn't have done it.' For Charles the confession was reminiscent of that delivered by George Washington when he owned up to his father that it was he who had chopped down a cherished cherry tree (actually, he had only mortally wounded it): 'Father, I cannot tell a lie, it was me' and, like Washington's father, he was more pleased by the honest admission than distressed at the loss of his precious bird.

The year 2002 was not one Harry can look back on with much joy. Apart from his personal troubles it also ended in tragedy when his dearest friend, Henry van Straubenzee, whom Harry called Henners, was killed in a car crash just before Christmas. Like Harry, Henry longed for a career in the army and he was bound for Newcastle to read business studies under the sponsorship of the MoD, before going on to Sandhurst to begin his army training. Having gone to Harrow from Ludgrove, he had returned to teach for a term at his old prep school and had arranged a Christmas party for the boarders. When the sound system packed up some time after midnight he and a friend went out to borrow a CD player. It was a foggy night and as they travelled back up the long, narrow drive, their car crashed into a tree – the only tree on the drive. Henry died instantly and his friend, who had been at the wheel, was badly injured.

Harry was distraught when he heard the news. The two had been the closest of friends since their Ludgrove days. Grief-stricken, he hardly spoke a word to anyone before arriving with William and Tiggy days later, on 23 December, at the small parish church where the van Straubenzees had hurriedly arranged a funeral. Memories of their holidays in

Cornwall, French cricket on the beach by day and barbecues at night flooded through his mind. He had lost both his great-grandmother, the Queen Mother, and his great-aunt Princess Margaret that year but their time had come and their deaths were not a shock. At the age of eighteen 'Henners' had his whole life ahead of him and Harry had looked forward to many more happy meetings, holidays even, with the best pal he ever had. In January he attended a service of thanksgiving held for his life at Harrow School before returning to Eton, a chastened man.

It was with little emotion that on 12 June 2003 Harry bade Eton – in an arranged photo call with his long-suffering housemaster Andrew Gailey – farewell, writing in the leaving book that his next stop would be Sandhurst. He may have had no regrets about leaving the college, but Harry was sad to be parting from many of the close friends he made there and he remains in touch with a number of them, who have all done well. Not one of them has a bad word to say about the Prince, although several noted that he left Eton with none of the ambition that fired them.

Five sometimes difficult years had come to an end and he was happy to be going home to a private celebration at Highgrove during which his father gave him the welcome news that he had authorised St James's Palace to announce that he would be the first senior royal for more than four decades to join the British Army. Harry was elated: not only was he now an Old Etonian but he was a candidate for Sandhurst, the Royal Military College. He was to achieve his childhood ambition by becoming one of 'Granny's soldiers'. Navy-devotee Prince Philip was not so thrilled although his own joyous experience of piloting helicopters undoubtedly had some effect on Harry.

Although his son had achieved the necessary A levels to be accepted at Sandhurst, and despite a public declaration that he was 'very proud of Harry', Charles was understandably disappointed when the results came through. Despite excelling in sports – particularly polo and rugby – and being made house captain of games, after five years at Eton Harry managed only a B in art and a D in geography – more than 90 per cent of Eton's pupils achieve grades A or B. He had dropped a third subject – history of art – after he got poor results in his AS exams the year before he left (his more academically inclined brother had achieved an A grade in geography, a B in history of art and a C in biology). And this was despite the efforts of an admiring teacher who subsequently claimed that she had helped Harry cheat to get the results he did manage to muster. Sarah Forsyth said that Eton's head of art, Ian Burke, had asked her to prepare text to go with some of Harry's work for an expressive project in which pupils are required to explain some of their work and relate it to that of great artists. She shocked everyone associated with lauding the Prince by saying that she assumed she had been asked to do it because Harry was in fact a weak student and that his academic failings were well known at Eton. Adding insult to injury she claimed that a teacher who marked his entrance exams had been desperate to find points

Loving Mum. This was said to be Diana's favourite picture of herself with her youngest son. It was taken in Majorca during a royal holiday.

Just one of the boys. Harry arrives for a school carol concert at St Matthew's church in London.

New beginnings. Just ahead of his third birthday, Harry pauses for the photographers as he arrives at nursery school, complete with Thomas the Tank Engine school bag.

Mum with 'Uncle Ken'. Inspector Ken Wharfe looked after Harry and William before becoming Diana's personal protection officer.

Starting early. At the tender age of ten Harry undertook his first public engagement, saluting officers parading at the 50th anniversary of VJ Day in London.

Favourite nanny. Harry films a happy Tiggy Legge-Bourke at Cirencester Park Polo Club.

All is well. Diana took Harry and William to the Thorpe Park amusement centre, having invited photographers to show they were the survivors of her failed marriage.

The saddest day. Flanked by his father, Prince Charles, and uncle, Earl Spencer, Harry walks behind his mother's funeral cortège.

TOP LEFT  Shape of things to come. Harry gets his first ride in a tank during a visit to the barracks of the Light Dragoons in Hanover.

TOP RIGHT  Comrade-in-arms. Harry with Lt Col Bill Connor, the American officer who befriended him and witnessed his bravery on his first tour of Afghanistan.

LEFT  Love in progress. A proud Harry strolls with Chelsy Davy after receiving his helicopter pilot's wings from his father.

BOTTOM  Posh and Becks. Third-in-line to the throne with soccer star David Beckham in Johannesburg where, along with Prince William, they were promoting England's bid to host the World Cup.

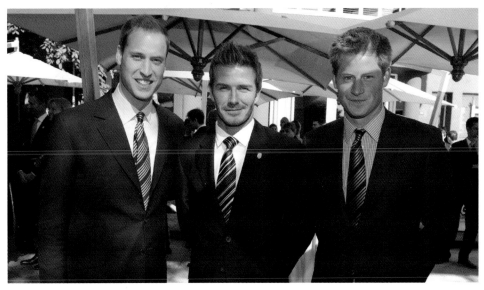

LEFT  In Diana's footsteps. Harry being shown a minefield in Tete Province, Mozambique and taking the opportunity to promote the HALO Trust, Princess Diana's favourite charity, which has cleared more than a million mines.

RIGHT  Family group. Harry, with his brother and sister-in-law, the Duke and Duchess of Cambridge, and the Queen, enjoys a light moment during the Diamond Jubilee celebrations.

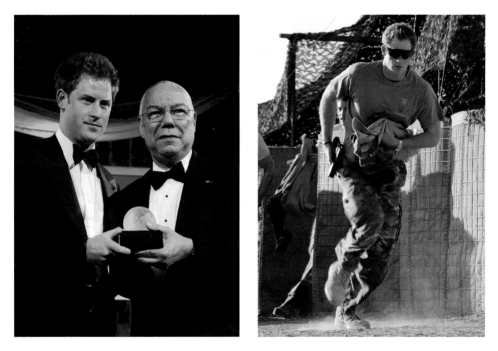

LEFT  Proud moment. Harry receives the Distinguished Humanitarian Award from former US Secretary of State, Colin Powell, at the Atlantic Council's Annual Awards Dinner in Washington DC.

RIGHT  Ready for action. Captain Wales races from his VHR (very high readiness) tent to his Apache helicopter at Camp Bastion in Afghanistan.

Pointing the way. Prince Charles looks on while his father signals a landmark to Harry as they travel down the River Thames on board the *Spirit of Chartwell* during the Diamond Jubilee Pageant.

LEFT Caring Prince. The Prince is greeted by a young boy at the St Bernadette School for the visually impaired in the Maseru district of his beloved Lesotho.

RIGHT Supporting the groom. The royal brothers at Westminster Abbey on William's wedding day.

My hero. Harry duplicates Usain Bolt's trademark stance after 'beating' him in a race in Jamaica.

Waiting for the flame. Harry joins the Duchess of Cambridge to receive the Olympic torch at Buckingham Palace.

for which he could award marks. She went on to suggest that Harry's work, which had featured in newspapers and included two screen prints inspired by Aboriginal designs, had actually been finished off by Burke.

Ms Forsyth claimed that, unbeknown to Harry, who trusted her, she had on 16 May 2003 secretly recorded him admitting that he had written 'about a sentence' of the disputed text. She was sacked for going public with the information but later won a claim for unfair dismissal although the tribunal hearing her case decided to reject her claim that she had done some of his written work for him, allowing a Clarence House spokesman to snatch victory from the jaws of defeat by announcing: 'We are delighted that Harry has been totally cleared of cheating.'

There had been one bright spot on the horizon as Harry cleared out his study at Eton: he had excelled in the school's Combined Cadet Force and been promoted to the highest rank of cadet officer. Although, unlike his brother, he failed to win the Sword of Honour awarded to the school's leading cadet, he led a detachment of forty-eight cadets as parade commander in the Eton Tattoo in front of a crowd of hundreds which included his clearly proud father and an assortment of the army's top brass. If he had entertained doubts before about his ambitions to join the army – and for a while he thought about joining his friend Guy Pelly at the Cirencester Agricultural College – then that experience set his life-long dream in concrete: he was going to be a soldier.

His army life would have to be put on hold, however, and

not just for the traditional gap year. Despite having passed with flying colours the army's pre-Regular Commissions Board assessment to test his aptitude for a military career, his father had decided that after the shocking surprises and disappointments of his Eton years, Harry must go away for two years – far away, to work hard 'in his own best interests'.

Just as all this was happening, James Hewitt – who had encouraged if not inspired Harry's military ambitions – released a statement that really set tongues wagging. The former cavalry officer emphatically announced that he was not Harry's father:

> I can absolutely assure you that I am not. Admittedly the colour of his hair is similar to mine and people say we look alike. I have never encouraged these comparisons and although I was with Diana for a long time I must state once and for all that I'm not Harry's father. When I met Diana he was already a toddler... I have to say he's a much more hand-some chap than I ever was.

There were some who failed to accept Hewitt's declaration. One intellectual, who sees Charles regularly, says:

> I know what the official line is but I still find the resemblance extraordinary. Quite recently I was sat at a table with James Hewitt and, never mind his hair, when you look into his eyes it's like you are looking into Harry's; there is not a scintilla of difference.

Hewitt's declaration certainly disappointed those who had sought to profit by proving the contrary was true. One European tabloid newspaper had engaged an attractive blonde – Harry's type! – to ensnare him in a honey trap, probably in Spain where his reputation as a lover of the night life was growing. Her job was to get close enough to him to run her fingers through his hair and snatch a strand or two. The 'evidence' would be examined for its DNA which would then be compared to Hewitt's. Scotland Yard's Specialist Operations department was alerted and the plot was thwarted, although not before Britain's most senior police officers had been briefed and a worried Charles had consulted his lawyer, Fiona Shackleton.

And as for Hewitt's announcement, as far as Harry was concerned it meant nothing. Prince Charles, his real father, had beaten Hewitt to the punch. Aware of how cruel gossip can be at such an upmarket establishment as Eton – where parents all claim to be privy to what goes on in the very top circles – Charles had summoned his younger son for a heart-to-heart meeting prior to his start at the college and warned him that he would hear such rumours and to assure him they were not true.

Harry listened to his father's difficult speech without interrupting. He had always looked up to Hewitt, a war hero, a real-life tank commander in the First Gulf War and a likeable man. At one stage in his life he had been something of a mentor to the boy, who longed to follow in his soldiering footsteps – and Charles knew it. It was, by the account relayed to me, one of the hardest moments in the heir's life, for in his candid explanation it was impossible to conceal that Diana really had been in love with the dashing Household Cavalry officer. Despite the pain it caused the Prince to deliver the message, he handled it with great courage.

Harry thanked him for that but he hung on to his admiration for his mother's soldier lover until Hewitt subsequently sold his story of the affair, an error of judgement that allowed a slavering tabloid-reading public to lap up the sordid details.

# 8

# COMING OF AGE

Harry had hoped that after five arduous years at Eton, interspersed with his wild breaks at Highgrove, he would spend much of his gap year playing polo in Australia – he was already a member of the Beaufort and Cirencester clubs and given a season or two's further experience was expected to join Britain's elite group of 100 professional players. His father, however, had other ideas. Certainly he would be going to Australia but as a £100-a-week jackaroo (and his father would allow him not a penny more), a farm labourer, not as a fledgling polo star. Disappointed by the poor academic grades Harry had attained and concerned that he was still not over his wild days, Charles (who regarded himself as an academic despite having achieved no better than average results as an undergraduate) told him he was sending him off to far-flung corners of the world for not one gap year but two. In year one he would be rounding up cattle, shearing sheep and fixing broken fences on a farm Down Under, and in year two he would be doing even harder manual work 'somewhere in Africa', putting off his much anticipated entry into the army until 2005, even though he had already passed the pre-Regular Commissions Board assessment with flying colours, virtually assuring him of a place at Sandhurst Military Academy.

They got the wrong idea in Australia, too. Newspaper reports and television shows were deluged with complaints about the anticipated £240,000 cost to them of helping his own protection officers guard the Prince. Public opinion was that his stint as a farmhand would be no more than a glorified holiday, as it might have been had Harry had his way.

Alas, the stint did not start well. No sooner had he got to know his five fellow jackaroos on the 40,000-acre Tooloombilla station in north-eastern Australia than he realised they were not the only company he would be having in the outback. Reporters and cameramen arrived in droves, all hoping to get the scoop of the 'spoiled Prince' getting humiliated down on the ranch. At one point he threatened to end his Queensland country experience and seats were booked for him and his bodyguards on an early morning flight out of Roma airport. 'I can't do what I came here to do so I might as well go home,' he told one of his new farmhouse friends. The negative PR backlash of such a move, however, was clear to see: the Australian press had licence to label him a whinging Pom and Prince Philip sent word that at home his quitting would be likened to Prince Edward's walking out on the Royal Marines because of the discipline he simply could not take.

It took a call from Buckingham Palace to oblige Queensland's Premier, Peter Beattie, to make an official statement: Harry was still on the property – but a prisoner in the ranch house, restricted to watching videos instead of getting on with the work he had been sent to do, so leave him alone. Nevertheless a trip to the nearby Mitchell rodeo had to be called off when it was realised that, despite the Prime Minister's plea, the army of newsmen threatening to descend on them was simply too large for the local security forces to handle.

Even his influential employer/hosts, Annie and Noel Hill – Annie had been an Earls Court flatmate of Diana's and her husband was the son of the wealthy polo star Sinclair Hill, who was Charles's polo coach – could do nothing to stem the media ambush. Press secretary Colleen Davis's pleas for the journalists and photographers to leave him to get on with his work also fell on deaf ears. She was later replaced by the lofty but softly spoken Paddy Haverson, an army colonel's son who had managed to end the feud between Alex Ferguson and David Beckham when he was press officer at Manchester United (although that was by prior arrangement).

It took a heartfelt appeal from Charles's former equerry Mark Dyer, who was a sort of male Tiggy during Harry's stay, to bring the charade to an end. 'I've got a young man here in pieces,' he told the hunting pack. After agreeing that there would be later photo opportunities the newsmen backed off, freeing Harry to get on with his chores, rising at seven each morning and working through till early evening with a two-hour break for lunch when the Australian heat is at its fiercest – 40 degrees in the shade.

And that, as it turns out, was the moment Dyer – himself a hard-living ex-Welsh Guards officer – became Harry's hero for life. The Prince could see that Dyer was not only a great diplomat, but also that no one would mess with him. Within days the Prince was able to slip into a bull-riding competition in the tiny nearby town of Injune (population 362). He wandered up to the ticket booth and paid his $10 entrance fee to gain admission to the Queensland Rodeo Association state finals. Then, sitting on a grass hill, he videoed the event and – aware that his father was scrutinising reports of his activities – sipped a soft drink rather than the beer most around him were enjoying.

He declined an invitation to ride a steer but good naturedly accepted some friendly ribbing; Jamie Johnson, president of the Injune Rodeo Association, called him 'a useless pommy jackaroo like all of them that come out here'.

Harry had been warned by his father in advance that when speaking to people he should do his best to avoid any trace of upper-crust English accent. When he was in Australia many years earlier Charles was being driven through the outback when he spotted a gang of labourers working on the road in the blistering heat and seemingly hundreds of miles from anywhere. He ordered his driver to stop so he might step out of the limousine and speak to them. It was, to say the least, a stilted conversation: once they had told him they had been away from their homes for weeks he asked them, 'And what about your wives?' Unfortunately the Windsor pronunciation of 'wives' left them nonplussed and after he had repeated the question three times to the puzzled group, one of the gang turned to his fellows and said, 'I think he wants us to wave,' and a red-faced Charles, watched by his policeman, the aptly named Paul Officer, stood on the roadside facing a handful of men waving at him just as the crowds had done in Sydney.

Two months after the media fracas, Harry honoured the deal Dyer had made for him. The media were allowed to film and photograph the nineteen-year-old as, dressed in open-neck blue shirt, jeans, donning a brown Akubra hat, he rode a chestnut horse called Guardsman and guided a herd of thirty Shorthorn and Shorthorn Charolais cattle around part of the property. It was a very different Harry from the young man who had arrived in the country just nine weeks earlier and sulked his way through a media baptism by fire. He had also been able to indulge his twin passions of polo and rugby, travelling to Sydney to lead his Young England team to a 4–6 victory over Young Australia Polo. Next he was in the stadium to witness the successful World Cup campaign of the England rugby team, joining his cousin Zara Phillips and her future husband Mike Tindall for an appropriate celebration in some of the city's wilder bars.

There was no longer any danger of 'whinging Pom' accusations. At home, after Mark Dyer had called him with an extremely favourable report of the second son's transformation, Prince Charles celebrated the success of his plan with champagne, declaring, 'It's working.' His boy, it seemed, was becoming a man. Alas, if he thought the troubles were fixed then he would have another think coming in the months to follow: his high-spirited son's hard-drinking, partying days were far from over.

For the time being, however, all seemed well and Charles was much relieved for he had problems of his own to deal with. Still bereft at the loss in March 2002 of his beloved grandmother, Queen Elizabeth the Queen Mother, he had consoled himself with the thought that he could perpetuate her memory by moving from St James's Palace into her London residence, Clarence House, just as she had wished. Then one of his closest friends, Emilie van Cutsem, had asked him: 'What about Camilla?' The Camilla Question remained unresolved despite the fact that she had been divorced from her husband, Andrew Parker Bowles, for years and had even discussed the subject of marriage to Charles with the then Archbishop of Canterbury, Dr George Carey. It would be improper, his closest friends counselled, for him to be living in sin in his grandmother's old house. Van Cutsem told him: 'You must decide whether to marry her or let her go.' After the house had been renovated at great public expense, however, Charles and Camilla moved in together and shared a bedroom but he did nothing about their marital status.

The most insurmountable obstacle standing in the way of their marriage was not the attitude of the Queen or Prince Philip, his brothers and sister, the Anglican Synod or its members, but the implacable opposition of the Catholic

Church, of which she was very much a member. Catholic hostility to divorcee Camilla led to an embarrassing incident when the ecumenically minded Prince was invited to attend a service at Westminster Cathedral in early 2004. Camilla wanted to accompany him and a phone call was made on her behalf from St James's Palace to the cathedral. The monsignor who took the call said he would have to refer the request to the Archbishop. The reply to the Palace was that the Archbishop could not agree to such a suggestion. Charles had to make the visit to the cathedral on his own.

The truth was that Charles needed his mistress more than ever, as a couple of moments of Goonish farce at the royal European premiere of film *Cold Mountain*, starring Nicole Kidman, in a wintry London in 2003 had demonstrated. When Charles was being introduced to members of the cast in the traditional pre-screening line-up, it became apparent that he had no idea of the identity of the shortish, shaven-headed chap in a suit who introduced him with such easy familiarity to Kidman, Jude Law and Ray Winstone. Charles chatted to each of the stars in turn, starting with Winstone. When he reached Kidman, Charles asked whether she had been in the movie *Enigma*. Realising he had mixed her up with Kate Winslet, Nicole smiled: 'No.'

Charles added: 'You've done a bit since then … *Moulin Rouge*.'

'Yes,' replied Nicole, growing increasingly uncomfortable, 'a few things.'

As the man who had been making the introductions

hovered at his side, the Prince whispered to an aide: 'Who is this chap?'

'He,' the Prince was informed, 'is Anthony Minghella, the director of the film.'

'Oh God,' said Charles, 'the ice-cream man from the Isle of Wight!'

This was a reference to the trade formerly practised by Minghella's hard-working parents. 'Charles had not done his homework,' the aide admits. 'That's the sort of thing Harry could have helped him with. He was always up to date with such things and would have made sure his father knew exactly who he was meeting had he been there.' With Harry absent, Charles needed Camilla by his side.

On 13 February 2004 Harry was despatched to the Kingdom of Lesotho, a 12,000-square mile landlocked enclave totally surrounded by South Africa, which it supplies with water from the huge quantities garnered by its lush mountain region. Although Lesotho (which translates as 'the land of the people who speak Sesotho') is also rich in diamonds, 40 per cent of its people live below the poverty line and it has the third-highest rate of AIDS in the world. Charles chose it as a country badly in need of the kind of charitable work Diana had undertaken in the latter years of her life. Harry would learn that AIDS was responsible for the colossal number of orphans he would encounter during his stay in the country and, more importantly, that he could bring smiles to their sad faces.

Upon his arrival, Harry was met in the capital Maseru by Lesotho's Prince Seeiso, the brother of King Letsie III. The country's government is a modified form of a constitutional monarchy, the Prime Minister is the head of government and the monarch serves in a ceremonial capacity only. But this was no royal tour even though Seeiso stayed with him for much of his time there and introduced him to many of the people. Hard work lay ahead. Just outside the town of Mokhotlong, Harry was handed a set of tools and told to get stuck in with those labouring to create the foundations for a new health clinic. He hardly had time to draw breath before he found himself working as part of a gang on a road bridge over the Sanqebethu River.

He helped dig trenches to divert water away from the crop fields at Ha Moeketsane and spent time sowing vegetable seeds for the garden at an orphanage. It brought back to him another saying he had heard from a counsellor at the Featherstone Lodge rehab when an addict was bemoaning the fact that he was low on self-worth: 'If you want to regain self-worth go out and do something worthy.'

Accompanying a doctor on his rounds in the village of Matsieng, he saw the horrifying extent of the AIDS pandemic that gripped much of the country. The young Prince could not do enough for the victims. When his working day was over he taught the children to play touch rugby and painted their barren rooms for them. He discovered that, in addition to those suffering as a result of AIDS, there were children known locally as 'herd boys', boys as young as five who had been sent by their families to look after livestock in remote locations on their own. These children have to fend for themselves and many do not survive.

To draw attention to the efforts of the British Red Cross in Lesotho he made a television documentary, *The Forgotten Kingdom*, which also raised more than £500,000 for the cause. Then, in partnership with Prince Seeiso, he founded a new charity: 'Sentebale [Forget me not – a veiled reference to his mother and her charity work], the Princes' fund for Lesotho'. The charity had four programmes: one to provide management advice and funding to care for children who are orphaned or disabled; another to arrange regular camps for children aware of their HIV status; a third to make education available to children who live in remote mountainous areas and finally what Harry calls the Letsema network – a collaborative online network encouraging people to congregate and 'discuss topical matters concerning children in their care'. One of his main problems has been to raise international awareness of Lesotho's plight and, as a remedy, he came up with a number of promotional ideas including the Sentebale Polo Cup which moves to a different location around the globe each year.

Pledging to support the cause for the rest of his days, Harry said with obvious conviction:

I met so many children whose lives had been shattered following the death of their parents – they were so vulnerable and in need of care and attention. It's time to follow on – well, as much as I can – to try to keep my mother's legacy going. I believe I've got a lot of my mother in me and I think she'd want my brother and I to do this. Obviously it's not as easy for William as it is for me. I've got more time on my hands to be able to help. I always wanted to go to an AIDS country to carry on my mother's legacy.

Not everyone took him at his word. His heartfelt statement fell on deaf ears, for example, when it came to the *Daily Express*'s acerbic columnist Carol Sarler. She wrote a piece describing him as a 'horrible young man ... a national disgrace who rarely lifted a finger unless it's to feel up a cheap tart in a nightclub'. She described his gap year as a space between no work whatsoever at school and utter privilege at Sandhurst. As for his spell in Australia, she claimed he had spent it 'slumped in front of the television waiting to behave badly at the next available rugby match' and in Lesotho she said he was spending eight lavish weeks, during which 'he has reluctantly agreed to spend a bit of the trip staring at poor people'. Harry's new press guardian, Paddy Haverson, replied in detail pointing out that Sarler had, in effect, used her poison pen to put down a diligent, hard-working young man without having a clue as to what he was really like or what he was doing during his gap years. The Palace had had enough, just as the *Daily Express* would have done had anyone dared to describe one of their own in similar terms.

A leading London psychiatrist who had once treated his mother, says:

Forget the critics: I think the Lesotho experience turned young Henry's [he insists on calling him by the name he was christened with] life around. For the first time in his life he saw desperate poverty, terrible suffering. I remember Diana telling me how she took him to visit the poor and the prostitutes in London in the hope that it would stir his conscience, but they were brief visits to places surrounded by wealth and luxury. He would not have been able to understand why those surrounding these unfortunates could not take care of them, plus he was obviously aware that there is a welfare state and no one in the UK need die of hunger or lack of any medical treatment. In Africa he saw people who had nothing and little chance of getting anything. Now that did wake his conscience and I think if Diana were alive today she would be greatly relieved by this turnaround in him.

His subsequent insistence on going to war and living under those dangerous and uncomfortable conditions in Afghanistan also speaks volumes about wanting to gain experience outside his upbringing. To be honest, I think he was bored with the way the royals live and what they expect the world to provide for them. He never consulted me, of course, but from a distance I can see nothing in him of the terrible paranoia poor Diana suffered. There were times when I thought she might end her life; Harry lives his to the full. Now she couldn't do that and I suspect that she would have been unwell whoever she was married to. Prince Charles may have exasperated her, but take it from me he did not cause her underlying illness.

The unfortunate orphans of Lesotho were not the only ones Harry met during his stay in Africa for it was there that he re-encountered the girl who was to become the love of his life: Chelsy Davy, a girl who had first aroused his interest when they met during her time as a student at Cheltenham Ladies' College, close to Highgrove and its Club H. Chelsy was a lively blonde just a year younger than Harry and the attraction was as instantaneous as it was mutual. A close friend says: 'Because she is so attractive Chelsy has had many male admirers, but from the way she talked about Harry we all believed that this was the one she would end up marrying.' It has to be said, though, that Harry was not the only thing Ms Davy had on her mind: as fiercely ambitious as she is intelligent, she was heading for a degree in philosophy, politics and economics from the University of Cape Town and had her sights set on a career in law. Fresh from his ditch-digging tasks, Harry was overawed by this particular beauty's intellect, but their love of clubs, parties and vodka meant they had a great deal in common. During their early courting period, Harry got to know her parents when he went to stay with the family in Durban and once he had won Mr and Mrs Davy's confidence the couple went off to stay in their seafront apartment at Camps Bay where the relationship developed despite the chaperoning presence of Chelsy's brother Shaun.

In a letter home to a former school friend Harry wrote that Chelsy was 'the love of my life – this one's unreal'. Initially Chelsy was puzzled by his insistence that they keep their fledgling romance a secret: she soon found out why. They had been enjoying a peaceful relationship until the day they let their guard down and were photographed kissing at a polo field in Durban in 2004; from that moment on

Chelsy discovered what it was like to be public property and how the fledgling relationship was destined to change her life. Gone were the days when they could camp out and watch the wildlife on exotic safaris. From the moment she followed him back to the UK, however, Miss Davy felt at ease in royal circles. She would become close friends with the Duchess of York's daughters Beatrice and Eugenie, and Prince William's wife-to-be Kate and her sister Pippa Middleton. Her Facebook pages read like a who's who of British society. She accompanied Harry to royal weddings and enjoyed nights out sipping vodka with him in London's most exclusive – and expensive – nightclubs. She shared Harry's annoyance when they were shadowed by the paparazzi, whom Harry called 'the tossers' – a phrase he had learned from his mother. It was to be a tempestuous affair, however, and several times they walked away from each other only to be subsequently reunited. Clearly devoted to her, Harry describes Chelsy as being as gaffe-prone as George Bush 'but better looking' and says it was the Essex-girl mentality in her that forced him to take her to the *X Factor* studios even though he had no great regard for the programme's creator Simon Cowell, who had once had the audacity to say to him, 'If you ever get tired of running the country, you can come and work for me.'

Although happy that his daughter had met 'someone', Charles Davy found himself the recipient of some unwelcome press attention when a newspaper claimed to have uncovered many misdeeds including an unsavoury friendship with the internationally despised President Mugabe. Davy vehemently denied all the allegations made against him and asserted that he had never even met Mugabe. In any event, Davy had other things to worry about when his royal guest started a major security alert by leaving the family ranch without informing anyone after having drunk 'one too many'.

It was July before Harry returned to the UK and revealed to his father that he was in love. Charles listened attentively but reminded him that he had his final Sandhurst entrance exams to study for and encouraged him to help out on a Duchy of Cornwall farm and to train with the Rugby Football Union as a rugby development officer. Charles was pleased that his son seemed to have changed his ways: Lesotho had made a difference; younger people were now his focus. He was told that girlfriends and what he called 'emotional baggage' would have to take a back seat. But Harry could never stop thinking about Chelsy and the two remained in close touch by telephone.

Meanwhile, James Hewitt wasn't having the best of summers: to Harry's amusement his mother's former lover was arrested in July 2004 at the Cactus Blue bar in Chelsea on suspicion of possessing cocaine. The former cavalry officer, nicknamed Timeshare for his many dalliances, was with TV and radio presenter Alison Bell, who was also accused. Hewitt was locked in a cell at Notting Hill police station to sober up before he could be interviewed the following day. He could have faced a jail sentence of up to seven years if convicted, and Ms Bell (a former girlfriend of Prince Edward) a life term for the even more serious offence of supply, but the authorities smiled on the pair, letting Hewitt off with a warning (though he lost his gun licence after police found a disassembled shotgun on his living room floor) and Bell without charge.

Harry did not see a great deal of his father that summer. Charles had taken Camilla to Birkhall, the Queen Mother's former house on the Balmoral estate. Rupert Lendrum, who worked as Charles's major-domo at St James's Palace, Clarence House and Highgrove, as well as Birkhall, says that the Scottish house is by far the Prince's favourite. 'It's a very big house, very big but not grand in the sense that some royal homes are,' he says.

He worked terribly hard on the boxes of stuff we sent up to him during summer. He starts at breakfast and is often still at it at midnight. Sometimes we would think twice about including something in a box and think does he really need to read this, perhaps I should just ring him up and say 'Look here, sir...' but he likes to see everything in writing so the boxes just swell.

No one at Clarence House is sure of the exact date in the autumn of 2004 when Charles made his decision, but make it he did. He was going to marry Camilla and as soon as possible. It would have to be a civil ceremony since the Church of England – of which he will one day be the Supreme Governor – disapproves of remarriage of divorced people in church. In addition, a high-placed official of the Catholic Church pointed out that Camilla was not only a divorcee but the husband she divorced in 1995 was still alive. Clarence House, nevertheless, said the ceremony would take place in the Windsor Castle chapel, St George's (a statement it later had to revise as the pair married in a civil ceremony in Windsor Guildhall before a service of blessing at the castle chapel). Camilla would never be Queen but maybe that was no bad thing. Meanwhile, Queen Elizabeth is said to have sighed deeply when asked if it could be made known that not only was she very happy for them both but that the marriage had her blessing.

Charles broke the news to Harry on his return to the UK. It was never going to be an easy task for a man to tell his son that the woman blamed for the break-up of the marriage to his mother was to become his stepmother. But she had been that in all but name for a long while and she made Charles happy. What's more, Harry had grown to like her, to love her even, and was bound even closer to her by the public criticism and negative comment she had received: 'She's not a wicked stepmother, she's a wonderful woman,' he said in one emotional outburst. And he meant it.

After the historic father–son chat and a brief discussion about how and when the marriage would be announced, Harry decided it was time to rejoin the real world and he took himself and William off to the Chinawhite club in Mayfair. Somehow a glamour model, one Lauren Pope, managed to inveigle herself into the VIP area where she made a beeline for the princes, leaping on to Harry's lap and planting kisses on his cheek. For once he did not welcome the attention from a young woman, probably anticipating the publicity it would create for the Page 3 girl who was later to join the cast of the bawdy television show, *The Only Way Is Essex*. Sure enough she subsequently gave interviews claiming that he spent hours chatting with her and later telephoned her for a date. Harry's friend says: 'Sorry, Miss Pope, but you are definitely not the Prince's type. This was never going to be a Cinderella moment.'

There were more nightclub incidents during his UK stay as this was, after all, the double-gap year, the extended period in which Prince Charles hoped that Harry would get his wild days out of the way. But now, it was time for him to go back to work.

If Charles was burying himself in his work in the hope that the issue of his recent engagement to Camilla would go away, then he needed to think again. At a New York dinner party Prince Andrew had let his fellow diners know in no uncertain terms that he was not enamored by the thought of Camilla becoming his sister-in-law and perhaps Her Royal Highness or, heaven forbid, Queen Camilla, but the gap between brothers had never been wider. It was clear that no matter what the public or Prince Andrew might think, Prince Charles needed her at his side. This was one battle Andrew would have to fight on his own. Harry was acutely aware that his father and uncle were not on the best of terms. On hearing of unsavoury goings-on in New York, Charles had asked his youngest brother to use a useful show-business contact he had in Manhattan to investigate. The information that Prince Edward brought back about certain individuals did not please Charles, and Harry had to put up with his father brooding over the matter at a time when he was doing his best to get his own life together.

In September Harry breezed through his Sandhurst exam but just as Charles was beginning to believe his younger son's wild days really were over, the young Prince found himself back in trouble. After the highly successful summer PR offensive, he 'lost it' leaving the West End nightclub Pangaea, close to Piccadilly, at 3 a.m. on an October night. Despite his awareness of the part pursuing paparazzi had played in his mother's death, he seemed, up to this point, to have found acceptance in the knowledge that the photographers would always be on his tail. That night, however, acceptance seemed to have deserted him. He had failed to accept the rejection of an aspiring actress called Anne-Marie Mogg, whose stunning appearance had attracted his attention. He made the mistake of sending a flunky over to ask her and her friend Josephine to join him at his table. The flunky bungled it by saying, 'Harry would like to invite you to join him – that's Harry as in Prince Harry.' Ms Mogg declined the invitation declaring, 'I wasn't going to give him any special treatment because he was a royal. Don't get me wrong, he's a very good-looking guy. He's much taller and stronger-looking than I thought from his photographs. If he hadn't been a royal I probably would have gone over.' No way was this one going to be a groupie and Harry's mood blackened as he downed his vodka, failing to appreciate the joke when his male companions chided him about being too shy to approach her himself. Finally he left the club at around 3 a.m. in a foul temper.

Outside he climbed into the car that had been waiting to transport him the short distance home when his eyes focused on Chris Uncle, a photographer working for the Big Pictures agency. 'Suddenly he burst out of the car,' says Uncle,

and lunged towards me as I was still taking pictures. He lashed out and then deliberately pushed my camera into my face. The base of the camera struck me and cut my bottom lip. At the same time he was repeatedly saying, 'Why are you doing this? Why don't you leave me alone?'

Another photographer, Charlie Pycraft, told BBC News that Harry had indeed attacked Uncle: 'He was half-way getting into the back of the car when he suddenly reacted and lunged at him, grabbed his camera and pushed him against the wall.'

While the Prince used his best soldier-speak expletives during the altercation, his protection officer, helped by the two club doormen, pulled him off and pushed him into the back of the car which then sped away. Giving Harry's version of events the following day a Clarence House spokesman said that even though it was Uncle who sported the evidence of a cut lip from the altercation, it was the Prince who had been hit in the face. Harry was fortunate that Uncle did not press charges for assault. No one is on record as saying whether he was inebriated on that occasion, but then again, who sits in a nightclub until three in the morning without consuming a fair amount of alcohol? Certainly not Harry Wales.

Once more, it was time to move on and the Queen made her feelings known to Charles, suggesting he make it clear to Harry that he was a royal not a selfish, arrogant movie star. He was into his second gap year and there were more good works to be done … and, yes, more nightclubs, at safe distances from London, deserving of a royal visit. So off he went, this time to Argentina, but Harry's insatiable appetite for the wild life – something most twenty-year-olds would appreciate –was to get him into trouble yet again during his stay there. He had arranged to stay on the El Remanso (the Backwater) estate with friends Mark and Luke Tomlinson (sons of Prince Charles's friends Simon and Claire Tomlinson). The estate was owned by Major Christopher Hanbury, polo patron, racehorse owner and for two decades an aide to once the world's wealthiest man, the Sultan of Brunei. El Remanso's own polo grounds were still under construction so Harry planned to practise each day at the nearby La Alegria estate but residence at Hanbury's spread ensured him close proximity to the world's best polo player, Adolfo Cambiaso, from whom he expected to learn much.

Alas, his plans were thwarted by a knee injury which prevented him from riding let along playing polo. Instead he made frequent visits to the nearby town of Lobos where he drank beer and played pool with men who lived and breathed horses specially bred for polo, before moving on to the clubs favoured by local girls. He became extremely popular with the townspeople, who marvelled at his lack of airs and graces but the popularity did not extend to those charged with protecting him. According to one newspaper report the adventure-seeking playboy Prince 'escaped on a motorbike with four Scotland Yard bodyguards having to chase him. For the police Harry became a real headache.'

Frustrated by being unable to ride, he tried on more than one occasion to slip away with his friends on fishing trips but, to his annoyance, the over-enthusiastic local police insisted on following him. The final straw came when a newspaper reported that a murder suspect had told a journalist that underworld characters were planning to kidnap Harry when he next visited the Bar Nievas in the one-street town of Salvador Maria, a rough bar frequented by hoodlums and bandits. The bar could not have been more different than the London night spots Harry had become used to where champagne can cost £1,000 a bottle. With its bare walls and crude wooden tables, Omar Nievas's establishment discourages women customers, preferring to serve their card-playing menfolk the local Quilmes beer at thirty pence a bottle.

The Nievas security scare was enough and Argentine authorities told Harry's detectives they could no longer guarantee his safety in their country. What was always thought to have been planned as a six-week 'working trip' was to be cut short, with the media throughout South America reporting that the Prince was being sent home in disgrace. After the Buenos Aires daily *Página 12* claimed that Harry had returned to his hosts' estate from one night of partying in town in 'quite bad condition given his uncontrolled consumption of alcohol', it was agreed that this was time to call it a night. Despite obvious heightened security at Ezeiza airport at the start of his journey home, Buckingham Palace insisted he was returning on exactly the date that had been scheduled. Whichever way, that particular party was over. And anyway, Christmas was coming.

It was a quiet Christmas with his father and brother under the Queen's roof at Sandringham – the traditional break Diana dreaded each year. The princes stayed for the traditional New Year shoots but sped off to Highgrove as soon as good manners would allow. Harry was presented with an opportunity to redeem himself. The earthquake beneath the Indian Ocean that exploded into being on Boxing Day morning just off the coast of Indonesia was the longest-lasting faulting ever known. It caused a series of tsunamis in the area that killed more than 230,000 people; Indonesia, Sri Lanka, India and Thailand were the hardest-hit countries but the devastation spread across large swathes of the eastern hemisphere.

After watching a documentary about the pitiful plight of the tens of thousands of children orphaned, the brothers asked what they could do to help. They were told there was a warehouse at nearby Warmley where volunteers were preparing and packing hygiene packs for the Red Cross to despatch to the Maldives where more than 15,000 people had been made homeless. The princes wasted no time in joining the volunteer force. Harry said later: 'It's been by far the worst thing I've ever seen. We're not exempt from what everybody else does. We just wanted to be hands on. We didn't want to sit back.'

Alas, his halo slipped a bit just twenty-four hours later. Harry had been invited to join 250 guests at a party at the Chippenham home of the Olympic triple gold medallist Richard Meade to celebrate the twenty-second birthday of the showjumper's son, also called Harry. It was a fancy dress party with a colonial theme and Prince William delighted others by dressing as a lion. It was Prince Harry's choice of costume that caused a furore: he went as a Nazi to try and outdo his devil-may-care friend Guy Pelly who said he was going as the Queen.

Harry had on a jacket with the German flag on one arm and when he removed it, it revealed that he was wearing the desert uniform of General Rommel's Afrika Korps with a badge of the Wehrmacht on the collar. Most of those present – many of them, like Prince Charles, members of the Beaufort Hunt – would have kept quiet but one of the guests took a photograph and sold it to *The Sun*, which published it a few days later under the front-page headline HARRY THE NAZI. The picture showed the third in line holding a drink and smoking a cigarette while bedecked in a shirt altered to look like a German uniform by the addition of the collar flashes and an eagle insignia on the chest. The part of the amateur-ish ensemble which caused most offence, however, was a red, white and black swastika armband. He'd hired the outfit from

Maud's Cotswold Costumes in nearby Nailsworth where no questions were asked although, apparently, eyebrows were raised. No one has been able to explain how he managed to leave Highgrove without anyone spotting him so attired – Prince Charles was still in Scotland where he had seen the New Year in. But it is a sign of Harry's determination not to be overruled by his brother that William was unable to persuade him that the outfit was, at least, unsuitable for a British prince – and a potential British Army cadet at that – to wear, even to a fancy dress party.

The incident caused international outrage in the Jewish community which was preparing to mark the sixtieth anniversary of the liberation of Auschwitz, and there was even a call from a former armed forces minister for Harry to be stripped of his place at Sandhurst, saying that the picture showed he was unsuitable for the prestigious military academy. Fortunately that didn't happen but Harry was obliged by his father to make a humiliating formal apology, albeit via a press spokesman, who said the Prince was very sorry if his poor choice of costume had caused any offence or embarrassment to anyone. The Conservative leader Michael Howard said he should have made the apology in person rather than through a spokesman. A leading Jewish figure said his father – who had already made him atone for the offence by swilling out the pigs on his farm – should compel him to attend a forthcoming ceremony at the death camp Auschwitz later that month.

Never mind death camp, for Harry it was clearly time for boot camp.

# 9

# SOLDIER BOY

The obvious answer to Harry's problems was to get him into the army at the earliest opportunity. That was his wish in any case. Whereas his brother's choice of toys in the days of the Highgrove nursery were usually games, puzzles and Dinky cars, Harry's most treasured possessions were a complete set of lead toy soldiers and, ironically, the model of a Panzer tank, developed in Nazi Germany in the late 1930s. He would play noisily with those for what seemed like hours while William pitted his early affinity for business against his mother over a game of Monopoly, neither boy paying attention to the wooden rocking horse (a present from Nancy Reagan) which stood in the corner alongside a miniature antique piano that had been a christening gift for Harry from Barry Manilow.

His favourite choice of garb as a small boy was the little soldier's uniform James Hewitt had run up for him by his regimental tailor prior to one of the highlights of his early years – a visit to Combermere Barracks, the Windsor home

of the Household Cavalry. It was there, clad in the miniature flak jacket, army trousers and beret, which Hewitt had
shown him exactly how to position, that he decided on his
career plan: clambering on a real tank (and a British one!) he
declared, 'I'm going to be a soldier when I grow up.'

Fascinated by the vast array of weapons displayed in a gun
cabinet in the Cavalry Museum, he pleaded to be allowed
to hold one but Diana forbade him, saying there would be
plenty of opportunity to do so in the future.

She was not wrong, although she underestimated Harry's
determination to enter his desired Service: when Hewitt said
it would be nice for Harry to one day join his regiment, she
replied: 'Yes, I'd like that too. But sadly this family goes into
the navy, which they regard as the Senior Service.'

Although in essence she was correct, Harry's father is
Colonel-in-Chief of twelve army regiments and the boy
was fully aware of the 'secret' wardrobe in which Charles's
uniforms hang and had frequently inspected his array of ceremonial medals. However, his grandmother's position as head
of all Britain's armed forces – the only person in the country
who can officially declare war and peace – offered some room
for flexibility on that point.

The miniature army uniform Hewitt had had made for
him was worn practically threadbare and his request every
Christmas for a replacement ignored, but Harry finally
acquired a second one when he accompanied his mother on
an official visit to the Light Dragoons Regiment at Bergen-
Hohne Barracks near Hanover on 29 July 1993 – a day which

should have been a joyous one for Diana since it was the twelfth anniversary of her wedding to Charles. Concerned, so she said, that her sons might fall out over who could ride the tank, she had left William at home and taken the son she said was 'into soldiers at the moment'.

Because the visit was an official one, Harry was immaculately dressed in his best school uniform for the benefit of the waiting photographers – but not for long. Not to be outdone by the outfit he'd heard Hewitt had had made, the Light Dragoons' quartermaster had sent to Kensington Palace for Harry's measurements and had camouflage fatigues made which the Prince duly turned out in, with a beret to match those worn by the soldiers his mother had just inspected and with camouflage paint applied to his face to perfect the look. He was in his element and duly clambered aboard the Scimitar tank for the ride he'd been promised. This made his visit to the Combermere Barracks look like tame stuff, for the Dragoons had arranged a mock battle with machine guns firing blank rounds at the Scimitar. When he could see through the multi-coloured smoke they had also arranged, Harry directed operations from the tank's turret. According to an observant reporter present at the time, Harry blotted his copybook on that occasion by waving to his mother from the tank instead of saluting her. But at least he was now in absolutely no doubt about what he wanted to be when he grew up.

Harry had his chance to use a real gun long before Diana would have wished. Charles introduced him at an early age to grouse shooting. He was just nine when he badly bruised his shoulder during a royal shoot. He had not held the weapon correctly – a mistake he was never likely to repeat. Two years later Prince Philip bought him a shotgun for Christmas, earning himself still more negative points from Diana.

Unlike their mother, neither boy had any qualms about hunting to kill. On one occasion Harry earned himself negative front-page headlines when, out on a shoot with his father at Sandringham, he misfired and almost felled one of the beaters, the men who were there to drive out the pheasants for the royal party to shoot.

Harry's agonising wait to join the army finally ended early in May 2005, four months after the public humiliation over his choice of costume for the fancy dress party, but first he had a wedding to go to. Prince Charles was to marry Camilla in a civil ceremony at the Guildhall, Windsor on 8 April. Well, that was the plan; in the event the wedding was switched to the following day so that Charles could represent the Queen at the funeral of Pope John Paul II on what was originally intended to be his and Camilla's big day. It was Harry in best mischievous form who chided his father that the worldwide television interest and the crowds thronging the streets on the Saturday were really there to celebrate the union of local lady Grace Beesley to one Fraser Moores half an hour before the heir to the throne wed the woman he had loved for more than thirty years.

And, however the Queen felt on the day about her eldest son marrying his mistress, it was Harry who made her laugh by imitating the kind of facial expression she famously adopts when confronted with something she disapproves of.

Covering the wedding for Fox News from the roof of a building that housed a branch of the Threshers booze stores on the ground floor, I mentioned to my co-host, one John Scott, how intolerant Charles was of anyone who drank too much. That had, unfortunately, brought him into conflict on more than one occasion with Diana's mother, Frances Shand Kydd. She subsequently lost her driving licence through a drink-driving offence she blamed in court on me for writing her a letter which caused her 'considerable distress'. At the time I was writing, with Dominic Midgley, a book called *Diana On The Edge* that examined the Princess's psychological problems; one expert had suggested that anyone who suffered from both bulimia and self-harming had almost certainly been abused as a child. I wrote to her mother to ask if this had been the case. Alas, it caused her to have one too many, after which she unwisely went for a spin in her car and was arrested for driving under the influence. She never forgave me and it is unlikely she ever forgave her royal son-in-law for his occasional expressions of negative opinion. When she died in June 2004 Harry and William flew to the Scottish Isle of Seil for her funeral, but Charles stayed at home.

When he finally stepped through the doors of the Royal Military Academy in the Berkshire village of Sandhurst on 8 May 2005, as the most senior member of the Royal Family in living memory to enter training there, Harry was under no illusions about the discipline and fortitude he would have to display, particularly in view of the 'spoiled toff' reputation concomitant with being a prince. The first five weeks were going to be difficult for a man who enjoyed the kind of freedom and benders he had become accustomed to. A senior royal aide says he was instructed by Charles to tell the Sandhurst commandant, Major General Andrew Ritchie, not to spare the rod:

> But that was one instruction from HRH I purposely did not carry out. It was apparent that Sandhurst was not the kind of place where anybody got spared the rod. I only met Sergeant Major Vince Gaunt once but it was clear he was not going to let up on discipline for anyone – not even an heir to the throne.

Sandhurst is where all officers in the British Army are taught the qualities of leadership. It's the equivalent of the Britannia Royal Naval College at Dartmouth, which Harry's father, grandfather and uncle Andrew attended, and the Royal Air Force College at Cranwell. More than 80 per cent of officer cadets are university graduates and no one can pay to get in although some sons of wealthy foreign potentates have been known to try.

Charles drove his son there just as he had driven him to Eton on his first day. The playful punch he gave him on the arm as he dropped him off at the Old College training centre in Camberley seemed to signal: 'Get your act together, you're a man now.' But Harry knew he had to do more than most if he was to make a success of this longed-for career since he would be closely watched twenty-four hours a day.

Nevertheless, once the heir to the throne had left, Harry became just one of the 270 recruits joining that day for the 44-week course and that's exactly the way he wanted it: although the college was special, he was a normal recruit. Of the three companies, he was told he would be attached to Alamein and become a member of a thirty-strong platoon. After enrolling he picked up the keys to his room and a red name badge with just the word 'Wales' printed in white capital letters. Just as there were no 'HRH's at Mrs Mynors' school when he first entered aged three, Harry noticed the same went for Sandhurst. From this point on he was Officer Cadet Wales. The room he was to call home for the foreseeable future was even more modest than the one he had been allocated at Eton and this time there was no maid to keep it clean and tidy: he was required to provide his own ironing board and to place such items as his toothbrush and paste with exact spaces in between, much as servants had done for him in the past. Even his bed had to be made perfectly with the corners turned back and the blankets folded into a neat block. Everything had to be in perfect order for inspection at 5.30 each morning: 'I was never up this early unless I was going to bed this late,' he told a fellow cadet, whom he also told that for the first time in his life he had learned to use a lavatory brush – something a royal maid had once revealed his grandmother was a dab hand at. Just a photograph of his mother – the same one he had kept in his room at Eton

– propped on the simple bedside table would define him to visitors – not that there were likely to be many of those. Though thirty-two female cadets joined the same day there was no mixing of the sexes – the women trained in a separate platoon and their rooms were out of bounds. And anyway, there was always Chelsy – with whom he had just enjoyed a romantic break – waiting in the wings. But what, he asked himself, would she make of his almost shaven head? She hadn't seen him with his Michael Owen cut at Eton.

Harry had more to contend with than the lack of female company. A fellow cadet was obviously determined to fill the boast back home that he had given the third in line to the throne a beating; he chose his off-duty moment after a group – including Harry – had enjoyed a few beers. 'He picked on the wrong man, unfortunately,' says one who witnessed the fight. Harry let him have it where it hurts most and he was never picked on again. 'Harry always fought to win and he didn't mind fighting dirty, either,' explains Ken Wharfe, who took many a punch in his private parts when he had charge of the Prince as a child.

No mention was made of the incident when he gave an interview on his twenty-first birthday that September to Sky News, BBC Radio and the Press Association. His interviewers had to agree that he was a different man from the one they had encountered in the past; a serious, dedicated soldier. Despite his assertion that 'I am who I am. I'm not going to change,' he clearly had. This did not appear to be the party Prince of old, but a fast-maturing, well-disciplined adult whose days of drinking and brawling were over ... or so it seemed that day. He said that in certain circumstances he had been treated even more harshly than other recruits – 'But it did me good'. He was determined to serve on the front line when the time came and gave the frequently repeated quote: 'There's no way I'm going to put myself through Sandhurst and then sit on my arse back home while my boys are out fighting for their country.' And speaking for the first time about the Nazi uniform incident, he did what many had expected at the time and delivered a personal apology: 'It was a very stupid thing to do and I learned my lesson... That was then and this is now. It's something I will never do again. It was a stupid thing to do. I think it's part of growing up.'

It was during his first term at Sandhurst that Harry was appointed a Counsellor of State on his twenty-first birthday that September, ousting Prince Edward. He would serve in that capacity by standing in for the Queen when she visited Malta two months later to attend the Commonwealth Heads of Government meeting and by all accounts he loved being up there, as he put it, 'with the top guys'. There were more honours to come: a few months later he was appointed as one of nine new Commodores-in-Chief of the Royal Navy: Commodore-in-Chief, Small Ships and Diving. The growing responsibilities seemed to mature him.

The proudest day of Harry's life was probably 12 April 2006. The Duke of Edinburgh, Prince Charles, his stepmother the Duchess of Cornwall, his brother and his proud and loving former nanny Tiggy (now Mrs Pettifer) all turned up for his passing-out parade at which he and the other 219 graduates were inspected by his grandmother. The Queen smiled at him and Prince William saluted him. Only one important person in his life was missing: Chelsy had arrived in London but stayed away from the ceremony in order to avoid being a distraction at the extremely formal event. She would see him later at the Sandhurst ball and she would be with him when, at precisely midnight as tradition demanded, he removed the velvet cover from the new officers' pips on the jacket shoulder of his perfectly tailored £2,000 mess suit. Via another tradition he became a second lieutenant as he climbed the steps to Old College. As a Blues and Royals officer he would receive a salary of almost £22,000 a year. He deserved the honour heaped on him: he had behaved perfectly for forty-four weeks and responded to the strictest discipline without a murmur of dissent. At the ball even he was dazzled by Chelsy's stunning appearance in a backless turquoise satin dress and with her hair pinned up to emphasise her long neck and tanned back. There was a round of applause as the couple kissed passionately on the dance floor. It was a sign of the change in him that, although each cadet had been allowed to invite nine guests, none of the friends from his wayward days were there – just Chelsy and William. Outside they watched a fireworks display, ate hamburgers smothered with onions and washed them down with champagne. He posed for photographs with anyone who asked, returning a bottom pinch one girl had audaciously carried out.

To add to his joy Clarence House announced in effect that

Cornet Wales was on his way up in the military world: he was to serve in an armoured reconnaissance unit as part of his training to become a troop commander. He would be in charge of eleven men and four tanks and the likelihood was that he would get his wish to serve in a combat zone – probably Iraq or Afghanistan. Harry Wales was going to war.

It was not, however, that simple. Even as he continued his post-Sandhurst training there were rumours that his promised posting to Iraq would not materialise. The army denied them and Harry apparently insisted – though this has not been confirmed – that he would quit his beloved army if his regiment was sent without him. There were protests from members of the public too – why had he been trained at great expense for a job he might never be allowed to carry out? It gave General Sir Richard Dannatt, Chief of the General Staff, sleepless nights but he finally made up his mind: on 21 February 2007 the Ministry of Defence made it clear that Harry's wish was to come true. The Ministry's announcement read:

We can confirm today that Prince Harry will deploy to Iraq later this year in command of a troop from A Squadron of the Household Cavalry Regiment. While in Iraq Cornet Wales will carry out a normal troop commander's role involving leading a troop of twelve men in four Scimitar armoured reconnaissance vehicles, each with a crew of three. The decision to deploy him has been a military one. The royal household has been consulted throughout.

Harry's godfather Gerald Ward said he was disappointed by the announcement: 'I fear for anyone's life in that situation. It is very naïve of the Ministry of Defence to spell out the work he might do and the type of vehicles he may drive.' He went on to venture that the good relations the Prince of Wales enjoyed with Muslims across the world would serve Harry in good stead.

The news was, however, received with joy by Harry ... and bitter glee by the enemy. Abu Zaid, commander of the Malik Ibn Al Ashtar Brigade declared: 'We are awaiting the arrival of the young, handsome, spoiled Prince with bated breath. He will return to his grandmother but without ears.' He had, he said, spies inside the British bases who would notify insurgents whenever and wherever the Prince arrived. No wonder Harry told those bidding him farewell at a London nightclub that he was 'shitting himself'. The regiment he had chosen to join specialised in the highly dangerous operation of scouting out enemy-held terrain in light armour and was particularly exposed to ambushes and roadside bombs.

The Army High Command had to think again, however. General Dannatt was forced to announce on 16 May that he had changed his mind. The chilling threats, along with intelligence that a crackshot enemy sniper, already responsible for killing six British soldiers, had already been assigned the job of assassinating the Prince, made the risks altogether too great. The Prince would not be going to Iraq, where his onetime hero James Hewitt had served, after all.

Harry was devastated, although in response to General

Dannatt's declaration that he had proved himself to be an officer of determination and undoubted talent, he made it known that he fully understood and accepted the reasons for the General's about-turn: his presence on the battlefield would put the lives of those around him at even greater risk. He did his best to explain that when he was allowed a brief meeting with other members of his regiment as they prepared to depart for Iraq. For their part his men said they would happily accept the increased risk to themselves if they could have him as their troop leader.

'That seemed to cheer him up but privately he was in pieces, not helped by those critics who said he shouldn't have joined the army in the first place if it was only to enhance the Windsors' glory,' says a well-informed source. 'He went out and got blotto.' Prince Philip joined the chorus of disapproval by saying that Harry should never have been allowed to join the army in the first place: the navy would have provided a 'far more secure environment'. General Dannatt responded by blaming the media for its criticism of what it had described as a 'cock-up', pointing out that during his long army service, the Duke of Kent had not been allowed to go to Northern Ireland during the troubles there since he, as the Queen's cousin, would have been an obvious target for the IRA.

Harry showed that he was still contemplating leaving the army if it meant sitting on his 'arse back home'. 'I feel,' he said 'that if I'm going to cause this much chaos to a lot of people, then I should bow out, and not just for my own sake, for everyone's sake.' It was at this point that he was privately assured he would see active service but next time there would be no publicity ahead of his deployment. The MoD gathered the media's most senior executives – owners as well as editors – to get them to agree to a complete news blackout when the time came for Harry to go to war. Although one or two argued that this amounted to press censorship the majority persuaded them to agree to what amounted to a demand rather than a request although it fell short of the kind of D-Notice issued during Prince Andrew's service in the Falklands War.

Harry, his deployment to Iraq on hold indefinitely, was obliged to join his brother in a holding unit of the Household Cavalry while William was training to fly helicopters. To distract himself from the bitter disappointment, he had to find other things to concentrate his active mind on. There were, for example, royal matters to attend to.

As the tenth anniversary of Diana's death approached, Harry learned that his press office had been inundated with requests for him to bare all to the media. So in April 2007 he persuaded William that they should accept one of the many invitations Clarence House had received for both princes to be interviewed on television principally about their mother. They chose the American network NBC and the fortunate interviewer was one Matt Lauer who travelled to London to perform his privileged task in the princes' familiar surroundings, Clarence House. Lauer began by reminding them that since one of Diana's main concerns was that they be able to live as normal lives as possible, would she be happy with the result ten years later? While William hesitated over his response, Harry dived in: 'I think she'd be happy in the way that we're going about it but slightly unhappy about the way other people were going about it.' And in response to a remark Prince Andrew had once made to them – 'Look, you're not normal so stop trying to be normal. You've got certain responsibilities.' Harry looked somewhat bemused as William made his response: 'Obviously we know we have certain responsibilities. But within our private lives and within certain other parts of our lives we want to be as normal as possible. And yes, it's hard because to a certain respect we never will be normal.'

Lauer, clearly unaware of how close the two of them are, and always have been, probed Harry about their relationship with each other.

You can't ask [us] that because I'm his brother so I see a different side of him… He enjoys himself more than people think… But as long as we want to be fools we can… You know he works very hard. He's definitely the more intelligent one of the two of us.

William smiled and said of his brother, 'Oh, he's a wild thing all right.'

Harry was back in serious mood when he said how slowly the ten years had passed for him:

It's weird because when she passed away there was never that time, there was never that sort of lull. There was never that sort of peace and quiet for any of us due to the fact that her face was always spattered over the papers the whole time. Over the past ten years I personally feel she has been … she's always there. She's always been a constant reminder to both of us and everybody else. And therefore I think when you're being reminded about it, it does take a lot longer and it's a bit slower… You know when people think about [her], they think about her death. They think, you know, how wrong it was. They think whatever happened. I don't know, for me personally, what happened, you know, that night. Whatever happened in that tunnel, no one will ever know. I'm sure people will always think about it the whole time. I've never stopped wondering… There's a lot of people wondering, I'll never stop … I can't ever stop [the public fascination] ever ending. I think there may be certain sort of times when there's nothing to write about or when they're working towards something new. But I think people will always have a fascination about her… You know, it still upsets me now, the fact that we didn't have as much of a chance as other children to spend time with her.

Among the many nicknames Diana gave them was Wombat for William and Ginger for Harry, which the Queen regarded as a little unfair. As he grew older Harry's hair turned to the sandy colour it is now, and no one could call him ginger these days. Harry makes the point that his mother

wasn't always herself in front of the cameras. She was more natural behind the scenes when there was no one else there and she could be herself. I don't know whether it's the right thing to say, but she was quite good at acting. She wasn't acting as though she was trying to be someone different. But very much trying to appear as normal as she could in front of the cameras which she hated so much.

They said they knew when she had been placed under pressure or chased down the street by the mood she was in when she came home to them. How upset she was when she was criticised about her body – especially when it was insinuated that she had cellulite: 'For any woman it's outrageous that these people sit behind their desks and make such comments … there were many times when we had to cheer her up and tell her that she was the best thing ever.'

'After our mother's death,' said Harry,

there was so much of us being in the public eye and then seeing stuff on TV and in the papers saying 'Oh, they show no emotion', that sort of stuff. But that's our public side. If we don't feel comfortable crying our eyes out in front of thousands of people, then that's our problem. You know, we've got each other to talk to… We are both very grateful that each of us has the other's shoulder to cry on when required.

Of the negative publicity he had received over incidents like smoking marijuana in his Eton days, drinking and brawling with photographers, Harry said people generally seemed pleasantly surprised when they met him and said, 'Oh, you're so not what I thought you were. They believed what they'd read … [what's written] is just poisonous.'

And when Lauer compared their fame to that of a pop star or a sporting celebrity, Harry delivered a surprising response, pointing out the difference between them and people who strive for fame: 'If you're born into it as we were, I think it's normal to feel as though you don't really want it [whereas] they choose it or they're just so naturally talented at a sport and they've got to deal with it like David Beckham,' at which point William – known to be less of a Beckham fan than his brother – interrupted, 'But he likes selling himself, so he's fine with it.'

Both princes agreed they were very guarded about people they chose to befriend, that they didn't want sycophantic people around them. However, Harry was quick to point out: 'But at the same time you've got to understand that it's just as difficult for our friends as it is for us… There's a massive element of trust. Our friends have to put up with a lot when it comes to us.'

When it came to his relationship with Chelsy Davy and their recent holiday together in the Caribbean, Harry avoided mentioning her by name in his reply but admitted his unwanted fame made relationships difficult: 'You always find yourself hiding somewhere and doing something that you don't really want to be doing. Why? Because you just don't want to get photographed doing [what you'd like to be doing] because of what will be written about it.'

Perhaps there was a suggestion of his intention of eventually settling down with her when he answered a question from Lauer about what he would do and where he would be if he wasn't a prince but a plain ordinary citizen. Lauer got the same response as a number of Harry's friends had given me when I put the same question to them about Harry: 'I'd probably live in Africa. I'd like to spend all my time out there. As a job I'd probably be a safari guide… If I became normal tomorrow, then I'd help Lesotho more.' But, he said with what sounded like just a tinge of regret, 'I feel abnormal.' (A Palace source attempted to qualify that by saying 'Yes, he loves Africa and I'm sure that given the chance to live and work there he would have taken it, but he's very conscious of the fact that he has a royal role which requires him to live in England.')

In what seemed like a veiled reference to James Hewitt, Paul Burrell and one or two others of their ilk, William declared: 'Harry and I are both quite upset about it, that our mother's trust has been betrayed and that even now she's still being exploited. There's always people out there who want to make money. And that's their certain choice and method to do it this way.'

The time was fast approaching for decisions to be made – both by the MoD and by Harry – about where his military options lay. Suggestions by some minions that he be sent to Bosnia or 'somewhere in Africa' as part of a United Nations peacekeeping force were dismissed by Harry as cop-outs. He wanted to be on the front line of a war zone or he would find employment elsewhere. 'He could make a fortune as a mercenary,' someone declared at a meeting chaired by General Dannatt. Nobody laughed. This was a now-or-never situation. Having reached his agreement with the media bosses that in no way would the enemy be alerted, it was decided that he would serve in a conflict zone – Afghanistan – but in a new capacity: he would be retrained as a battlefield air controller. But no one could know other than the couple of dozen media executives sworn to secrecy in return for a certain amount of access to Harry, though nothing was to be published or televised until he had returned from his tour of duty. 'You could be risking his life if this got out,' they were warned. For the first, but not the last time, he was referred to as a 'bullet magnet'.

However, it seemed pretty obvious that he was bound somewhere for action when he flew to the British Army Training Unit at Suffield in Alberta, Canada, an area used for British armoured vehicles to practise operations with live ammunition just like the equipment his regiment were using in Iraq. The people at Clarence House were happy, Chelsy was happy. What mischief could Harry get up to in the backwaters of Canada? They hadn't reckoned on the Calgary Cowboys bar where Harry flirted outrageously with a provocatively dressed barmaid/hostess called Cherie Cymbalisty to whom he called himself Gary and in the next breath asked her if she was wearing any underwear. Despite a necking session the 22-year-old declined his offer of a trip to the nearby barracks but – according to her – the next morning she claims he sent the following text message to the mobile phone number she had given him: 'What happened to you last night babe? U disappeared. We waited for you outside coz apparently u were keen to come back to party?! Loser. Guess you didn't have the stamina, hey?!!!! We went all night and u were v missed X.'

When it was reported, Chelsy got angry: 'her' man was at it again. Once more their relationship was seriously strained.

It had been Harry's idea to stage a massive concert in memory of his mother's death some ten years earlier. On 1 July 2007 it would have been Diana's forty-sixth birthday and the Queen had suggested a private dinner for relatives and a couple of dozen close friends at Buckingham Palace. But Harry had other ideas. He persuaded William – who normally did his best to honour his grandmother's wishes – that a quiet palace dinner was no way to celebrate such an occasion: Wembley Stadium should be the venue and they could have not dozens but tens of thousands of people there to share the day at a big concert. In the event 63,000 turned up in person and an estimated 500 million watched it in the 140 countries it was transmitted to. The princes delivered a 'night of energy and fun' to remember Diana's *joie de vivre*. The Queen watched it on TV and later told Harry he had been right to choose the public option; she was beginning to see that his forward thinking was pointing the Royal Family in a new, modern, direction. It was a direction she could never expect Charles to follow.

'This event is about all what our mother loved in life – her music, her dancing, her charities and her family and friends,' Harry told the massive audience. 'She would have been the first up and out of her seat.' Then he added mischievously: 'When we first had the idea we forgot we would end up standing here desperately trying to think of something funny to say so we'll leave that to the funny people ... and Ricky Gervais.'

On a more serious note he addressed a special message to his Household Cavalry squadron serving in Iraq, which was listening to a live simulcast: 'I wish I was there with you. I'm sorry I can't be. But to all of those on operations at the moment – stay safe.'

An anticipated comeback appearance by his once favourite group, the Spice Girls, failed to happen. Their non-appearance, however, did nothing to dampen the spirits of the massive crowd who had paid £45 each for their tickets (the profits were to be divided between three charities – Sentebale, the Diana Memorial Fund and Centrepoint) for there was a vast array of entertainment to come, provided by Sir Elton John, Duran Duran, Status Quo, Sir Tom Jones, Lily Allen, P. Diddy, the Black Eyed Peas, Fergie, James Morrison, Joss Stone, Natasha Bedingfield, Andrea Bocelli, Sarah Brightman and Donny Osmond. Not forgetting Diana's love of dancing there were performances by the English National Ballet, of which she was a patron, as well as a medley of musicals created by Andrew Lloyd Webber.

Just two months after the fun and games of the massive

Wembley concert, Harry found a more sombre occasion to honour his mother's memory. Needless to say the Guards Chapel at Wellington Barracks in Knightsbridge could accommodate only a tiny fraction of the number who attended the Wembley event, but 500 people packed the chapel for a special service to mark the tenth anniversary of Diana's death. Despite the difference in numbers Harry said he felt 'a hundred times' more nervous walking up the aisle to the strains of 'The Londonderry Air', than he had facing the 63,000 crowd at Wembley cheering on Status Quo.

Because the organisers feared that ever-sensitive William might break down while addressing a congregation that included his grandmother, grandfather, father (without Camilla, whom Diana had always referred to as 'his lady') and the Prime Minister, it fell to Harry to make the toughest speech of his life and he did it with great aplomb. He spoke of Diana's 'unrivalled love of life, laughter, fun and folly' and pointed out that she had been 'our guardian, friend and protector ... never once allowing her unfaltering love for us to go unspoken or undemonstrated'.

The Queen, with William at her side on the front pew, blinked when her grandson said of the woman who had been stripped of her royal title:

She will always be remembered for her amazing public work. But behind the media glare to us, just two loving children, she was quite simply the best mother in the world. We would say that, wouldn't we? But we miss her. Put simply, she made us and so many other people happy. May this be the way that she is remembered?

It was moving stuff and many gathered outside the chapel wept as Harry delivered with great dignity the most moving tribute to the late Princess anyone could remember – a far cry from the bitter eulogy Charles Spencer had proffered at his sister's funeral.

It was at the brothers' request that the Bishop of London made an appeal in his address for the gossips to cease their endless repetition of stories about Diana's amorous adventures:

> It is easy to lose the real person in the image, to insist that all is darkness or all is light. Still, ten years after her tragic death, there are regular reports of 'fury' at this or that incident and the Princess's memory is used for scoring points. Let it end here. Let this service mark the point at which we let her rest in peace and dwell on her memory with thanksgiving and compassion.

Sporting his regimental tie, Harry stood with his head held high as the congregation sang his choice of closing hymn, 'I Vow to Thee, My Country' (a favourite of Diana's), before launching into a specially stalwart rendition of the national anthem.

Those assembled in the chapel – and they included the singing knights Elton John and Cliff Richard – had seen a new Harry emerge that day and, had they not felt it inappropriate, they would surely have given him a standing ovation. As it was he got something even better: in a rare public display of family affection the Queen, dressed in vivid purple for the occasion, gave him a hug.

It gave him the strength for what lay ahead: the inquests into Diana's death, an inquiry which delved into the darkest corners of her troubled life. The Bishop of London's words had fallen on a number of deaf (though in many cases eminent) ears.

Harry made a pledge to himself from the outset that he simply would not read newspaper reports of the hearing into both his mother's and Dodi's deaths in the Paris tunnel. Just as well; the 'evidence' presented – much of it at the instigation of lawyers acting for Dodi's father Mohamed Al Fayed – included the most personal details of Diana's life and health. There was even a shocking allegation that their maternal grandmother, Frances Shand Kydd, had called her a 'whore' for her involvement with Muslim men, but then Mrs Shand Kydd was not a well woman at the time and those caring for her were concerned about the level of instability she displayed from time to time.

☙

The two princes survived the inquiries, recriminations and emotional hand-wringing that surrounded the tenth anniversary of their mother's death. The pair had supported each other throughout and grown extremely close during the ensuing decade. They had also galvanised royal reputation and prestige in the eyes of an intrusive and demanding twenty-first century public, as well as providing a touchstone for what had, at times, been a much-beleaguered monarchy.

The morning after the July 2007 bombings in which fifty-two people lost their lives in central London, an extraordinary scene was witnessed by a man well known in royal circles:

I was walking down Bury Street and about to turn into St James's Square when I spotted Harry and William walking towards me. They were being quite noisy and making exaggerated gestures with their hands which made it quite obvious that they wanted to be noticed. But what shocked me was that there wasn't a close protection officer in sight – and this was less than twenty-four hours after the carnage which had taken place nearby; Blair and his Cabinet had got out of London almost immediately and yet these two heirs to the throne were out walking the capital's streets. I telephoned someone I knew who is close enough to the Royal Family to know what on earth was going on and he said, quite calmly, they were 'princing'. He explained, 'It was a deliberate exercise to demonstrate to the people that there was nothing to worry about. It goes back to the kings and princes Shakespeare wrote about who led their armies into battle rather than send other mortals off to do it while they sought refuge in their castles.'

I have also noticed over the years how close they were to each other. I don't believe they've had a fight in their lives. These two are true friends.

# 10

# HIS OWN MAN

It was the Queen who, after a conclusive meeting with General Dannatt, had given Harry the news that he was going to Afghanistan. He could not have been more pleased. After a slight period of depression following the cancellation of his Iraq deployment, this was exactly what he wanted to hear. This time the MoD had done its homework and General Dannatt was sure that the deal he had struck with the media leaders would work, that they would honour their part of the compromise deal by not writing or saying anything until he had returned safely home, provided they were allowed access to the Prince in the war zone.

Having packed his kit into his Bergen rucksack, Harry slipped out of the UK on 14 December 2007. At RAF Brize Norton in Oxfordshire, he joined surprised comrades aboard a C-17 transport carrier aircraft for the twelve-hour flight to Afghanistan. This was the real thing so, determined to follow the instructions he had been given, he slipped out of his sleeping bag as the plane approached Kandahar and put on his body armour and helmet in case the aircraft came under attack on landing.

After collecting his ammunition he joined special forces soldiers in a Chinook helicopter headed for what was then Forward Operating Base Dwyer in Helmand Province, the most dangerous place on earth. He had made it to the front line and he had his grandmother's persistence to thank for it: without Her Majesty's approval his deployment would never have happened

Even in the theatre of war he could not resist an opportunity to flirt and he chatted up Michelle Tompkins as she piloted a Harrier jet over snow-covered mountains. His commanding officer teased him that if he continued that line of conversation with the first woman he had come across since bidding farewell to Chelsy in London, he'd better get a room.

Talk about the opposite sex – members of which were clearly in short supply from this point on – was the favourite pastime during the limited breaks he and his fellow soldiers got. Girly magazines were passed around and one pilot focused his on-board camera to reveal a picture of a topless model taped to the outside of his aircraft, not knowing that it was an heir to the throne he was entertaining. But then, at that stage, few of the aircrews he communicated with were aware of his identity. To them he was just another voice, albeit, as one said later, 'rather a plummy one. Although he was obviously trying to tone it down.'

'It's just me and him [the pilot] having good banter and

obviously when the aircraft comes in you know you've got them on task for three hours and yet you're looking for just one or two [enemy individuals] digging a trench. It can get quite tiring,' Harry told one interviewer.

> If you're just saying 'Yep, go to this point' and putting the radio down and just staring at the screen it sends you insane. So I think it's good to be relaxed on the net and have a good chat, but when things are pretty hairy then you need to obviously turn on your game face and do the job.

Dave Baxter, with whom he formed a close friendship said, 'He's a really down-to-earth person. To be honest I don't think anyone here thinks of him as third in line to the throne. You just take him at face value.'

But for all the fun and camaraderie, this was real war, a bitter war and there was danger around every corner. A number of men came close to breakdown and Harry was always the first to comfort them: 'Think of the folks back home,' he said to one. 'You will see them again; focus on what a wonderful moment that will be and don't forget, they're longing to see you too.' The same could be said of Harry's family, who had by now all been let in on the secret the Queen, Philip and Charles had kept to themselves at Sandringham on Christmas Day. His camp frequently came under attack from mortar shells and machine-gun fire. He was under no illusion that mortal danger snaked around every corner as he patrolled the bombed-out streets of Garmsir turning it from a lively community into a ghost town, with those inhabitants who had not fled constantly aware that any friendly contact with the British soldiers could bring the ultimate punishment if the Taliban spies in their midst spotted and reported it.

How he must have missed the chilled cocktails at Boujis when the daytime heat left him parched, for the bottled water specially flown in was strictly rationed and even a prince used to having just about everything he wanted had to make do with his meagre share – one bottle a day. Often the desperate men drank foul-tasting chlorinated water from the local supply, the Prince included. What fresh water could be spared, Harry and his men took to the locals, sharing what they could really have done with themselves. There was as much danger associated with such an action as there was generosity. Any one of those smiling Afghans could have been a suicide bomber. He was taught to watch for tell-tale signs – a man sweating profusely, wearing too many clothes in the heat, walking with leaden feet, or with something protruding from his body – all showed that he was a potential killer.

But the danger and the discomfort are what he had signed up for. Tired of the royal pampering that dominated his early life, he wanted adventure and was getting it in large measure. There were no privileges and he had to stand in line for his weekly thirty minutes' use of a satellite phone to call home. This was the Harry Wales he had longed to be, not the 'spoiled toff' who got waited on hand and foot at home. His mother had said too that she longed for 'normality' but would she ever have accepted it to such an extreme? Perhaps serving as a nurse in a field hospital instead of visiting in a smart suit with a Gucci handbag tucked under her arm? No, Harry was his own man and no one – not even desperate Diana – had gone this far to secure the sanity that normality provides. Royals, as Prince Andrew had once said to him, could never be normal: 'We live in a different world.' Using the 'thunder-boxes' – metal containers to collect bodily waste which when dried out was burned with kerosene to provide some warmth when temperatures plunged at night to ten degrees below freezing – Harry was proving his uncle wrong.

There were times when the lives of his men as well as his own were in grave danger and, as such, it was imperative that Harry kept his wits about him at all times. When the Taliban launched one particularly relentless attack on FOB Delhi, he was ready; having monitored their movements with sophisticated surveillance equipment for the previous forty-eight hours he had the foresight to realise that their movements from bunker to bunker demonstrated preparation for a major attack on his base. He called in an American F-15E fighter plane whose pilot he had become familiar with during previous attacks on the garrison. First he despatched the aircraft to a point where its engines could not be heard by the enemy, who would therefore think they were safe to resume their attack. Alas, they had not allowed for Harry's careful planning and determined concentration. As they emerged from cover to complete their attack, the Taliban fighters were surprised by the emergence of the lethal American jet Harry had kept waiting in the wings. His action saved many lives and wiped out a number of increasingly skilled enemy fighters. It was not until some time later that Captain Ben Donberg learned the identity of the man who had called him in to carry out such a successful sortie, but the compliments he heaped on the caller were the same as he would have lavished on any soldier who had carried out his work with such proficiency.

Harry repeated military buddy Bill Connor's sentiments when he said in a subsequent interview:

> It's somewhat like I can imagine the Second World War [Connor had actually said the First World War] was like. They poke their heads up and that's it. I call the air [aircraft] in and as soon as the air comes in they disappear down holes or into the bunkers. My job is to get air up. They check in on me when they come into the [restricted operation zone] and then I'm responsible for their aircraft making sure they don't get taken out by the shelling… It's a piece of piss really.

Whatever he wanted to call it, the Prince was in mortal danger every day of his life during his spell in Afghanistan. He had two very narrow escapes: once when a drone aircraft spotted a Taliban landmine his convoy was only metres away from striking and on another occasion when the Taliban managed to land a 107mm Chinese-made rocket fifty metres from the spot where he had dug in following a warning only seconds before it exploded. But if he was ever scared, he never showed it. In all his ten weeks in combat he never displayed anger until he was eventually given the information that his recall was due to a leak by the Australian women's magazine and a crazy blogger who had let the world know of his presence – and that included the Taliban, who were now certain to do all they could to catch and kill him. 'He said you were a bitch and that Drudge was a bastard,' wrote one sat next to him on the homeward flight to the magazine editor. He never got a reply.

General Dannatt had called the Queen and told her, 'It's time to pull him out.' She agreed: 'Please bring him home safely.' Within minutes the order had been conveyed to Helmand.

Harry had his suspicions about the recall when he heard of the decision by chance as he monitored radio conversations that did not mention him by name but seemed to have been about him. His fears were confirmed when the six SAS guardian angels arrived from Helmand in the Chinook that had been kept on standby for just such an emergency. 'Sir', as he was called (such a welcome change from 'Your Royal Highness') was given less than an hour to pack his possessions and hand over his high-tech equipment to another JTAC. At that point still unaware of the reason for his recall, he was flown to the coalition airbase on the outskirts of Kandahar and transferred to an RAF TriStar passenger jet for the journey back to RAF Brize Norton where it had all started just ten weeks earlier. He was not given the details until the aircraft was safely out of Afghan airspace and even then his thoughts were with two seriously injured soldiers lying close to him, both sedated. 'Those are the heroes, not me,' he said. 'The ones who have lost limbs and will never be able to live a normal life again.' After a brief stop at Birmingham airport to take the badly injured to Selly Oak military hospital, the TriStar touched down at Brize Norton. There were no smiles on their faces when Charles and William welcomed him home. 'Got your Christmas card the other day,' he said to his father. Charles merely nodded. Harry was sullen as he stepped into the car for the short journey home to Highgrove, where he stayed in the bath for more than an hour before feeling able to interact with them.

It was from Highgrove that he telephoned Chelsy and told her he was on his way to Africa; would she be there for him? Would she! And then he was back in the air again, this time headed for Botswana. There, he and Chelsy picked up a rickety houseboat which took them along the Okavango Delta and the now happy pair set off into the sunset, cooking their own meals as they went rather than revert to the kind of royal service he at least was used to. The romance was back on; for a few days Helmand was a place in the past. They could not have been in a better setting: the area Chelsy had chosen spans more than 10,000 square miles of forests, flood plains and magical deserted islands. No Taliban in sight. It was a romance the people at the palace were beginning to take seriously: this was a woman who could comfort a much-depressed and angry prince. It had not escaped their attention that he was calling her 'wifey' and she him 'hubby'.

Back home the third in line to the throne (at the time of writing) had been pilloried as a playboy who brawled with photographers after over-indulging in nightclubs and who chose to display himself in a Nazi uniform at a costume party, but he had returned from the Afghanistan front line as a hero, although he hated the description. WHEN HARRY MET TALI trumpeted the *Daily Star*, one of the tabloids that had made the most they could out of any previous misdemeanours. Like the men who served with him, he had risked his life in head-on clashes with the enemy; his behaviour had been faultless throughout and the British media were united in their praise. Now it was time to live up to the title he had been born with and he began to carry out official engagements, winning hearts in the process just as his mother had done.

Back from Africa, and after taking Chelsy to his cousin Peter Phillips's wedding to Autumn Kelly – where she met the Queen for the first time – a mellowed prince travelled to Wales for a full day of official engagements. It was not the kind of work he wanted to do and he would certainly have preferred to be back with his regiment in Afghanistan, but no one would have guessed it from his friendly demeanour. For his first port of call he chose Cathays High School in Cardiff, which had raised thousands of pounds to help buy equipment and a herd of cows at £500 each to provide milk for the pupils at Molapo High School in Lesotho.

When the pupils lined up he picked out twelve-year-old red-haired Matthew Taylor to chat to. Matthew revealed

afterwards: 'He said to me, "I'm ginger – gingers love gingers."'
Not an unusual remark for a man who had always been teased
about the colour of his hair and could empathise with others
who might have suffered similarly.

He went on to meet staff and patients at a children's hospital and, as the day went on, he clearly warmed to royal duty,
although he had made it clear when he started his army
career that he did not envy his brother having to take it on
as a full-time job one day. In the evening he was joined by
his friend Prince Seeiso at what was billed as a Lesotho
Links Conference.

'I can't wait to get back to your country,' he told Seeiso. He
didn't have long to wait: less than a fortnight later he was
once again Africa-bound and this time he took his brother
with him to witness the work he had started with the poor
and the sick in Lesotho through Sentebale, the charity he had
set up in both their names (he was already patron of three
UK-based charities: Dolen Cymru, which promotes activities that links health organisations in schools and villages in
Wales; MapAction, which employs a team of skilled volunteers to monitor humanitarian disasters worldwide; and
WellChild, which is dedicated to the needs of sick children).

Although it was serious business, fun was not excluded on
the princes' visit: one night Harry, having sampled the local
rum, persuaded William to dance with him and William
rarely refuses any request from his younger brother to let
himself go. Harry encourages William to take risks, even
engaging in some very non-royal banter in public: 'But

the banter gets a lot more fruity when we're in private,' admits William.

Harry was now back in the UK and ready to embark on the next stage of his military career. The news that he wished to follow his brother, father and uncle in flying military helicopters was revealed in October 2008 as Harry was made an honorary Air Commandant at RAF Honington. After passing the initial aptitude test, he undertook a month-long course and having passed that he proceeded to full flight training early in 2009.

He was based for a while at the Defence Helicopter School at RAF Shawbury on the Welsh borders where, coincidentally, William had also been sent after his training on fixed-wing aircraft. For several months the brothers shared a cottage close to the base. 'For the first time and the last time, I can assure you of that,' Harry said when they held a press conference. Harry, it appeared, had been constantly nagged by his brother for neglecting his clearing-up duties, although he did do most of the cooking. William also light-heartedly complained that he was kept awake at night by Harry's snoring – a habit he seemed to have picked up from their father since Diana told him as a small boy that that was the reason she and Charles slept in separate rooms. At the same media gathering Harry also took great delight in pointing out that William was losing his hair: 'That's pretty rich coming from a ginger,' William retorted. It was all in good fun and clear to those assembled that no offence was intended and the brothers remained the very best of friends.

Their special brand of humour led to the discovery of their mobile phones being bugged. William once left a jokey message on Harry's cell phone using a high-pitched voice and a South African accent to pretend to be Chelsy giving him hell for visiting a lap-dancing club. The story appeared in reporter Clive Goodman's column in the *News of the World*. That, and the reporting of other messages left on their phones, convinced them that their messages were being hacked (Goodman subsequently went to prison for the offence) and the Royal Protection Service was informed. Because the messages also gave details of their movements, the police called on the services of the anti-terrorism squad who quickly established that their phones were being hacked and eventually led to the newspaper – the biggest-selling in the world – being closed down by its severely embarrassed owner, the outspoken Rupert Murdoch. The leak had been sealed and Harry was soon able to send his brother messages again without fear of them being published in a downmarket tabloid. But it was an uncomfortable time for all concerned, 'especially because Harry was known to leave intimate details of his love life on trusted friends' phones', according to a member of the royal household. Diana had long been of the opinion that her calls were bugged and had adopted the code-name 'Julia' as well as, none too artfully, encoding 'Highgrove' as 'Low Wood'. It fooled no one at GCHQ, which monitored and recorded all her telephone conversations as part of its operation to guard national safety.

After leaving Shawbury in October 2009, Harry moved

to the Army Air Corps (AAC) base close to the Hampshire town of Middle Wallop to begin the eight-month first half of his required training course. There he had to pass his flying assessment in order to determine which of three different helicopters he should train to pilot: the multi-purpose Lynx, the five-seat Gazelle – both used for reconnaissance purposes – or the ultimate 'war machine', the Apache, very much an attack aircraft. He says now that he had never been more focused: he desperately wanted to be at the controls of an Apache, not only the most sophisticated of the three but the one that would assure his return to front-line service since the army had already decided that it was no longer safe for him to be on the ground. Harry revealed later that his preference was to serve with his men as regular infantry, but at least now he had an ambition that he could fulfil, providing he passed the rigorous training process.

So dedicated was he to his new role and the prospect it offered of him returning to war that Harry's twenty-fifth birthday passed uncelebrated: in no way was he going to disobey his unit's ten-hour 'throttle to bottle' rule preventing pilots from drinking, despite the fact that this was the day on which he came into the first instalment of his multi-million pound inheritance from his mother's estate – much of which had come from his father in the divorce settlement. The interest on his share alone gave him £300,000 a year 'pocket money', part of which he donated secretly to Sentebale. Another plus was that the Queen granted him and William their own royal household – one which would take precedence over even Prince

Andrew's. With offices in St James's Palace it would take care of the young princes' public, military and charitable activities. To the princes' delight Jamie Lowther-Pinkerton – who had been their secretary since March 2005 – was put in charge. Lowther-Pinkerton, who had proved to be a good friend and wise mentor, was equally delighted; he enjoyed working with them. 'Prince Harry has his moments,' he said,

> but even with old Harry and his wild moments, the guy's instincts are absolutely 100 per cent brilliant... People used to say, 'You really must find something for young Harry to do.' Now they say, 'God, you've got to find somewhere where the country can really capitalise on Harry,' which is so great.

In her wisdom, Her Majesty appointed Sir David Manning, former British ambassador to the US, to oversee the whole operation and report to her if any matter needed superior attention. Sir David, she knew, would ensure that not a penny was wasted in the new household. Showing their trust in Manning, Harry and William also appointed him as a trustee of their Royal Foundation, a group charity they conceived in 2009 which took over the Diana, Princess of Wales Memorial Fund when it was wound up three years later. One of the foundation's aims is to promote the welfare of those serving in the armed forces – a cause close to both princes' hearts. Their support for various charities did not always require their participation as patrons. When Harry started wearing a Help for Heroes wristband, the cause's takings soared.

Harry did well in his exams and was presented with his flying brevet (wings) by his father on 7 May 2010 at a ceremony at Middle Wallop, a ceremony during which he switched his Blues and Royals Officer's Service Dress cap for that of the Army Air Corps' sky blue beret with a Blues and Royals badge. But the big news of the day for Harry was that he had been selected by Army Air Corps commanders to train as an Apache pilot. Harry declared:

> It is a huge honour to have a chance to train on the Apache, which is an awesome helicopter. There is still a huge mountain for me to climb if I am to pass the Apache training course. To be honest, I think it will be one of the biggest challenges in my life so far. I am very determined though, as I do not want to let down people who have shown faith in my ability to fly this aircraft on operations. It is a seriously daunting prospect, but I can't wait.

In a far less formal note he wrote to a fellow soldier over there: 'Afghanistan, here I come, better warn the Taliban.'

First, though, Africa once again beckoned. He and William set off for a six-day, three-country visit, their first official overseas tour together, in June 2010. They began in Botswana working for the charity Tusk Trust, of which William had been patron for five years despite never having had an opportunity to visit the country. His patronage of this particular charity had been Prince Charles's idea since it taught thousands of children each year about the essential needs of conservation if the country was to survive. In the presence of supportive media, they witnessed and praised the work of four youngsters from the UK who were working on a Tusk project to turn a disused quarry into a nature reserve. Then, once the accompanying journalists had left, the princes sat down to an informal lunch with the volunteer workers, 'keeping them in stitches of laughter', says a royal retainer who was required to stay with the party.

For a short while the brothers split up: Harry couldn't wait to get to his beloved Lesotho while William remained briefly for more formal activities. The reception Harry got was tremendous and he was delighted to see how the money Sentebale had already raised was being used to help AIDS orphans – a cause his mother championed despite the Queen's view that it was not an appropriate one for a senior royal to be associated with. Many of the children he had talked to and played with on his earlier visit were delighted to see him. He had promised he would return and here he was. When he joined Harry in Lesotho, William was clearly impressed by the effect his brother was having on the country: everywhere they went Harry was hailed as a hero. It was Harry who had got Sentebale launched, despite William raising money for what was officially their joint charity and both having helped raise £300,000 for that and similar causes with an incredible endurance test (unpublicised) riding motorbikes 1,000 miles across the inhospitable terrain of South Africa's Eastern Cape the previous year.

Their stay was concluded on a flat note when they watched

a pathetic performance by England's side in a football match in Cape Town. The England team could manage only a 0–0 draw against Algeria and were booed off the pitch. In the circumstances William was not keen to go to the players' dressing room when the match ended but Harry persuaded him they should go down 'to cheer the players up'. Although David Beckham did his best to receive the royal brothers gracefully, other players, including a frustrated Wayne Rooney who had had some unkind words to say to the booing fans before he left the pitch, were in no mood to be cheered up. When William tried to find something complimentary to say to the team, Harry, whose preference is for rugby anyway, interjected: 'Oh, they'll really enjoy being told how to play better by a posh soldier.'

Even if the footballers were not exactly hailed as heroes on their return to the UK, Harry and William received ample praise for their work with the poor and the sick during their brief African expedition. Just as all seemed well in his life, however, everyone was reminded of Harry's past reputation as the bad boy of the Royal Family: a video diary filmed during his Sandhurst days emerged showing him describing a fellow officer as 'our little Paki friend' and later calling a colleague wearing a cloth on his head 'a raghead'– typical soldier parlance, perhaps, but less palatable from the Queen's grandson. Considering that he had put his past behind him and had just risked his life for his country he was somewhat disgusted when he had his knuckles rapped by the Prime Minister for the playful remarks (Cameron said the remark was 'completely unacceptable'). 'Actually Cameron was only teasing him,' explains a senior Downing Street official. 'He had to say something to him and it seems Harry took it the wrong way. The PM was very grateful to him for the work he had done in Afghanistan and I think the Prince now knows that.'

Harry's initial annoyance over the PM's reported comments came in a period when he was still angry about evidence given by Hasnat Khan at a belated inquest into Diana's death. Despite, or perhaps because of, his intense dislike of Dodi Fayed, the Prince was shocked to learn that Khan had received many death threats during the courtship of his mother, which had begun after she sent flowers to him at the hospital where he worked. Anonymous hate mail included cut-out photographs of the surgeon with a noose around his neck. Could this have been the work of a jealous rival? Harry, according to a source close to him, had his own theories.

In April 2011 he was promoted to captain within the Army Air Corps in recognition of time served in the armed forces. Captain Harry Wales was also awarded the trophy he had most wanted in his life: his Apache Badge. Now he could fly the lethal machine without an instructor and was ready for a further eight-month weapon course in order to become a fully operational Army Air Corps pilot. The 'Apache Conversion to Type' course would involve intense ground school train-ing, day and night flying and intensive work on a simulator at RAF Wattisham in Suffolk. He and his fellow students would need to undertake fourteen-day flying sorties testing their ability to fly in cloud and congested airspace. Before progressing on to the night-time flying phase, however, Harry was tested using a cockpit blackout system known as 'the Bag', an exercise preparing him for flying on the night-vision system displaying thermal imagery into the helmet mounted display over his right eye.

Awesome stuff, but first he had a wedding to go to. As a clear signal of the growing admiration he had for his mentor Mark Dyer, before setting off for Wattisham the morning-suited Prince acted as an usher at the former royal equerry's wedding to his Texan bride Amanda Kline in the Welsh town of Abergavenny. He had grown close to Dyer since the former Welsh Guards officer took him under his wing during the drugs scandal of 2002 and was greatly impressed by the way he handled the press invasion during his 'virtual rehab' gap-year sojourn in Australia. Clearly moved by the ceremony and, in jolly mood, he told one guest at the reception afterwards: 'Gosh, this is so lovely it makes me want to get married too and have lots of kids.'

But as Chelsy, the only serious candidate to be his partner for life, might have thought of a boy with such a roving eye, the trouble was choosing a girl he could settle down with from the multitude of eager contenders waiting in the wings.

# 11

# GIRLS, GIRLS, GIRLS

As Harry Wales discovered early in life, there are lots of advantages to being a royal, but there are disadvantages too. Many young sons of wealthy parents have all the material things their hearts desire – fabulous homes, luxurious holidays and servants to ensure their every need is taken care of. In Harry's case there is an added bonus: there are few desirable women in the world who would not like to be a princess. He has had his choice of a multitude of such delectable females and quite a few of them, it has to be said, were the daughters of women who would give anything to be related by marriage to Her Majesty the Queen. But there was one big problem he had to face that would not trouble his contemporaries: how was he ever going to know if the girl he eventually chose would be the right one, marrying him for the right reason?

But Harry's first love was not a girl chasing his fame and potential fortune. From the moment he set eyes on the beautiful Laura Gerard Leigh, a nice St Mary's Calne girl, during his troubled time at Eton (where she was said to be a regular visitor) he fell head-over-heels in love. Prince Philip, wary of the dangers of Harry falling for a misfit, was particularly delighted when he learned of the budding romance between his grandson and the granddaughter of the close friend he called 'G' – Colonel William Gerard Leigh, who had served in the Life Guards throughout the Second World War and was a much respected figure in the polo world.

The Gerard Leighs' close connections with the Royal Family promised a match made in heaven. Alas, much as she liked him, Laura was not as besotted with Harry as he was with her though she enjoyed his attention, his sense of humour and his gracious hospitality. On their many summer evenings out the pair talked endlessly about their mutual love of rugby (she attended the Six Nations tournament with him) and horses – especially polo horses. But, as he admitted later, his passion for the beautiful girl at his side was never fully reciprocated. Letters he wrote professing his love for her failed to receive the desired answers. Romantic Valentine cards from Harry were answered with jocular ones from Laura.

A contemporary at Eton says:

Harry was heartbroken. I believe he turned to drinking copious quantities of vodka at that time because of it. I was going through a similar experience myself so I knew how he felt. We both thought more about our loves than we did our suffering studies. Laura wasn't interested in titles and prospects – her father was a multi-millionaire stockbroker so she didn't have to care about money, just love, real love, and sadly, from what I witnessed, as much as she liked Harry she decided she wasn't in love with him.

The match ended when both set off for their respective gap years. According to Harry he tried to keep the fire in his heart burning, but once they were apart there was little or no response from the girl he had fallen so deeply in love with.

And then along came Margaret – that's her middle name, she declines to be identified any further – a totally different girl from Miss Gerard Leigh. Unlike the rich and often-spoiled women he met in nightclubs and parties, 'Margaret' was an ordinary girl he first glimpsed on a visit to her shop where he had called in to pick up groceries during his time at school.

He was very nice, very polite and at first I didn't even recognise him. After we'd been chatting for a few minutes he asked me if I would join him for a drink later. I told him I had a boyfriend but he was very persuasive and I agreed to see him at a pub in a nearby town – another girl who worked with me whispered in my ear, 'You know who that is, don't you? It's Prince William's brother, it's Prince Harry.' I was stunned, the closest I had ever been to anyone famous was when Kenny Everett came to an event in our town and I plucked up the courage to ask him for an autograph.

I didn't want to be seen with Harry by anyone who knew me or, more importantly, someone who would tell my boyfriend, so we met up in this pub and I had cider and he had a beer. He was really lovely although I don't think he really knew how to [behave] with someone from the other side of the tracks; all his friends were upper class, privileged people. Also, I felt so guilty because I knew my boyfriend would have been very upset if he knew. We talked for more than an hour – he asked me about my job, whether I had any hobbies, and when I said I had to go because I needed to catch a certain bus, he asked me for my mobile number and I gave it to him; he didn't offer me his but he did ask me not to talk to anybody from the newspapers about him and me which offended me a bit so half-jokingly I said to him, 'OK, on condition you don't talk to them about me,' which made him laugh.

Anyway, he called me the next day and said he'd enjoyed my company and would like to see me again. We met on two further occasions and on the second he held my hand and kissed me and said he thought he was falling for me. I felt awful, I liked him a lot but I knew it wouldn't come to anything and that I risked losing the boy I'd been courting for nearly two years. I was also embarrassed because there was a man who was obviously his minder hovering in the background.

Harry called me several times after that but I had to tell him I couldn't see him again. He was pleading but I knew it was wrong. I could never be part of his world. I cried buckets after that last call but he never rang me again. He'd said he understood. I wrote it all down in my diary – including the cheeky remarks he made to me – but I destroyed the diary on the night before I married my boyfriend, a marriage which is very happy, I'm pleased to say, and we have two lovely children.

Margaret's story says a great deal about Harry's genuine compassion. The Prince that she encountered was not a royal playboy but a young man who would ultimately give his heart to whomever he was attracted to, regardless of their position or status in life. As Margaret herself sums up their brief romance:

> I still think about Harry. He's such a lovely man, a true gentle-man. I never talked about it before except to a girlfriend who I know called you. Please don't let anyone else contact me. It's long been my secret and I guess his too. I've read all about his affairs – well, his girlfriends – in the papers and I hope he's happy but none of them seem like the kind of girl I believe he needs. Glamour and nightclubs may sound very attractive but the Harry I knew, albeit briefly, needs real love and he doesn't seem to have found it.

Prince Philip might well have approved of Margaret after his fears that Harry's position in life might be used for all the wrong reasons were realised when a Hollywood publicist decided to link the Prince with a young starlet he was anxious to turn into an international celebrity. The girl was one Hilary Duff, an up-and-coming actress who had just appeared in *Lizzie McGuire* and also had high hopes of becoming a sing-ing star. The hype merchant helping her on her way claimed that Harry had made a series of telephone calls to her and that the pair were 'keen to meet up soon'. Duff herself said: 'This is just like a fairy tale and he's my Prince Charming.' She even sent the bemused Prince an autographed poster for her movie, a film he had never seen since the picture was aimed at fourteen-year-old girls. The ambitious PR campaign bandied it about that Harry had initiated contact with Duff: 'He pulled a few strings and was able to get his private telephone number to her. He was thrilled when she called him. They've just started talking on a regular basis. It's a case of puppy love for both of them.' Duff soon forgot Harry when she married the real man of her dreams, a professional hockey player called Mike Comrie.

Although there can never be a replacement for the first love in anyone's life, he was to find brief consolation in the arms of two others: TV presenter Natalie Pinkham, a friend of his cousin Zara Phillips, and Beaufort polo club assistant Jo Davies. If there was one girl who certainly had nothing to gain from publicity linking her with Harry it was Pinkham, a talented broadcaster who fascinated him with her love of extreme sports like bungee jumping, canyoning, sky diving, paragliding, scuba diving and rock climbing. Similar to him, she was a keen supporter of good causes and received acclaim for walking on fire for the Motor Neurone Disease Association. But Pinkham announced that she was suing a newspaper (not *The Sun*, which had first printed it) for publishing a photograph of the Prince kissing her cheek and cupping her breast which had been taken three years earlier, alleging a current romance. Pinkham, who was introduced initially to Harry by her ex-boyfriend, former England rugby team captain Matt Dawson, claimed the picture was from her own private collection and represented 'a flagrant breach of copyright'.

No such litigation was brought to bear by the delightful Ms Davies, at twenty-seven then eight years Harry's senior, who made light of her kiss with Harry. Then assistant manager at Cirencester Park Polo Club, she joked, 'What can I say? It's all a bit silly really. We're just friends.' Her embarrassment was not diminished, however, at the publication in the national press of a topless photograph of her (well, she was using oranges to cover her modesty) taken for a charity calendar.

It was, however, Chelsy Davy who eventually captured his heart. On his twenty-first birthday (15 September 2005) he surprised even his father by going public and declaring that Chelsy was his girlfriend. In the spring of 2006 they spent a fortnight on a getting-to-know-you holiday and, following her return to the UK on a six-week break, they stayed at Highgrove at weekends and a borrowed cottage on the Lulworth Castle estate during his leave from a tank-driving course at Bovington in Dorset. To their friends it sounded bliss: this was surely the real thing. They were together constantly until, on the evening of 20 May, he decided to have a night out on his own after watching a show headlined by Ozzy Osbourne and Lionel Richie. On the other side of town the same thought had crossed the mind of Catherine

Davies, a 34-year-old married (though separated from her husband) mother of two. Their paths crossed at the Art Bar in Walton Street, Knightsbridge. One can only imagine how Chelsy felt when she subsequently read Mrs Davies's account of what followed: 'Hi, I'm Harry,' said the Prince, thirteen years younger than the woman whose cleavage had transfixed him. In what seemed like no time at all he invited her to join him on a club crawl, travelling in the back of the Range Rover with his two armed protection officers in the front.

After some horseplay at the club Boujis they went to a house in Chelsea, retiring to the kitchen where he made her a bacon sandwich. To cut a long story short, they ended up enjoying some horseplay, partly in an empty bath after Mrs Davies had said she would like to see the rest of the house. Shortly after, she claims he gave her 'a long and lovely kiss'. More than that she declined to reveal in the account of her night with the Prince, which she sold to a newspaper, except to say that at 3 a.m. one of his protection officers drove them to her home in Battersea where Harry bade her a polite farewell with a kiss on the cheek. Catherine had just one souvenir of her unusual encounter with the Prince: a photograph a friend of hers had taken on a mobile phone of the two of them sitting in the bath.

It was probably Harry's roving eye that caused Chelsy to split from him the following year. Although he was clearly in love with her and teased her mercilessly as only two people so close to each other can, he found it hard to be faithful. There was even talk of her finding a goodbye text message on his mobile phone from 'Margaret', who by now must have acquired his number. Harry's decision to go to Paris for the Rugby World Cup final in October 2007 instead of turning up for Chelsy's twenty-second birthday celebrations proved a bridge too far and she let it be known that they had split because she 'needed space'.

Harry's response to Chelsy's choice was to go party-hunting although it has to be said that the girls who followed were never to be serious contenders for his heart. When Sir Richard Branson's son Sam told him the heavenly Australian singer Natalie Imbruglia was planning a fancy-dress celebration for her thirty-fourth birthday in February 2009 at his father's nightclub, the Kensington Roof Gardens, Harry made it known that he would very much like to be there. Recently divorced (from husband Daniel Johns), Imbruglia was more than happy to have one of the world's most eligible bachelors – dressed in a surgeon's outfit for reasons best known to himself (one of his more mischievous chums says he had gone as a gynaecologist and called himself Dr Goldfinger) – grace her gathering.

Well aware that royal presence would do her no harm, Imbruglia later boasted that she had both a prince and a princess at her party, for Harry's cousin Beatrice also turned up with boyfriend Dave Clark who happens to work for Branson's Virgin Galactic company. However, there was never any question of a romance: as a friend of the singer confides: '[Natalie] gets on very well with Harry but she tends to go for rock musicians rather than public schoolboys.'

Someone with no objection to public schoolboys is Astrid Harbord, with whom Harry was spotted leaving Chelsea haunt Raffles within weeks of his split from Chelsy, seeing him safely home to Clarence House after yet another celebratory night. Astrid (an old friend of Kate Middleton's) and her sister Davina are from a noted family with aristocratic connections. Their father Charles Harbord was an Old Harrovian and the family home was a splendid residence in Wiltshire – until, that is, Harbord shot himself dead in May 2012 at the rented apartment in Dorset to which he and his wife Sarah-Juliet (née Blandy) had been obliged to move eighteen months earlier when his extravagant lifestyle caught up with him.

Dubbed the Hardcore Sisters by *Tatler*, Astrid and Davina are known to enjoy a good party – and it doesn't have to be in the Chelsea/Mayfair areas that Harry normally frequents on London nights out. So when they decided to celebrate Davina's twenty-seventh birthday at a rave on the third floor of a dilapidated venue in Whitechapel – an area of east London notorious for high crime rates and drug problems – the Prince had no qualms about accepting an invitation, despite the fact that the property had been repossessed. According to neighbours, police had been called to the premises on a number of occasions to break up fights which had broken out between drunk and drugged guests. It was known to be a matter of concern to his royal protection officers that Harry was determined to go and join in the 'fun' at the party labelled 'Dress 2 Sweat'.

Techno was pumped out to 400 revellers at the event, which was organised by a group of students from Leeds, a number of whom were known to Chelsy: the Who's Who guest list included Prince William's former girlfriend Arabella Musgrave, the daughter of Cirencester Park Polo Club manager Major Nicholas Musgrave.

Harry's attendance at the rave was subsequently criticised by Dai Davis who was in charge of royal security until 1998. He said,

> We are at the severe end of severe danger according to the Home Secretary. What is the point of the taxpayer spending £50 million on protection for the Royals when officers are unable to prepare for events like this in a venue that is incredibly difficult [to police]. My concern is that if you are being protected the onus is for you to look after yourself to some extent. That responsibility seems not to be taken seriously and it puts Harry and his officers in a dangerous position.

Royal aides had already advised him to keep a distance between himself and the blonde socialite hostesses. He had, it seemed, developed a taste for a clubber lifestyle and had no difficulty in finding similar events known to the affluent attendees as 'raavs'.

Harry swears he went home alone on the night of the Whitechapel raav. The same may not be said, however, for the night he met fun-loving television presenter Caroline Flack that June. The *Daily Mail* reported that she might have spent a night with Harry at his 'private London apartment'. If ever there was a party-loving girl it is Miss Flack: her many friends include actor James Corden, One Direction star Harry Styles, Robbie Williams (who entertained her with a beans-on-toast supper at his apartment), Dec Donnelly, comedian Russell Brand, Jordan Stephens of Rizzle Kicks, Johnny Lloyd of Tribes and Ozzy and Sharon Osbourne's son Jack, with whom she was reported to have shared a hot tub at his Los Angeles home alongside another girl – Caroline enjoys the company of a number of close female friends.

It was way back in 2005 when she found out that a colleague at the Poker TV channel (none other than the aforementioned Natalie Pinkham) knew Prince Harry, that she set her sights on meeting the most famous one of all. It took four years for her dream to come true but the one-time presenter of Sky 1's *Gladiators* show achieved the near-impossible shortly after breaking up after a year with Holloways drummer Dave Healy ('the absolute love of my life'). It was in 2009 that she met her Prince Charming at a charity poker event.

The two briefly became close and when she posted 'Caroline loves Jam…' on her Facebook site it was mistakenly reported that she had given HRH the codename Jam 'because he has jam coloured hair and is really sweet'. She was, however, able to put the record straight when she explained that Jam was the joint nickname she had given to one of her closest friends Josie and her boyfriend Sam.

A confidant of Caroline's says:

She and the Prince are like chalk and cheese but perhaps that's where the attraction lay. He was fascinated by her wild carefree attitude and rock-chick lifestyle. He was never really her type though. She normally goes for cool, grungy indie musician types. I'd never known her to date a non-celebrity. The main criterion is fame and they don't come much more famous than HRH Harry.

It took a royal advisor to convince Harry that the association would do him no good and that word of it had already reached Chelsy, whom he still regarded as 'the best thing that has ever happened to me'. Miss Flack found herself being reported as 'well and truly dumped'. 'These are just silly stories in a very serious world,' says the *Xtra Factor* presenter.

> 'When you think of the real stories – people around the world dying of starvation, being killed in conflicts, born into poverty – when you think what I did: I went out with a younger guy [she was referring to Harry Styles] and I am the front page news. It's just absurd.

The warning he received from the Palace was enough for Harry Wales to proceed with caution that summer. Apart from enjoying the company of PR advisor Stephanie Haynes, who worked for the Italian fashion house Armani at the time, he seemed to be taking his royal position more seriously. Despite being his type (an easy-on-the-eye blonde) it was not Stephanie's physical attributes that attracted him to her.

Although she was just six years his senior he regarded her as a mother figure and found her to be the best media advisor he had ever encountered. This was important since he was well aware that newspaper reports of his escapades since their split meant he stood little chance of winning Chelsy back unless she saw – or rather read – that he had changed his ways.

Whatever Ms Haynes advised him seemed to pay off, for by July the couple were secretly meeting again following Chelsy's return from a holiday in Portugal, and when Harry – by now on his best behaviour – celebrated his twenty-fifth birthday at Raffles (where a methuselah of vintage champagne costs £9,000), Chelsy was the star, not to say the surprise, guest. It was after all the first time they had been seen in public for more than six months. The couple spent most of the night together in deep conversation in the club's VIP room while the Wagabees – WAG wannabes – could only look on enviously.

The reunion was a delicate matter and, apart from a joint appearance at a West End pub to celebrate the successful completion of his helicopter course, they kept it out of the public eye. But not for long. The world, they decided, needed to see they were back together and it was Harry who chose the venue and the occasion for their public display: Twickenham Stadium where England were playing Australia early in November of 2009. Prepared for the inevitable throng of photographers, Harry did his best to look like any other member of the crowd, dressing in a blue beanie, a casual jacket, black zip-up top and jeans. Chelsy opted for a bright blue jumper, leather jacket and gold scarf. No one was going to miss them. As it happens, the English team were beaten by the Australians but the result gave the love of his life the opportunity to comfort him in front of a massive audience.

Although the Queen's rules forbade Harry from taking Chelsy to Sandringham for the traditional Christmas gathering, they enjoyed advance yuletide celebrations. Nothing revealed their reconciliation more than a joint Christmas e-card sent to their friends: it featured Harry and Chelsy's faces – along with those of her brother Shaun and her best friends Kirsten and Pegs – superimposed on a 44-second segment of video footage which featured a group of elves dressed in green tunics and striped stockings. When the card was played the group broke into a breakdance to the tune of a jazzed-up 'Jingle Bells' soundtrack with Harry as the undoubted star.

The card was fun but the thought behind it was serious: the third in line was back with the girl he loved. Chelsy was sure that he had mended his ways. What's more, he would be reunited with the Davy family on a beach holiday in Mauritius just as soon as he could get away from the Queen's formal festivities at Sandringham.

꽃

It had been early on an October morning in 2010 that Harry received the call that proved him wrong about William's intentions regarding Kate Middleton. 'How do you fancy being a best man?' his brother asked. William had proposed to Kate on the balcony of an isolated log cabin they were sharing miles off the beaten track during a holiday tracking elephants, hyenas, buffalos and leopards in Kenya. They had made a 24-hour stop at the Rutundu camping area (a hideaway he had visited two years earlier) staying in a small lodge that didn't even have electricity. A four-poster bed was the only luxury and guests, including William and Kate, were advised to bring their own food and drink. For two weeks William had been carrying in his rucksack his mother's diamond and sapphire engagement ring – for which Charles had paid £28,500 almost thirty years earlier – to slip onto his sweetheart's finger. And, in anticipation of an acceptance, he also had a bottle of – albeit warm – champagne to celebrate. He was not disappointed by her positive reply, although he made no mention of the historic event that had occurred in Cabin 5 when, on departure, he simply wrote in the guest book: 'Thank you guys! Look forward to the next time, soon I hope.'

When the engagement was announced the following month Harry said he was delighted to be getting a sister, 'which I always wanted'. Somewhat less tactfully Charles said, 'Well, they've been practising long enough,' and there was even a note of impatience in the Queen's response when she added, 'It has taken them a very long time' after expressing her delight at the 'brilliant news'.

Once the news had been absorbed it was time for public attention to be re-focused on the still-eligible Prince: who would be on Harry's arm at the wedding on 29 April? It was, of course, Chelsy, the love of his life, and they looked to all the world as if they would be the next royal couple at the altar. Alas, the reunion turned out to be all too brief and after yet another serious disagreement (over what this time no one will say), it was Harry's turn to look elsewhere for a bride of his own – not easy for a man who has a fondness for fabulously attractive women but must find one to fit comfortably into the Royal Family. His dreams seem to have come true just two months after William and Kate's wedding when he re-met Florence Anne Marie Brudenell-Bruce – they had vaguely known each other for years – a woman stunning enough to model lingerie for La Senza and yet one who had heritage suitable to become Her Majesty the Queen's daughter-in-law and sister-in-law to a future queen.

The impeccably mannered aristocrat is a descendant of the Earl of Cardigan who led the Charge of the Light Brigade against Russian forces during the Battle of Balaclava in 1854. Privately educated (like Chelsy) at Stowe School in Buckinghamshire before graduating with a degree in history of art at Bristol University, she is the daughter of Old Etonian Andrew Brudenell-Bruce, a wine merchant, and his French wife Sophie, an exotic painter.

And she is also the sexiest woman Harry had ever dated. Known to her friends as Flee, she had previously been involved with Formula 1 racing driver Jenson Button, featured in a Bollywood movie, played a corpse in an episode of the TV detective drama *Lewis* and posed for risqué modelling shots in her underwear. What more could a man ask?

Less of a party girl than some other of Harry's female acquaintances, Flee spent much of her 2011 summer romance with Harry in private trysts at her home in Notting Hill, west

London where he did the washing up after each meal and called for a minicab when it was time to go home, rather than have a royal limousine turn up outside. This looked like the real thing – it certainly put paid to nonsensical reports that he had become romantically involved with Pippa Middleton, as well as confirming that Flee was free of her entanglement with the upper-crust (and grandly named) Henry St George, son of the fabulously wealthy financier Edward St George.

Alas, the relationship lasted a mere two months, with Harry's nearest and dearest declaring that he did not want to be tied down. Plans for him to join Flee on holiday in Ibiza were suddenly cancelled. The only certainties are that Harry was certainly not ready to give up his army career and settle down and Flee, at that time, still cherished the dream of moving to Hollywood and becoming a movie star, although she subsequently returned to the arms of Henry St George and in January 2013 the couple announced their engagement.

Flee had once been the face of the designer fashion label Aspinal and her successor in that job, Mollie King, who sings with the group The Saturdays, found herself linked with the Prince in April 2012 after matchmaker-in-chief Zara Phillips (friend of another Saturdays girl, Una Healy) intro-duced them. Although King says she went out with him a few times, it turned out to be yet another 'we're just friends' situation which neither caused Harry any grief nor the rising girl band any harm – a repeat of the situation in 2010 when he was said to have fallen for Scandinavian rock singer Camilla Romestrand, who fronts a band called Eddie The Gun. Harry was obliged to point out that his stepmother was the only Camilla he had learned to love.

Harry's much proclaimed longing to be a 'normal' human being is greatly frustrated by his failure to have a normal love life but he is the first to admit that he is often helpless when it comes to the female temptation pushed his way. One circle of girls ensconced in apartments in Kensington, Chelsea and Belgravia, and known as the Harry Hunters, developed their own signal system, circulating text messages which would read something like 'H@M no C' – gibberish to most but to the recipients it meant 'Prince Harry is at the club Mahiki without Chelsy'. When one Mahiki regular, seemingly fuelled by cocaine, told him about the coded messages, he simply responded (according to her), 'Wow, bring it on.'

Harry's choice of friends is believed by his father to have much to do with his often wild behaviour. They are almost, without exception, fellow clubbers. It was his best friend, Guy Pelly – then promotions manager of the club – who introduced him to Mahiki, a venue close to the Ritz Hotel which sells Treasure Chest cocktails at £300 a shot. One of the first to become a Mahiki regular, Harry's presence attracted huge attendance and queues were known to grow round the corner once it became known that the club had royal patronage. Even the so-called *Tatler* set girls – those with double-barrelled names who often employee PR men to keep their names in the society columns – are content to stand in line when there's a chance of bumping into the party Prince.

Another of his favourite late-night haunts is Raffles

on the King's Road. It is conveniently located close to a friend's Chelsea home where the party often goes on until breakfast time and bouncers have been known to turn away 'unattractive' women. Chelsy's favourite, though, was always Chinawhite, just off Oxford Street and a regular haunt of the young, rich, famous and, of course, glamorous.

In many of the places he favours, the Prince is rarely presented with a bill. An exception is Boujis, where he once ran up a tab of more than £10,000 after treating complete strangers to £200 bottles of champagne. According to a reliable Buckingham Palace source he got a lecture from the Queen for flaunting his wealth after news of his huge bill leaked out – something his brother has never had to face. It didn't stop Harry: similarly large amounts of royal cash were spent at his other favourite venues: The Brompton Club (subsequently bought by another of his close friends, Piers Adam), The Box and Whisky Mist, where his attendance is always welcomed.

Whichever nightspot he was at, Harry was never short of company, especially of the female kind. But Chelsy, the very antithesis of all things Middleton, was the only one who truly tugged his heart strings: 'He doesn't know what to do because she's the only one he's ever wanted to settle down with and she's just not interested in being a professional princess,' says one close to the Prince.

I saw him cry one night in The Brompton because, although he was surrounded with beautiful girls who would have done anything for him, it was Chelsy he wanted to be there. She's not bothered about the Harry Hunters, she treats them with the contempt they deserve, and let's face it, she has a busy social life of her own. She's not born aristocracy, as Kate Middleton was not either. To the true bluebloods around here, both women are regarded as nouveau riche.

Without naming Chelsy, Harry came close to detailing the problem to an American TV host when he said: 'As any girl would tell you, it's sort of "Oh my God, he's a prince. No thank you."' And on his chances of marriage he sadly explained the problem: 'I'm not so much looking for someone to fulfil the role, but obviously, you know, finding someone who would be willing to take it on.' Clearly Ms Davy was not such a candidate. Nevertheless, he sent her indirect messages, announcing that he was '100 per cent single', but Chelsy was not fooled by his bid to challenge her to call him for yet another reconciliation. She had a life of her own to live and his responsibilities were too great to support a tender romance.

The tug-of-love was not over yet, however.

Had he given in to his various affairs, Harry could have been married several times by now, but he is cautious in that regard; his father had reminded him that a previous royal Henry – King Henry VIII – had one of his wives beheaded simply because he wanted to marry another woman. The killing apart, though, Harry may have more in common with his amorous red-headed ancestor than he realises.

# 12

## WITH FLYING COLOURS

No one was more surprised than his father when Harry passed his Apache flying test. For someone who had limped through his academic career at school and college, it was an extraordinary achievement. Harry had said himself a few years earlier that although his dream – after repeatedly viewing the Tom Cruise movie – was to become a *Top Gun* pilot, he did not feel he was bright enough for the role.

The new-found application to learning – something he had abysmally failed to demonstrate at Eton – was astonishing. Apache helicopters cost £46 million each and are among the most advanced and complicated war machines ever conceived. Learning to fly them and use their highly complex weaponry requires the kind of brainpower few believed Harry possessed, yet he had amazed his instructors with both his dedication to study and his natural and instinctive flying ability.

He had spent several weeks of his training flying the gunship though the precarious French Alps. Nicknamed the 'flying tank', the aircraft is so sophisticated it can detect, classify and prioritise 256 potential targets in seconds, but that's of no use unless the man at the controls can absorb and act on the information it delivers. The Apache is no robot; it requires a man at the controls capable of using the 30mm cannon firing 625 rounds a minute, the CRV-7 point-and-fire rockets and four air-to-air missiles on receipt and interpretation of signals received in front of his right eye on the helmet display unit.

Harry was trained to act as the aircraft's co-pilot gunner, operating the Apache's arsenal of weapons from the front seat while behind him sat the pilot. He was now qualified to embark on missions that would involve targeting the Taliban in support of ground troops under attack from insurgents. With its payload of laser-guided Hellfire missiles the Apache can target buildings being used by the Taliban for cover, reducing them to rubble. For enemy out in the open, Harry could operate the Apache's 30mm chain gun using his helmet-mounted display as the aircraft flew at 205mph in all weathers from arctic cold to desert heat and by night as well as day.

Harry was not just good at it, he was declared one of the two best young airmen to have fulfilled the course; he was a true Top Gun.

Charles was justifiably proud of the son whose lack of application had so exasperated him during his schooldays and, in the way that such fathers do, before he went to bed on the night the results came through, he wrote his son a letter of fulsome praise.

Harry celebrated in his own way: he had a date with four soldiers and a great deal of snow and ice. When he heard that four servicemen who had all been seriously injured in Afghanistan were planning to walk to the North Pole, he asked if he might join them.

Although they had pledged to make the trek with as little able-bodied help as possible, he pointed out, he had after all agreed to be patron of their Walking With The Wounded charity, founded to raise funds for the re-education of wounded servicemen and women, so he surely deserved a place in the team. His wish was granted but his father did not approve. He explained that he had had no training for such a dangerous venture; the trek would take the men through an area populated by polar bears and where night-time tempera-tures dropped to -45°C. But Charles knew better than to try and talk his younger son out of anything he had set his mind to. So, with less than four weeks to go to his brother's wedding, Harry set off with Private Jaco van Gass, whose arm was amputated after he was hit by a grenade; Captain Martin Hewitt, whose right arm is paralysed after a bullet went through his shoulder; Captain Guy Disney, who lost a leg to a rocket propelled grenade; and Sergeant Steve Young whose back was so severely damaged by an IED blast that he was told he might never walk again – all determined to reach the most northerly point of the world to highlight the plight of the 1,700-plus service personnel injured in Afghanistan since the conflict began.

With preparation in Norway, it would be a four-week

mission, covering 200 miles of the frozen Arctic Ocean by foot, pulling their equipment in sledges weighing more than 100kg. Needing to get back to the army as his leave had finished, Harry was able to spend just four days skiing across the ice with them, sleeping at night in a tent he called his 'pleasure dome' and where he kept them amused with jokes, some of which would have made royal courtiers cringe. 'He's so down to earth,' recalls Jaco van Gass. 'I was very surprised at that; he helps out with absolutely everything.'

Such was the effect of his spirited encouragement that despite a start delayed by gales in Norway, they were ahead of schedule after hauling themselves and their sledges twelve miles on Harry's final days with them.

He was as reluctant to leave them as the Arctic was to let him go – cracks in an ice runway at Borneo Ice Airfield delayed his homeward flight by forty-eight hours. On his return he admitted: 'I took part in only a small section of the trek, but I know full well how physically demanding what they are doing is. The spirit and determination of these lads is second to none. They are true role models.'

And when the team reached the North Pole just thirteen days into their trek across the polar ice cap and three days ahead of schedule, Harry was the first to congratulate them via satellite phone, telling them they were 'showing off' by getting there early and urging them to enjoy the champagne he had provided them with for 'the magic moment when you make it'. An aide confides: 'They may not have been together long but they became his buddies. One of the first things he did when he got back was to add them to his personal Christmas card list.' He had clearly had the 'Diana effect' on the expedition since his participation helped raise the anticipated financial target by several times, so when the charity announced that the brave four planned to tackle Mount Everest next, he promised to go with them as far as the base camp, 17,000 feet up.

In a rare 'I was wrong' admission, Charles congratulated his son on his 'pluckiness' and before he went to bed on the night of 14 April – the day his son received his Apache Flying Badge – wrote him the letter of praise which Harry treasures to this day. Just two days later Charles had further reason to congratulate him again when Harry was promoted to the rank of captain.

Within days of returning from the Arctic, Harry got to work on the best man's speech he would deliver at his brother's wedding breakfast. He was required to submit the final version of it to Palace courtiers, but first – in a telephone call that went on until the early hours – he read it to Chelsy who had flown from her South African home specially to attend the wedding with him. Although she says she found many of his anecdotes hilarious, Chelsy advised him to take out a number of the racier ones – including a reference to Kate's 'killer legs'– reminding him that his grandmother would be there and that she would not take kindly to the sort of humour traditionally delivered by the best man on such an occasion.

It came as no surprise to Charles that his plea to his younger son to 'behave' on the night before the big day went unheeded. After dining with his brother and stepmother at Clarence House he moved on to the nearby Goring Hotel, which the Middletons had taken over in the days prior to the wedding, and he was, as expected, the life and soul of the party. He not only joined those celebrating in the bar but remained there until 3 a.m. when he made a spectacular exit leaping from one of the hotel's balconies and – worryingly considering what lay ahead – landed awkwardly on one ankle. 'He was showing off,' says a friend.

> He told me – and I tried to talk him out of it but he was, as you say, in full flow – that it would be quicker to make the 6ft drop than go inside and down the stairs. Actually, it was a bit of attention-seeking but that's Harry when he's pissed.

So no wonder he looked a little jaded, with squiffy hair, as he stood at his brother's side in Westminster Abbey just a few hours later. Thankfully there was no chance of him having forgotten the ring: aware of the possibility (because his military trousers have no pockets) an aide had had the tailors, Kashket & Partners, sew a special pocket for it into a gold-embroidered cuff attached to the jacket of his Blues and Royals uniform.

At precisely 9.30 that evening, following a three-course meal for 300 washed down with vintage champagne, Harry delivered the perfect best man's speech and the humour was indeed tempered. The Queen had declared that morning that in future Prince William and his bride would be known as the Duke and Duchess of Cambridge and Harry went no further than to make frequent references to 'The Dude and Duchess' during what was largely a moving address in which he described William as 'the perfect brother' and Kate as 'the sister I always wanted'. Even the Queen laughed when he added, 'William didn't have a romantic bone in his body before he met Kate so I knew it was serious when [I heard him] cooing down the phone to her.' Then he did a high-pitched impression of Kate calling William 'Billy' and his brother calling her 'baby'.

And that's as far as he went, thanks to censor Chelsy.

❦

Despite his dislike of the media, Harry used an American television programme to let the world know that he had warned army chiefs in no uncertain terms that he would quit the force if he was not redeployed to Afghanistan in his new – and even more dangerous – role as an Apache helicopter pilot.

Although it had trained him for the job, the army knew that such a lethal machine as an Apache with the third in line to the throne at the controls was bound to ensure that the Taliban, well equipped with surface-to-air missiles, would make it their No. 1 target, but Harry was determined that his training should not be wasted. 'You can't train people and then not put them into the role they need to play... These people [who said I shouldn't go] live in a ridiculous world.'

A source close to Prince Charles says he was 'uncomfortable' with the idea that as an Apache pilot Harry would be flying missions on which there was a certainty that he would be required to take human lives. But Harry reminded him that during his previous term in Helmand in 2007 he had not only ordered aircraft to bomb Taliban positions but had personally pumped out rounds from his .50 machine gun at Taliban soldiers advancing on JTAC Hill, so it was too late to worry about causing fatalities: this was war and however unpleasant it might seem, killing the enemy was a big part of the job. Anyway, Charles had been deeply moved when, in a speech at *The Sun* Military Awards, Harry had singled out the relatives of those left behind when members of the armed forces went to war:

> [For us] there aren't many idle moments, we're busy. We can focus entirely on the job we're doing, on the job at hand. Those we leave behind often have no such luxury. The strength and courage it must take to see your husband or your wife, your father or mother, son or daughter, head off into the unknown – and to support them doing it – I can hardly even imagine.

Charles sent him another note saying he had been 'moved to tears' by Harry's thoughts for those – now including himself – left worrying at home.

This time the Prince had a special reason for being desperate to return to the war zone: the Taliban had killed one of his closest friends, Corporal Liam Riley, who trained with him in Suffolk, Canada. Not one to normally show great sorrow in public, Harry was close to tears when he described Liam Riley as

> a legend – I remember him so well from the time we spent together in Canada. He was a really special man who got us all going in the right direction. It was a privilege to have worked alongside him. It is incredibly sad that Liam died alongside his friend Lance Corporal Graham Shaw. My heart goes out to their loved ones.

It was further proof of his great loyalty and concern for those he grew close to – men at least.

It was, however, several months before Harry was despatched to the US and he spent one of his last evenings in the UK dining with Chelsy at her Belgravia home, doing his best to rekindle their romance. For all their disagreements and his various flirtations, she was the one he loved at that time and he asked her to trust him, to wait for him.

And then, on 7 October, he was gone: off with nineteen other British airmen to the California Naval Air Facility at El Centro (population 40,000), close to the Mexican border to undertake over two months the final training exercise of his Apache Conversion to Role course. This paved the way for a second tour of duty in Afghanistan. The Americans, who named the operation Exercise Crimson Eagle, had chosen the location (it's where Tom Cruise filmed many of the scenes for his *Top Gun* movie) because it replicated the brutal terrain of Afghanistan: vast stretches of desert that run sharply into soaring mountains and reach temperatures in excess of 110 degrees. Ground skimming and night flying made it doubly dangerous but since his main tasks would be to seek and destroy Taliban tanks and positions and assist in secret missions to kill and capture Taliban leaders, as well as providing air cover for ground troops, he had to be ready for anything. From El Centro he would move on to Gila Bend, Arizona where Apache students undertook live fire exercises on the Barry M. Goldwater Air Force Range complex. The real thing ... but not quite.

Although the MoD top brass had warned Harry that there would be precious little free time during such an intensive course, he managed to find some and just a few weeks after his arrival in the US he rode into Las Vegas astride a 1600cc Harley Davidson motorcycle hired to him by one Dan Dvorak after a twenty-minute test in Scottsdale, Arizona, six hours' riding time away. The parking valet boy who took care of the Harley when he rode into the five-star Wynn Hotel says,

> I had no idea who he was even when he took off his crash helmet, bandana and sunglasses so we had a bit of banter and I said to him, 'If you're looking for any female company while you're here, just come to me.' How crazy was that? This was Prince Harry and he needed no help from me to find a girl.

Harry had spent the previous fortnight at the one-horse town of Gila Bend with only one bar in the Best Western Hotel;

he was ready for some bright lights and action. Accompanied by four of his new military friends, he found exactly what he wanted on his first trip to Sin City at the Encore Hotel. In the hotel's LasXS nightclub he sipped vodka cocktails and danced with a blonde dressed in a revealing cream blouse and knee-high black skirt. 'He danced seductively with her with his hands around her waist and zero daylight visible between their bodies,' according to *People* magazine which, to his annoyance, followed his every move around the town, noting, among other things, that he lost $300 on the gambling tables, was delighted to discover that the drinks in the casinos were free and never went to bed before 4 a.m. The magazine might also have noted that he jumped onto the lap of his security team at one point and got on his knees to dance with a brunette at another.

As if he needed reminding, Harry discovered, as his mother had time and time again, that anyone can make a fast buck out of what should be private moments when on another weekend off he headed for San Diego. There he was taken to a club called The Ivy where his favourite vodka cocktails were sold at a far higher price than he was used to paying. Detailed allegations that the waitress who served him spent the night at the Marriot Hotel where he was staying were sold to a local newspaper and subsequently circulated by a news agency. Harry was disgusted when the story made headlines across America but ignored advice to lodge a complaint, telling a fellow airman back at the camp, 'When you're me, it goes with the territory, I'm afraid.'

Many such stories are made up, as I learned during my research for this book, like, for example, the report about Chelsy warning the pop singer Cheryl Cole – who won publicity for her flirtatious remarks about Harry, despite never having met him – to stay away from her Prince. Ms Davy was alleged to have sworn that she was not threatened by Ms Cole and added that Harry 'doesn't like girls with tattoos'. In reality there was never any contact between the two women.

On his return from the American training exercise, Harry made a beeline for Chelsy, who had been offered 'a phenomenal sum of money' to write a kiss-and-tell book about their relationship. She was not remotely interested: for a start she had no need of the money and secondly she did not believe that the spark had gone out of their relationship even if Harry had hinted at it when he made the public declaration of being '100 per cent single'. Newspaper reports at the time described her as his ex-girlfriend; but was she an ex? The trusted source close to him was, on this subject, reluctant to be drawn but a friend of Chelsy's was less reticent:

> I think they love each other and eventually they will get back together. In fact – and she'll hate me for saying this – I believe they will marry – once she is convinced that his wandering eye days are over! One of Chelsy's arguments against settling down with him was that she hated the English weather and another was that his army career left him with little time for her anyway. But sooner or later he's going to leave the army and I know he loves Africa and would be quite happy

to spend at least the winters there. It would also allow him to devote time to working on Sentebale, which he is very passionate about.

Meanwhile, Harry had other things on his mind. He did much to illustrate that he was more than a London playboy when he delivered a stirring speech based on his experience of warfare that did much to silence his critics:

> It is often said of our armed forces that they are ordinary people doing extraordinary things. Well I don't buy that. Ordinary people don't run out under withering enemy rocket and heavy machine-gun fire to rescue a wounded comrade. Ordinary people aren't described by their platoon as being 'the rock' who held them together. Ordinary people don't brave monsoon conditions dangling on a winch line to rescue thirteen people, each in turn. For that matter, ordinary people don't put their lives on the line for distant folk, such as the Afghans, who need our help and are now turning their country round because of it.

Stirring stuff indeed and it earned him a standing ovation from those watching the transmission in Afghanistan, those who saw him not as a red-carpet royal but as a loyal comrade-in-arms who was proud of what they had all achieved together.

Loyalty, even when it means defying royal protocol, is a trait many of them referred to when asked what they most admire about Harry. Thomas van Straubenzee is particularly gracious in his praise for the Prince's loyalty – and with good reason: he was talking to Harry on his mobile phone when he was mugged in Battersea and had his BlackBerry stolen. Having heard the scuffle over his phone, Harry drove to the area in search of his friend. When he couldn't find him he went to the local police station where he found van Straubenzee at the desk reporting the crime. He gave a statement and offered to give evidence if the case ever came to court, which it did, but the mugger was sentenced to two years in prison without any requirement for Harry to fulfil his promise. 'That says a lot about Harry,' says his friend, 'any other member of the family would have thought twice about being caught up in a criminal case, but not Harry.' He has a special fondness for the van Straubenzees and only days before the mugging he had attended a carol concert in aid of a charity he helped set up to keep alive the memory of Thomas's brother Henry, the young friend Harry called 'Henners' who had died in such tragic circumstances.

Despite his appetite for young and pretty blondes, Harry has never yet been known to steal one from a friend, especially one as close as Thomas van Straubenzee. When on leaving The Brompton Club in west London, he discovered Vanners's girlfriend, Lady Melissa Percy, looking somewhat distressed, sitting on the club's rear entrance steps, he consoled her and phoned Thomas to alert him to the predicament. This is not how some of the tabloids interpreted it when they published paparazzi pictures of the Prince chatting to the shoeless girl. He was, as he always is in such situations, merely being the gallant knight, although he is rarely credited with the quality.

# 13

## THE PEOPLE'S PRINCE

Lest anyone thought his American experience had tamed his appetite for partying, Harry proved them wrong by celebrating the end of 2011 with his friend David Beckham in London, before moving on to Switzerland where he began 2012 by falling out of two nightclubs in his favourite ski resort, Verbier. After dining at his hotel with his friend Tom 'Skippy' Inskip he had gone to see in the New Year at the Farinet Hotel's Casbah Club where two blondes joined his table. He moved off a little after 1 a.m. for Guy Pelly's new bar, Public, where he was joined by soldier-turned-singer James Blunt, and his cousins Beatrice and Eugenie. Despite living up to his hard-partying image, he was able to steer clear when two fights broke out in the club.

On his return to the UK, however, it was back to the serious business of soldiering. On 8 February 2012, he was awarded the prize for being the best Co-Pilot Gunner during a dinner to mark the end of the Apache Training course. A return to Afghanistan was now beyond doubt.

As her Jubilee year dawned, it became increasingly apparent that the Queen needed the support of her husband more than she had ever done. Harry noticed the signs as Prince Philip's health showed signs of faltering – the Duke had been admitted to hospital after a heart scare over Christmas. More concerned than most, Harry said he did not believe that his 85-year-old grandmother could continue with her public duties without her husband at her side: 'Regardless of whether my grandfather seems to be doing his own thing, sort of wandering off like a fish down the river, the fact that he's there – personally I don't think she could do it without him.' His remarks, broadcast in a television interview, annoyed courtiers who warned him in a frosty meeting that he was forecasting an abdication in the event that Philip should die. Politely Harry reminded them that he was his own man and not their mouthpiece.

He made it clear that he often seeks Her Majesty's advice 'because she's always right'. But as the all-important year of 2012 was to prove, in many respects their roles were to be reversed.

Bitterly disappointed that he was not after all going to be able to join his Walking With The Wounded chums on their bid to climb Mount Everest, he called Mollie Hughes, the 21-year-old who was coordinating her own climb with the wounded soldiers, and asked her to break the news to them. He had badly wanted to go but the army had said 'no'. Like any employer growing tired of too-frequent absences even of such a favoured employee, the military top brass reminded him of his commitment to the service. No other soldier, they reminded him, could take off on excursions on a whim, even if they were in a good cause and, besides, he had already requested and been granted time off for the forthcoming celebrations to mark his grandmother's Diamond Jubilee, the Olympics and his first solo royal tour, which would take him to the Caribbean and South America. It was not enough to declare that he was hugely proud to be a British soldier, he was told: he had to do the work of one.

He did, however, get the time off afforded to all soldiers, and chose to spend one weekend with a bunch of chums in Transylvania looking for the Dracula he had been so fond of reading about in childhood-favourite horror stories. Aware that not all of those he was travelling with could afford the full fare, he was happy to fly with the budget airline Wizz Air and was grateful to Count Tibor Kálnoky for putting the whole bunch up with no charge at his home in Miclosoara. Alas, when they got there the vampire Count was nowhere to be seen.

The disappointment he suffered at being told he could not go on the Everest expedition was more than made up for when he arrived in the Caribbean as the Queen's Jubilee Year representative. He was fêted wherever he went in much the same way as his mother had been and, like her, it became apparent that he was destined to follow in her footsteps as the most popular royal of all.

Those who 'manage' the Royal Family had shaken their heads and tut-tutted when the Queen first made it known that she wanted Harry to go to Jamaica, Belize and South

America as her representative. After all, it was a vitally important year for the family; the almost-unique celebrations (only Queen Victoria had managed to reign longer than Elizabeth II) offered a fine opportunity to win back the popularity it had lost during almost two decades of royal scandal and only partially restored by Prince William's wedding.

Her Majesty's grandson was a good party man but an official royal tour of such importance, the men in suits asked?

Was he up to it? Most important of all, would he want to do it? After all, they argued, he had made it known that he had no wish to spend his life cutting ribbons and unveiling plaques as his brother was fated to spend much of his doing.

How wrong the courtiers were proved to be on all counts. Although utterly devoted to the army in which he served at the cost of a settled love life – Harry wanted desperately to do the bidding of his beloved grandmother who he had promised publicly to help out 'whenever she needs me'.

The concern of those whose job it is to insist that members of the most revered family in the world cannot behave as other men and women do, is understandable: could a repeat of past misbehaviour be expected when he carried Her Majesty's message to the hot spots of the Caribbean? Although his service career was thus far extremely successful, having overcome the learning weakness he had displayed at Eton, could he win over even those with strong republican leanings?

He could and he did.

Having discussed her advisors' doubt with the Queen in a half-hour meeting before setting off on the trip, he knew he was going with her blessing. 'She said to me, "I hope you enjoy it, now go and do me proud."' He was determined to do both.

From the moment he arrived in Belize, then went on to the Bahamas, Jamaica and Brazil, he charmed them just as Diana had done wherever she travelled. Even the Queen was amazed when Harry won over the 66-year-old Jamaican Prime Minister, Portia Simpson-Miller, who, only hours before meeting him, had said she wanted Queen Elizabeth replaced as her country's head of state and called for Britain to apologise and pay compensation for the 'brutal' years of slavery in the days of the Empire.

She changed her tune, however, after a hug and a kiss from Harry ('Well actually she hugged me,' he said later), who throughout the tour proved to be every bit as tactile as his late mother. 'He is a lovely man, really warm and great fun,' she wrote privately to one of her London-based officials.

What made the crowds truly fall for him was his sense of humour – fun was the nub of his forward planning and few can do fun better than Harry. As young choirgirls prepared for a solemn service at Christ Church Cathedral in Nassau, Harry – smartly dressed in his regiment's No. 1 tropical uniform – made them laugh by grinning at them and pulling faces. At a formal state banquet in Kingston, Jamaica, he said the Queen was sorry she couldn't be there 'so you're stuck with me' and, mimicking Bob Marley, added, 'but don't worry, 'cos every liddle ting's gonna be all right'.

He had the crowd cheering when he cheated in a race with his sporting hero, Usain Bolt, by taking off before the judges called 'Go', beating the fastest man on earth to the finishing line twenty yards away, although it has to be reported here that a usually reliable source says the pair had agreed the 'stunt' in advance. Whether it was a fix or not, film and television footage was seen by billions around the world with the two men performing Bolt's trademark 'lightning' gesture. The main beneficiary of that priceless piece of publicity was Puma, the sportswear makers' logo prominently displayed on the royal's tracksuit.

'The request to wear the Jamaican athlete's T-shirt was made by Harry himself but with the backing of the royal household and the Jamaican government,' says the Prince's press secretary. 'It was his way of signalling respect for the Jamaican team. The fact that the T-shirt contained branding was a coincidence and not a factor in the decision.'

Just as well, since had a deal been struck the Prince could have out-earned the huge sum Bolt receives from his multi-million-dollar advertising deals with Virgin Media ... and Puma.

Not that Harry had money on his mind when he was with his hero: so taken was he with Bolt that in a quiet and unpublicised moment, the Prince asked the fastest man on the planet to sign a napkin for him (probably the only occasion a royal has asked for an autograph since Princess Eugenie made a similar request of a TV star she fancied on a night out at the Goat In Boots pub on 'the beach' on Fulham Road, only to discover he had added a telephone number to his signature. According to the star's agent, she never got round to calling him.) Bolt laughed off the request.

The joy Harry's visit brought to those who turned out in their thousands to greet him was matched by the pleasure the tour gave him – for one thing he was fast becoming a fashion icon and the bright blue suede shoes he wore through much of the tour became so popular that the manufacturers were sold out within days of their first appearance on his feet.

From Jamaica he wrote to a soldier he had served along-side in Afghanistan to say 'this is one of the happiest times of my life – it's even better than meeting the Spice Girls, though that's a distant memory now. I hope all is well with you too. We must meet when I get home.' And he called one of his oldest friends in London to say he thought he'd 'really cracked it', that he'd 'got a real handle on the royal thing'. 'It must have been around three in the morning where he was but Harry was on the dog and bone [phone] whooping with joy, flying high,' says one of the few who, having known him for more than a decade, has Harry Wales's trust to speak frankly and without royal restraint of his friend. His reference to having 'cracked it' was taken as evidence that his plan to be a 'joyful royal' on the tour had worked. The friend wasn't the only person he called back home, however. A Palace source says, 'He was constantly on the phone to his brother who was always there to talk things through with him and give him advice when he needed it. It was very much William who gave him the confidence to go out and do a job he had not done before.'

With or without opinions and advice received from home, Harry had set out with the firm intention of enjoying as well as behaving himself. But even more importantly, he was going to hone his already considerable skills of communication with people at all levels – something his father had tried hard to do but never quite succeeded in. To Diana's son it came naturally.

It also came naturally to him to reverse some of the negative things Diana had said or done. Just a year after William's wedding, Harry turned up unannounced at Cothill House, a boarding school in Oxfordshire to watch a musical put on by the pupils. One of the stars of *Oh What A Knight* (a show written by the school's music teacher) was Fred Pettifer, the ten-year-old son of the princes' one-time nanny, Tiggy – now Mrs Charles Pettifer – who was also his godson. Both boys had relied heavily on Tiggy in the weeks and months following Diana's death even though they were painfully aware that the Princess, at the height of her suffering, had wrongly accused the nanny of being her husband's mistress.

Tiggy, who now runs the farmhouse bed and breakfast Ty'r in the Brecon Beacons and is one of the few women fly-fishing instructors in the country, was an enormous influence on Harry in his early years and the two remain on close terms – remember she had attended his passing-out parade at Sandhurst – but his appearance at Cothill House for Fred's stage debut surprised everyone including the other parents with whom he mingled freely afterwards.

But it went deeper than that. Harry and Tiggy knew what each had been through as the result of mayhem in the Palace and at Highgrove, which had once been homes to both of them. He talked to her at length about the sheer joy of his first solo royal tour and the privilege it had afforded him, but he went on to reveal that there was still much domestic strife behind the Palace walls. Because of his new-found and expanding influence within the family, its younger members chose him to go to with their problems – problems too great to trouble the octogenarian Queen with, and problems that Charles, more absorbed in matters of state, would pay no heed to.

Not long before his emotional reunion with Tiggy, Harry had been approached by a clearly upset Princess Beatrice. Her father had returned to Royal Lodge the previous evening in what she described as 'a filthy temper' and had begun 'throwing things around' saying his elder brother was treating him like a member of staff. One close to the young Princess says that during a tempestuous meeting Charles had told Andrew in no uncertain terms that he had to clean his act up and also to stop wasting public money. Charles had already incensed Andrew by withdrawing expensive 24-hour police protection from Beatrice and Eugenie on their nights out. 'What about when they are on official engagements?' Andrew had demanded. 'What official engagements?' Charles replied. 'My mother, my father, my sons and I can cope with those perfectly adequately.'

'For God's sake,' Andrew ranted, 'he's treating me like I'm Prince Michael rather than the monarch's second son.'

Alas, Harry had to tell his cousin there was little he could do to help. Acutely aware of the antipathy between his father and uncle, he was reluctant to get involved in family politics and in any event he knew his father was preparing for the day when he would take over the kingdom and was determined there should be no more scandal in the House of Windsor.

Beatrice got a similar response – although more gently put – when she went to William to see if he could help.

As for Andrew cleaning his act up, Charles had reminded his brother of the reports he had received some years earlier of his dubious activities in New York with some extremely rich friends: the paedophile Jeffrey Epstein and party girl Ghislaine Maxwell, daughter of the late, crooked media tycoon, Robert Maxwell. He had received information, not from the loyal (to their charge) royal protection officers, but via the American ambassador who had received a worrying report from a branch of the US secret service that was monitoring Epstein. Charles knew that Prince Edward was familiar with a New York socialite who had previously been a leading figure in the British music industry, and asked him to use the important contact.

Edward did as Charles asked and called his friend, saying that the family were anxious to know what their brother was up to mixing in such company. The heir to the throne was far from pleased with the response Edward conveyed to him and that was almost certainly a defining moment in what has been termed 'The War of the Princes', a feud that reached an all-time low in 2010 when the Duke's financially troubled ex-wife Sarah offered to sell introductions to him and his powerful friends (he was then Britain's trade envoy) in return for a payment of £500,000, claiming that Andrew himself had suggested the figure. The claim was strongly denied but Charles found it hard to contain his disgust at the actions of his brother's ex-wife. He became convinced that the same people who had set Andrew up with unsavoury company in New York were behind the 'Fergie sting' and he worried that his sons – particularly Harry, made vulnerable because of his penchant for nights out, might also become entrapped. That he should allow this row to be sustained in 2012 illustrates how seriously the heir was taking the 'Andrew problem'.

❦

No sooner had British Airways flight BA292 taken off from Washington DC's Dulles International airport bound for London Heathrow at a little after 11 p.m. on 7 May, than Harry fell asleep in his business class seat. It had been a long day: he had been in America for less than nine hours of a 24-hour special leave but was later to say that they were probably the most honourable nine hours of his life – so far.

As he boarded the 747 London-bound airliner a stewardess offered him a dinner menu but he politely declined it saying he had already eaten. That was the understatement of the year: he had just dined at Washington's Ritz-Carlton Hotel alongside his military hero, General Colin Powell – arguably the greatest soldier of his generation – who was about to present him with the Atlantic Council Award for Distinguished Humanitarian Leadership in front of an international assembly of distinguished guests.

Although there were three other recipients – including Ban Ki-moon, Secretary General of the United Nations – no one was left in any doubt that the event had largely been in Harry's honour. The girls outside the hotel entrance were screaming his name as they might once have done for the Beatles, but this was no occasion for teen idols. Indeed, his greatest female admirer that day turned out to be America's Second Lady, Vice-President Joe Biden's wife Jill, who was obviously (and somewhat embarrassingly) captivated by the young British royal.

On the outbound flight that morning Harry had, according to a travel companion, worried about whether he was worthy of the honour former US Secretary of State Powell was about to confer on him. He was scribbling into the speech he would deliver just a few hours later: 'For a captain in the British Army to be introduced by such a world-renowned soldier and statesman is truly humbling ... and a little terrifying... Genuinely, I don't feel that I have done nearly enough to deserve this award.'

On his arrival he had collected his modest set of luggage – one lounge suit for a reception that afternoon at the British embassy, a black tie suit for the evening's formal dinner, and a framed photograph he had signed for British ambassador Sir Peter Westmacott – before he set off for the embassy to spend time with the people he admires most: wounded veterans.

Powell introduced a note of humour into his speech of praise, acknowledging Harry's personal popularity in the US:

Apart from recognising his contributions to the humanitarian projects, I would be remiss if I didn't note that his presence has altered the normal demographic make-up of our audience: we have a record number of single young women here. You saw them outside. I also have to say the average age for an Atlantic Council dinner has dropped twenty-five years and [he added turning to Harry] for that we have to thank you.

Then, in a brief message that brought a tear to Harry's eyes, Powell added, 'Clearly the loving effort Diana made to teach her sons the importance of serving others has touched the hearts and souls of her two sons and continues her legacy.'

In his response Harry chose to pass the credit afforded him on to those veterans who had suffered for their cause:

It would be wrong of me to speak for these heroes, but not presumptuous of me to pay tribute to them: so many of our servicemen and women have made the ultimate sacrifice; so many lives have been lost and so many changed forever by the wounds that they have suffered in the course of their duties. They have paid a terrible price to keep us safe and free.

The events of that day would prove the highlight of what was already an incredible year in the life of Harry Wales. While the Queen's popularity soared to new heights as she toured her kingdom with Prince Philip, acknowledging celebrations held in honour of her Diamond Jubilee, and the nation had fallen as much in love with William and Kate as the two had with each other, it was Harry who emerged as the gleaming new star, for this was the year in which he was truly anointed the People's Prince. What had brought about this incredible change in the man once dubbed 'the royal rebel'? I have asked a man close to him who his main influences have been. The answer was: 'his parents'. Despite the differences between them, they had both contributed enormously to the way his life had shaped itself: Diana had taught him to be charitable, how to care for others less fortunate than himself; Charles had instilled in him a love of conservation, how to be concerned about the planet he lives on and how to do all he can for young people.

As his international popularity soared, a group of powerful Canadians said they wanted him as their king, *GQ* magazine made him their cover boy and named him the best-dressed member of the Royal Family, and dubious praise came from the late Boris Berezovsky, the oligarch who picked Vladimir Putin as Russia's leader. London-exiled Berezovsky described Harry as one of the brightest symbols of the modern civilised world and declared that if he had his powerful way again Russia would become a monarchy with Harry Wales as its head of state. As a further nod to his popularity it was declared that 'Harry' was now the name UK parents chose for their newborn boys more than any other.

But his outstanding achievement of the year was the work he did at home behind the scenes, work that went unpublicised: it was Harry who almost single-handedly did much to modernise the monarchy in the spring and summer of 2012.

It was, for example, he who persuaded the Queen not only to permit the Jubilee rock concert to be staged in front of Buckingham Palace but to sit through most of it sharing the music with many thousands of her younger subjects.

Knowing she would not be ready to join the audience until 9 p.m., Harry had talked the organisers into ensuring that Sir Elton John did not take to the stage before then for Harry knew that the singing piano player was one of her favourite performers after being introduced to his music by the Queen Mother who had frequently taken tea with him at his home in Windsor. Seated behind his grandmother for the concert, Harry leaned forward from time to time to tell her who some of the acts were and what they were singing about.

And it was after a plea from her younger grandson that Her Majesty overruled a decision by palace officials not to allow the band Madness to perform their hits 'Our House' and 'It Must Be Love' from the very rooftop of the Queen's London home.

Furthermore, he encouraged his father to deliver the line which stole the show when Charles paid tribute to his mother in his brief Jubilee concert speech. Traditionally the royals have always referred to close relatives in public by their royal titles (I once heard Princess Margaret – in response to the question 'And how is your sister, Ma'am?' – retort, 'Are you referring to Her Majesty the Queen?'), but Charles broke the mould when he looked at his mother and after describing her as 'Your Majesty', to the delight of the crowd, added after a well-calculated pause, 'Mummy...' Apparently Harry claims credit for the line and jokes about becoming his father's main speechwriter. Having used the same trick though at the Queen's Golden Jubilee in 2002, it seems Charles might well have been humouring his second-born.

But Harry's greatest achievement was to persuade his grandmother to take part in the spoof James Bond movie for the opening ceremony of the Olympic Games. When she was first asked to act out a scene with Bond actor Daniel Craig, the senior aide who put the proposal to her says he expected her to be shocked that he had even dared to do so. 'But she thought for a few moments and said, "I'll see what Harry says."'

By the insider account that reaches this author, Harry could hardly believe his ears when the idea was relayed to him: 'Go it for, Gran,' was his response. Even he could not have conceived a better progression for his royal modernisation work. The ceremony's producer Danny Boyle was stunned when he learned from Her Majesty's deputy private secretary Edward Young that she had agreed to be a Bond Girl for a night.

And so it came to pass that Craig, dressed in his 007 tuxedo, was filmed arriving at Buckingham Palace in a black cab and being escorted by a flunky through the illustrious corridors to the Queen's rarely seen study. Her Majesty remained working at her desk until the exact moment of his appointment arrived and then turned to receive him with the words, 'Good evening, Mr Bond.' It was a perfect delivery; there were no smiles, just an acknowledgment that there was a job to be done, a mission to be carried out and they both had a part to play in it.

Accompanied by her three Pembroke Welsh Corgis she then walked with Craig from the study and back along the corridor by which he had arrived. In the Palace courtyard the two were seen clambering into a helicopter – although by now the 'Queen' was being played by the actress Julia McKenzie, famed for her television role as Miss Marple. The scene concluded with stunt double Gary Connery – wearing an identical salmon-pink dress to that in which the Queen had received 'Mr Bond' complete with gloves and handbag – parachuting, knickers billowing, alongside Craig's double into the Olympic Stadium. Moments later the real Queen, wearing the same dress as she had been in the filmed palace sequence, received a standing ovation as she entered the arena with Prince Philip.

And where was Harry? At The Enterprise pub in South Kensington, laughing aloud with his friend Skippy, in whom he had obviously confided what was about to happen, although when asked later how surprised he was by the Queen's parachute jump, Harry said, 'What she does in her spare time is her business.' In excellent spirits and clearly not intending to drive home, he had downed generous quantities of sauvignon blanc to wash down a substantial steak topped with asparagus and a mango sorbet while his protection officer sank half a pint of Guinness at the bar.

Still in party mood, and clearly delighted with the success of the amazing event his advice had inspired, Harry set off the following morning to spend the weekend with his latest girlfriend Cressida Bonas, the 23-year-old daughter of fun-loving former model (and four times married and divorced) Lady Mary-Gaye Curzon. The two then joined the crowds attending the Womad festival at Charlton Park, the Earl of Suffolk's 4,500-acre Wiltshire estate. Back in party mood, Harry – with Cressida never more than inches from his side – amused his friends by wearing a duck-shaped hat; in response to a question from one of them, he was overheard saying he had 'absolutely no regrets' at learning earlier in the week that one of his old flames, the exotic lingerie model Florence Brudenell-Bruce, had returned to the arms of her long-term boyfriend Henry St George.

Harry had a helpful distraction: he was smitten by Ms Bonas from the moment he was introduced to her by his cousin Eugenie. She was just his type – tall, blonde and leggy. He knew that her impeccable pedigree was just what his Palace guardians would approve of – not that he had much time for their opinion. Her much-loved mother, Lady Mary, the daughter of veteran racing driver Earl Howe, a godson of Edward VII, was the 'It' girl of her day and a sporting woman by all accounts, Cressida being one of the five children she had by three of her husbands. Cressida's paternal great-grand-father, however, was of more humble stock: George Bonas was an impoverished butcher when he arrived in Battersea from his Midlands home.

Although she was working as a model for Burberry when she met Harry, Cressida once aspired to become an actress, an ambition that was almost certainly put in the shade by the possibility of becoming a princess.

A true blueblood (at least on her mother's side), she mixes in the very best circles. When she was studying at Leeds her boyfriend was Harry Wentworth-Stanley, whose stepfather George Milford Haven is a cousin of the Queen. She is also a close friend of the York set – Fergie as well as the Princesses Beatrice and Eugenie. In her teens she spent three years at the Royal Ballet School on Princess Alexandra's doorstep in Richmond Park, but according to a family friend,

> the pressure was too much. She decided she didn't want to go down the ballet route and her parents took her out and sent her to Prior Park College in Bath on a sports scholarship. She's a dreamy romantic whose reading taste rarely strays beyond the novels of Jane Austen and Nancy Mitford. In short she is very stable and a most suitable potential bride for the Prince. Intellectually she is probably his superior. Personally, I'd bet on her being 'the one' when the time comes for him to choose a bride.

Harry had been seeing Cressida for several weeks before deciding to unveil her in public at a midsummer night party to celebrate the London premiere of the latest Batman film, *The Dark Knight Rises*. Although they carried out the usual manoeuvre of arriving separately at the party – her on the arm of Harry's friend 'Skippy' Inskip – once inside they made no secret of the fact that they were together. And when they moved on to a second venue, Le Salon, there were plenty of witnesses to testify that they spent much of their time kissing and cuddling (although the Prince was highly amused to read the following morning that the girl in his arms was the model Cara Delevingne).

'I think Harry wanted Chelsy [Davy] to be sure she got the message that he had moved on,' says his talkative chum.

> But don't write Chelsy off, she was the love of his life for seven years and it wouldn't surprise me if she didn't re-emerge at some point in the not-too-distant future. His recent announcement that he was now 100 per cent single was, I'm sure, sent as a message to Chelsy – a message that if she wanted him back she would have to work for it.

Height and long blonde hair are not the only things 23-year-old Ms Bonas has in common with his on/off sweetheart. Like Ms Davy she went to Stowe (as did Florence Brudenell-Bruce) before also moving on to Leeds University. While keen to see the Prince settle down, some royal matchmakers had their doubts about whether the Bonas family was a suitable one for the Windsors to merge with: Cressida's father, Old Harrovian Jeffrey Bonas was once accused of being 'unreliable' by a judge in a court case over the £1.2 million he paid his first wife in the divorce brought on by his adulterous affair with Cressida's mother. The judge accused Bonas of hiding his wealth in offshore Isle of Man accounts.

So keen was Harry to watch Usain Bolt run for gold in the 2012 Olympics that he persuaded the organisers of a charity polo match he and William were committed to playing in to bring the match forward by half an hour so he could drive the 100 miles from Cirencester to reach the stadium in time for the 100 metres final. No helicopters for him; he was only too well aware of the negative publicity his uncle Andrew had brought on the family when he insisted on charter planes for foreign trips and helicopters to travel to golf matches – usually at public expense.

Ecstatic at Bolt's gold-medal victory – he ran the 100 metres in 9.63 seconds (the second-fastest time ever) – Harry decided a celebration dinner with his brother and sister-in-law was called for. Not for them a caviar and lobster feast at an award-winning restaurant in Mayfair but a home-prepared supper, albeit 'home' being Harry's place at Kensington Palace – a one-bedroom former staff apartment that he calls home until he takes over Nottingham Cottage when the Cambridges move into the late Princess Margaret's refurbished apartment in October 2013. He shopped for the food at the nearby branch of Marks & Spencer, scooping vacuum-packed steaks, a ready-cooked chicken, rocket salad and Cheddar cheese into his basket to the astonishment of fellow shoppers who were not used to standing in line behind a prince.

It was a shopping venture William would never have dared to carry out but it presented no problem for Harry, who has long hankered after a normal life. He told an old friend later that he and the Cambridges had 'shared a lot of laughs' as they watched ongoing coverage of the Olympics on television. William reminded Harry of how, straight-faced, he had told TV interviewer Sue Barker at an earlier athletics event how he and Kate would be running in the London marathon. When Barker – seemingly believing she had just got herself an amazing exclusive – asked if that was really going to happen, Harry burst her bubble when he responded, 'Well, they'll have to now, won't they?'

Harry is not the only one of Charles's sons with a sense of humour, though William's is usually expressed in private since he is well aware that anything said in fun by a future king is more likely to be taken the wrong way. He did nothing to detract from those who question Harry's paternity however, when during a visit to Bacon's College in east London the next day, he and Harry were asked, 'Are you two brothers?' William jokingly replied, 'We're not sure.'

Although he applauded all the athletes, it was Harry himself who proved to be the star of the show when he took centre stage on the closing night of the Olympic Games. Appointed by the Queen to be the royal figurehead for the spectacular farewell to the Games, it was his most important royal engagement to date. William had returned to north Wales to continue his day job as an RAF search-and-rescue pilot and the Queen and her husband had left for their summer sojourn at Balmoral, having agreed to step back and allow Harry to give the occasion the modern majesty it deserved. As the national anthem was played when he stepped on to the stage, 80,000 people rose to their feet. He did not disappoint them. Looking every inch king material, he made a stirring speech congratulating all the competitors and referring to the spirit of the Olympics as 'a magnificent force for positive change'. Once again his father, watching the ceremony on television at Birkhall, his own Scottish summer holiday retreat, had reason to be proud: here was a son who could shoulder a hefty chunk of the royal burden he himself had never been comfortable with.

So it was with Charles's approval that within hours of his final royal duty of the summer, Harry went off on holiday. With Cressida and a bunch of pals in tow including Inskip and Arthur Landon, who inherited more than £200 million from his father, a brigadier who was advisor to the Sultan of Oman, he set off for Necker, Sir Richard Branson's Caribbean island on which he had spent memorable holidays with his mother and brother. Enjoying absolute privacy, he was able to let his hair down as they celebrated the twenty-seventh birthday of Branson's son Sam. Pictures subsequently posted on Facebook showed members of the group wearing wigs and fancy dress and covered in body paint, lying passed out in the sand after nights of heavy drinking.

It was his next move that was to cause the problem. From out of the blue Harry received a call: how would he like to extend his break with a few days in Las Vegas? Harry and Inskip were up for it but others – including Ms Bonas – had commitments in the UK to return to. Having hurriedly

packed the small amount of clothing he would require, Harry
set off for the Nevada gambling city and duly arrived on the
afternoon of Friday 24 August – just twelve days after he had
brought that massive crowd to their feet with his stirring
speech at the end of the Olympics.

A Rolls-Royce had been sent to McCarran airport to
collect and whisk him to the Wynn resort hotel, where he
was taken up to a two-floor apartment in the Encore Tower
normally priced at $5,000 a night but provided without cost
for 'the British Prince' as the owner Steve Wynn referred to
him. The 6,000-square-foot apartment consisted of eight
rooms including three bedrooms, a billiard room and a bar
which could accommodate up to seventy guests as former
occupants the singer Beyoncé and her rapper husband Jay-Z
could testify. While other hotels offer little more than a box
of tissues on the dressing table, Harry discovered that the
Wynn had provided him with a complimentary 'intimacy kit',
a packet of condoms labelled with the message 'Have fun,
play safe'.

That night Harry went out on the town. He and his now
small group were followed from the XS club to a Frank
Sinatra-themed restaurant by a group of single – and available – young women, each resembling beauty queens. When
they got back to the hotel one of them asked where he was
going next; the third in line to the throne replied: 'Up to the
suite. Why, do you want to come?'

Of course she did and so did her friends. Once there, a
session of heavy drinking ensued until one of them – and

a Vegas investigator who inquired into the incident 'on behalf of certain parties in London' was unable to determine whether it was one of the girls or a member of Harry's group – suggested they spice up the proceedings with a game of strip pool, to which Harry said, 'Let's fucking do it!' The rules were simple: if you missed a shot you had to take off an item of clothing. By this time Harry was wearing only his shorts and a necklace which had been given to him by a Botswana shaman to protect him from evil spirits; it came as no surprise when he missed his first shot.

He either didn't notice or, more likely, didn't care when the camera phones came out and his nakedness was recorded for posterity. In the event several girls – including at least one who wasn't even there – offered to sell their stories … and their pictures.

The following morning the party continued for Harry. He was rejoined by Arthur Landon, who had flown from Los Angeles where he was working on a film. In a scene reminiscent of *The Hangover*, Harry, still drinking heavily, went to the Wet Republic pool party at the MGM Grand Hotel and the following night to the XS club where he encountered a group of Essex boys, one of whom tweeted, 'He kissed me on the lips. Haha! I can't describe how that night was with Harry!!' Having failed to locate one of his favourite singers, Jennifer Lopez, at a pool party the following day, the Prince, much the worse for wear, sought out the Olympic swimmer Ryan Lochte whom he challenged to a race in the pool, before diving in still wearing his jeans.

Clearly he is attractive to the opposite sex and never more so than when he is partying. 'I was in Vegas at the Encore before the pool incident and it was amazing to see the number of beauties who followed him around,' says American music executive Herb Goldfarb. 'If he didn't have another job this young man could have made it big in Hollywood. Take it from me; Prince Harry is Britain's answer to Brad Pitt. And he has an advantage – he's available!'

Alas, the Prince had no idea of the storm that was to break and, according to an aide, was 'deeply shocked' when told that not only had he been photographed in the nude with at least one disrobed woman but the grainy pictures were being posted on TMZ, one of America's most popular entertainment news sites which had paid $200,000 for just two of them.

Harry's unusual, to say the least, party was the kind of thing that goes on every night in Las Vegas, but was the Prince set up? His pal Arthur Landon denied that it was a friend who took the pictures and said that whoever had taken and sold them was abusing Harry's hospitality and that the mischievous act had 'put a real dampener on their trip'. But was he missing the point?

Although Harry has never revealed just who it was who invited him to a weekend at Sin City's Wynn resort in the first place, he blames no one but himself for what occurred there. He delivered the well-tuned line ('and he came up with it himself too', says the friendly Palace aide): 'It was a classic example of me probably being too much army and not enough Prince.' He added:

My father's always trying to remind me about who I am and stuff like that. But it's very easy to forget about who I am when I am in the army. Everyone's wearing the same uniform and doing the same kind of thing. I get on well with the lads and I enjoy my job. It's as simple as that.

However, there is good reason to believe that there is an anti-British-monarchy group constantly at work and always on the lookout for opportunities to besmirch the royals' reputations. There was the deliberate leak about the Duchess of York's extramarital affair with the Texan oil billionaire's son Steve Wyatt, and did the broadcast of Charles and Camilla's intimate conversation – Camillagate – really just happen to be heard by someone in Liverpool who was testing an electronic-honing device? And how about that revealing 'Squidgy' chat between Diana and James Gilbey? Was the acquisition of that and its subsequent broadcast merely a quirk of fate? Diana thought not and told Harry so when he asked on one occasion why the carpets in their Kensington Palace apartment had been taken up. She told him that anti-bugging experts were searching beneath the floors for the listening devices she was convinced had been planted.

Harry was never going to subscribe to the conspiracy theory. He was – and remains – a normal human being who does what many other men do, especially in the wild atmosphere that prevails in Las Vegas. Not for nothing is the town known to many as Lost Wages. Nevertheless he was crestfallen when he returned to the UK after performing so well on the Caribbean tour and at the Olympics, to receive a stern lecture from his father at Balmoral before setting off for the seclusion the grand Alnwick estate in Northumberland had to offer.

Harry Wales is a brave soldier as well as a deeply compassionate man and his fun-loving excesses should not detract from his enormous qualities. He loves children and works hard to support a number of charities that help the disadvantaged ones.

Not for nothing does he have the respect of fellow servicemen and women – 12,000 of them around the world posed naked for the cameras after the Vegas incident to demonstrate that they supported him, rather than condemning him for his uninhibited behaviour. His postbag at St James's Palace bulged with mail – more than 90 per cent of it positive.

In certain quarters he was criticised for choosing 'the wrong friends' – people who had become a bad influence on him. But Harry knows he is free to befriend whomever he wishes and he is too strong a character to be told what to do – or, indeed, what not to do – by any of them. In a discussion on the subject with his grandfather following his return from America he was told by Prince Philip 'familiarity breeds contempt'. He listened and nodded affirmatively, but paid little heed to the message.

Harry has done everything he can to be ordinary, to have a normal life. He shops at Marks & Spencer in Kensington High Street when he fancies a sandwich and in Ipswich he is a regular at the Tesco store close to his airbase. No other royal does that, with the exception of the Duchess of York, who has on occasions been spotted picking out special offers in her local Asda.

When he invited a pal to join him for lunch at the Waterman's Arms in Pembroke, west Wales, Harry took advantage of the pub's midweek 'buy two meals for a tenner' promotion. And during his US sojourn he loaded a trolley with frozen pizzas, beer and bananas at a Walmart supermarket. Inevitably, in the background, there is always the shadowy figure of a royal protection officer and, despite the ubiquitous baseball hat pulled down to hide his face, he is frequently recognised, stared at and followed by other shoppers surprised by seeing a royal in their midst. Being 'ordinary', when his life is shaped by what he refers to as 'an accident of birth', is no easy feat. However, Harry does not allow his position to get in the way of his desire to lead a near-normal life.

❦

Harry returned to Afghanistan in the autumn of 2012 to serve with 622 Squadron, 3 Regiment Army Air Corps in Camp Bastion. A far bigger base than FOB Delhi where he spent much of his first tour of duty, Bastion is home to 4,000 British troops (a number which will have halved before 2013 ends), 4,350 contractors and 2,000 civilians, and has spread to a town roughly the size of Reading. The Prince's new home was a shared room in an accommodation block made of modified shipping containers.

Harry's second tour of duty was always going to be quite different from his first: there was no secrecy this time around, no ban on media coverage and he posed – perhaps reluctantly – for photographers as he made coffee and stood in line to collect his meal. Unlike his previous tour when he shared a curried goat for his Christmas lunch with Lt Colonel Bill Connor, this time he had a proper seasonal meal and an accompanying cameraman was allowed to photograph him wearing a Santa hat complete with blonde plaits. He talked freely about the adrenalin rush he got each time he ran to his helicopter, adding: 'Once you're in the aircraft you've got to try and slow yourself down because otherwise you're going to miss something.'

Sometime after his return he was reported – many would say irresponsibly – by *The Sun* to have achieved the kind of 'success' his father had dreaded by wiping out a Taliban commander. Ignoring General Dannatt's earlier call for a blackout of Harry's activities in war zones and despite criticisms of press behaviour in the recent past, the Murdoch paper carried a story headlined HARRY KILLS TALIBAN CHIEF. According to the report, British troops had been tracking a vehicle in which they knew the enemy leader was travelling and they called for a helicopter.

We were on patrol and the Apache helicopters were called in. We heard this posh voice come over the radio and knew it was Big H. They were tracking a Taliban leader – he was commander level. The Apache then let off some Hellfire missiles and it's 30mm cannon and 'boom'. It was Big H all the way.

Needless to say, the MoD declined to discuss the matter.

Whether true or false, few reports could have more incensed the enemy to avenge the death of one of their own heroes by stepping up their efforts to capture or kill the British hero *The Sun* had deliberately named as being the man responsible. The report put the lives of Harry and his comrades even more at risk when a foreign newspaper followed up the report by apparently claiming that

> When he got back to the base he wasn't overjoyed but very serious and said something like, 'That's one for Liam [Riley]', his mate who the Taliban had killed nearly three years earlier. Then he collected a mug of coffee for himself and everybody was patting him on the back. We were all reminded that it was not information we should convey home but I believe Big H later called his father with the news. From what we've read before I think his dad would have received that particular news with mixed feelings, but, as H has said before, 'This is war.'

Harry let himself down somewhat when, in an interview he gave for transmission following his return, he made some ill-advised comments about killing Taliban fighters. He likened pressing the buttons which released his Apache's Hellfire missiles and 30mm cannon on scores of missions, to computer-game-playing off-duty, saying it was 'a joy ... because I'm one of those people who loves playing PlayStation and Xbox, so with my thumbs I like to think that I'm probably quite useful'. He compounded the offence by referring to destruction of his opponents as a matter of 'taking them out of the game'.

No one was shocked by the news that he had killed many of the enemy during his stint – after all, this was war and that is part and parcel of a soldier's job, especially when handed the controls of such a lethal machine as the Apache. But he seemed to be revelling in it, resulting in headlines such as I'VE KILLED TALIBAN FIGHTERS, SAYS HARRY (*Daily Telegraph*). His boast – and that's how it was perceived by many – raised fears for his safety and brought about an upgrade in his security. Among his critics was Dai Davies, a former head of the Metropolitan Police Royal Protection Squad who said:

> Purely from a protection point of view, I think it was highly inadvisable for Prince Harry to draw attention to himself. It may be the reality that he killed insurgents, but saying this publicly just increases the likelihood of some lunatic trying to take revenge on him. It does not seem to have occurred to this young man that he has responsibility not only to himself, but also to those who guard him.

And another former senior officer, Glen Smyth, added: 'I think it would have been better for Prince Harry to have simply said he had been deployed in an operational capacity and to have left it at that. What he has said has undoubtedly increased his value as a terrorist target.'

He further incensed his critics when he complained that life in the army was 'as normal as it was going to get... For me it's not that normal because I go into the cookhouse and everyone has a good old gawp, and that's one thing I dislike about being here.' A 'senior officer' who refused to give his name told the *Sunday Telegraph* that Captain Wales had adopted the language of a 'spoiled, truculent teenager' and sounded more like 'a disgruntled soldier than an Army officer'. Harry was learning yet again that you can please some of the people some of the time...

One of his close circle said the day after his comments about killing Taliban were broadcast:

> Oh dear, there's Harry going over the top again. It's a shame because he had done a brilliant job out there. He's bound to blame the newspapers for making so much of it but he has only himself to blame. I reckon he's going to be pretty cross, but not as much as his father. Someone should have been there to guide him when he gave that interview. He deserves better advice. It gave a totally wrong impression of the Harry I know.

A Palace source confirms that Prince Charles simply shook his head and said, 'This should never have happened. Harry needs some lessons in PR.' Following his subsequent return to the UK, Harry went to the Fulham home of his stalwart friend Mark Dyer before going to Highgrove for a man-to-man chat with his father.

However, the impression that he spent all of his precious spare time between his arduous duties engaged in war games on his PlayStation was totally misguided. Something he would have been justified in boasting about was how much of that time he sacrificed to sustain his work for Sentebale in far-away Lesotho. From the battlefield he had also laid careful plans for the charity to expand its work into other countries in need of similar help in his beloved southern Africa. Maintaining regular email contact with Sentebale's chief executive, Cathy Ferrier, from Camp Bastion, he urged her to help him come up with ways of raising more money since the £2 million a year it was collecting was inadequate to finance his ambitious expansion scheme.

Ms Ferrier says:

We have researched nine other countries in southern Africa which have similar problems to Lesotho, with a high number of orphans and high HIV infection rates, and we have a short list of four countries. We still have an absolute commitment to doing all we can in Lesotho but we want to take the programme to other countries because there is a huge unmet need.

One of the ideas Harry came up with during his second term in Helmand was to have a Sentebale garden at the 2013 Chelsea Flower Show to raise awareness of the charity and attract major sponsors. Not equipped with his father's horticultural skills, he made long-distance calls back home to ask Jinny Blom, a gold-medal winner in the field, to design a garden which was also to be a homage to his mother. Between sorties in his Apache, he pored over designs emailed to Camp Bastion. He asked Ms Blom to ensure that the garden included forget-me-nots, which would not only serve as a translation of Sentebale but also ensure Diana's memory would be recognised. He was delighted when she included a 'hearts and crown' motif on a stone-worked terrace and a Trifolium, a genus of herbs containing the trefoils or clovers, including the 'William' plant. The garden was also to include pollarded willows like the ones found in the damp valleys of Lesotho. It was an instant hit with B&Q who agreed to sponsor the garden, and Harry was shrewd enough to realise that it was likely to attract sponsors and donations for the charity itself. It was a brilliant move which ensured support for the suffering in Lesotho as well as paying tribute to Diana.

On his return to Afghanistan one of the first letters he had received was from his beloved Nanny (Olga) Powell wishing him luck but expressing her fears for his welfare. Alas, she died a few weeks later, aged eighty-two. His deployment prevented him from returning for her funeral and he did not send a wreath but urged all who knew and loved her as he did to make contributions to Sentebale.

Olga knew more of his secrets than most but always declined to divulge them even if she was offered substantial sums for her story. She did, however, give occasional talks to women's lunches and community events. On one occasion she said of Harry: 'He could be a naughty boy but the occasional clout soon brought him back into line.' Judging by the splendid way he has grown up – albeit belatedly – it must have been more than an occasional one.

'A naughty boy' might well have been the description Cressida Bonas applied to him after the Las Vegas episode but, contrary to reports at the time, she was never prepared to give up on him and, between carrying out his duties in Afghanistan, he telephoned her frequently from Helmand using a James Bond-style anti-bugging phone. The romance was seemingly back on and no one could have been more aware of it than Chelsy Davy; the two women had nothing to say to each other when they met up at the Henry van Straubenzee Memorial Fund Carol Concert in London early in December 2012. Chelsy had an unknown man on her arm but there was no sight of Henry Wentworth-Stanley, the ex-boyfriend Cressida had reportedly been reunited with. 'It's still a love match,' confides a talkative friend, 'but I would still put my money on Chelsy being the victor even though she once told me that marrying a prince was not the life for her. Only time will tell.'

Harry's own problems with women were swept aside when he received a call from his brother to tell him that the Duchess of Cambridge was pregnant. According to a fellow soldier, 'He was berserk with happiness although he couldn't tell us the reason at that stage – it was a "state secret", he said.' Even the huge bouquet of flowers he sent her had to be organised by a confidant in London. But when, eight weeks into her pregnancy, Kate was admitted to the King Edward

VII hospital in London after being taken ill with hyperemesis gravidarum – severe morning sickness – Harry knew he could break the strict silence that Palace potentates had called for prior to an announcement planned for Christmas Day and he sent her an open message: 'Get well soon, sis. I want to be an uncle soonest.' She immediately replied saying, 'I hope you won't mind if it's a girl. Since the times they are a-changing maybe you'll still allow her to join your potential family polo team.'

The birth of the royal baby pushes the People's Prince down from third in line to fourth in the line of succession – and he couldn't be happier. Knowing he will almost certainly never have to shoulder the awesome and tedious burden of kingship gives him the freedom to be the Harry Wales he always wanted to be. Quite apart from William's happiness in becoming a father, Kate's pregnancy had been the answer to his prayers. As Uncle Harry he will surely be the greatest role model the Royal Family has had for many generations. 'What a change in one man in a relatively short time,' says a courtier who guided me through the journey of Harry Wales, 'from hooligan to hero, and all within the space of a few years.'

Yes, Harry has changed and in the course of so doing has managed to achieve a large measure of the normality he craved earlier in his life when membership of the Royal Family made that dream seem impossible. He still likes his music (though Jennifer Lopez has had to give way to Beyoncé on the iPhone that goes everywhere with him), and watches *The Royle Family* and *Big Brother* (which he says he would like to appear on) on TV, although Tiggy managed to persuade him to extend his taste to include costume dramas such as *Downton Abbey*. *Tatler* said he was the coolest member of the Firm, but adds (in more vulgar terms than I repeat here) that this is like saying he was the most fanciable man in the Cabinet.

So where does he go from here? As my reliable source at St James's Palace admits, 'Even he doesn't know. Yes, he will leave the military in due course but I don't expect him to become his elder brother's deputy, just filling in when Prince William is unavailable. That's not His Royal Highness's way.'

Harry's dilemma is that he would dearly love to settle in his beloved Africa to work with those who truly need him – and during his February visit to Lesotho I understand he talked to Prince Seeiso about the prices and positions of available properties in the capital – but his grandmother has constantly reminded him that his place is in England, the country he says he does not particularly like. And what of his relationship with Chelsy? A close friend says that although Chelsy would have been happy to see him settle in her homeland, 'She has come to enjoy life in London where she now has a promising career and a wide circle of friends. She doesn't need Harry any more.'

Harry has found that difficult to accept. Let there be no doubt about it, Chelsy was the love of his life, but Cressida Bonas is more compliant, more able to fit in with his lifestyle. I believe the Queen may be a little anxious about her bohemian ways but Cressida is more likely to conform than Chelsy was and he loves her for it.

His love was demonstrated when she joined him for a romantic break at the Farinet Hotel in Verbier in February. Harry went out of his way to be photographed kissing Cressida on the slopes: 'I'm told that they talked of marriage but he wouldn't thank me for saying that,' continues his talkative chum. 'Fergie [the Duchess of York who was there with her daughters and former husband] was urging him to propose but "H" wouldn't go that far. That said, however, he's seen how happy marriage has made his brother and I think he wants some of that. I'm also informed that Cressida's mother has told [Princess] Eugenie she would love to see them settle down together, but the girl won't be rushed any more than he will. Harry is not one to be rushed; believe me, he still has a few tricks up his sleeve. He's special, he's interesting – watch this space.'

Of all the royals, Harry Wales is indeed the most interesting one to follow: in his short life he has produced many surprises and doubtless he will continue to do so. While Charles loves him deeply and dotes on his humour and wild enthusiasms, Harry's greatest achievement is to remain faithful to the memory of his mother. Diana would be so very proud of him.

# SOURCES

Prince Harry knew almost from the outset that this book was being written; indeed while explaining that – for the obvious reasons – he could not personally be involved, he sent his good wishes for the work in progress. It is to his immense credit that he forbade no one from talking to this author – a vastly different experience to that encountered when compiling a previous biography of Vladimir Putin.

A wide range of people helped put together this story of Harry Wales – from senior aides to humble members of staff, from aristocrats to bodyguards and protection officers, from friends of his to the not-so-friendly, from those who shared classrooms with him in boyhood to those he drank with (and still does) today, from girls he has loved and lost to soldiers who have served alongside him on the front line in Afghanistan.

Because some of them thought they might have said too much, they asked not to have their names attached to the fascinating stories they had relayed. For that reason the author decided to provide them all with a blanket of anonymity with the exception of those who were quite happy to be named – although it is unlikely that Harry would be critical of a single one: he knows that people in all walks of life talk and that does not dismay him. As he said of one of the interviewees: 'My secrets are safe with him, it's the people he tells who tend to be indiscreet.'

# INDEX

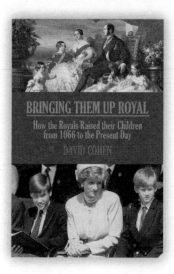

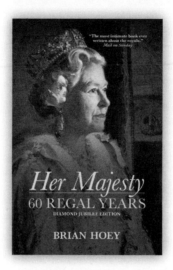

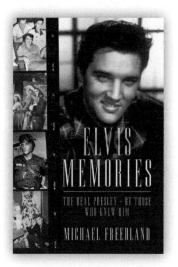